OBSERVATIONS *upon the* PROPHECIES *of DANIEL*, *and the* APOCALYPSE *of* St. *JOHN*

In Two PARTS

By
Sir *ISAAC NEWTON*

Watchmaker Publishing

1931

Copyright © 2011 Watchmaker PUB

ISBN 978-1-60386-402-2

To the Right Honourable

PETER
Lord *K I N G,*

Baron of *Ockham*, Lord High Chancellor
of Great-Britain.

My Lord,

I shall make no Apology for addressing the following Sheets to Your Lordship, who lived in a long Intercourse of Friendship with the Author; and, like him, amidst occupations of a different nature, made Religion your voluntary Study; and in all your Enquiries and Actions, have shewn the same inflexible Adherence to Truth and Virtue.

I shall always reckon it one of the Advantages of my Relation to Sir Isaac Newton, *that it affords me an opportunity of making this publick acknowledgment of the unfeigned Respect of,*

My Lord,
Your Lordship's
most obedient, and
most humble Servant,
Benj. Smith.

Contents

PART I

Observations upon the Prophecies of *Daniel*

PART II

Observations upon the *Apocalypse* of St. *John*

PART I

Observations

Upon The

Prophecies of *DANIEL*

CHAP. I

*Introduction concerning the Compilers
of the books of the Old Testament*

When *Manasses*[1] set up a carved image in the house of the Lord, and built altars in the two courts of the house, to all the host of Heaven, and us'd inchantments and witchcraft, and familiar spirits, and for his great wickedness was invaded by the army of *Asserhadon* King of *Assyria*, and carried captive to *Babylon*; the book of the Law was lost till the eighteenth year of his grandson *Josiah*. Then[2] *Hilkiah* the High Priest, upon repairing the Temple, found it there: and the King lamented that their fathers had not done after the words of the book, and commanded that it should be read to the people, and caused the people to renew the holy covenant with God. This is the book of the Law now extant.

When[3] *Shishak* came out of *Egypt* and spoil'd the temple, and brought *Judah* into subjection to the monarchy of *Egypt*, (which was in the fifth year of *Rehoboam*) the *Jews* continued under great troubles for about twenty years; being *without the true God, and without a teaching Priest, and without Law: and in those times there was no peace to him that went out, nor to him that came in, but great vexations were upon all the inhabitants of the countries, and nation was destroyed of nation, and city of city, for God did vex them with all adversity.* But[4] when *Shishak* was dead, and *Egypt* fell into troubles, *Judah* had quiet ten years; and in that time *Asa* built fenced cities in *Judah*, and got up an army of 580000 men, with which, in the 15th year of his reign, he met

---

[1] 2 Chron. xxxiii. 5, 6, 7.
[2] 2 Chron. xxxiv.
[3] 2 Chron. xii. 2, 3, 4, 8, 9. & xv. 3, 5, 6.
[4] 2 Chron. xiv. 1, 6, 7, 8, 9, 12.

and overcame *Zerah* the *Ethiopian*, who had conquered *Egypt* and *Lybia*, and *Troglodytica*, and came out with an army of 1000000 *Lybians* and *Ethiopians*, to recover the countries conquered by *Sesac*. And after this victory[5] *Asa* dethroned his mother for idolatry, and he renewed the Altar, and brought new vessels of gold and silver into the Temple; and he and the people entered into a new covenant to seek the Lord God of their fathers, upon pain of death to those who worshiped other Gods; and his son *Jehosaphat* took away the high places, and in the third year of his reign sent some of his Princes, and of the Priests and Levites, to teach in the cities of *Judah*: and they had the book of the Law with them, and went about throughout all the cities of *Judah*, and taught the people. This is that book of the Law which was afterwards lost in the reign of *Manasses*, and found again in the reign of *Josiah*, and therefore it was written before the third year of *Jehosaphat*.

The same book of the Law was preserved and handed down to posterity by the *Samaritans*, and therefore was received by the ten Tribes before their captivity. For[6] when the ten Tribes were captivated, a Priest or the captivity was sent back to *Bethel*, by order of the King of *Assyria*, to instruct the new inhabitants of *Samaria*, in *the manner of the God of the land*; and the *Samaritans* had the *Pentateuch* from this Priest, as containing the law or *manner of the God of the land*, which he was to teach them. For[7] they persevered in the religion which he taught them, joining with it the worship of their own Gods; and by persevering in what they had been taught, they preserved this book of their Law in the original character of the *Hebrews*, while the two Tribes, after their return from *Babylon*, changed the character to that of the *Chaldees*, which they had learned at *Babylon*.

And since the *Pentateuch* was received as the book of the Law, both by the two Tribes and by the ten Tribes, it follows that they received it before they became divided into two Kingdoms. For after the division, they received not laws from one another, but continued at variance. *Judah* could not reclaim *Israel* from

---

[5] 2 Chron. xv. 3, 12, 13, 16, 18.
[6] 2 Kings xvii. 27, 28, 32, 33.
[7] 2 Kings xvii. 34, 41.

the sin of *Jeroboam*, and *Israel* could not bring *Judah* to it. The *Pentateuch* therefore was the book of the Law in the days of *David* and *Solomon*. The affairs of the Tabernacle and Temple were ordered by *David* and *Solomon*, according to the Law of this book; and *David* in the 78th Psalm, admonishing the people to give ear to the Law of God, means the Law of this book. For in describing how their forefathers kept it not, he quotes many historical things out of the books of *Exodus* and *Numbers*.

The race of the Kings of *Edom*, before there reigned any King over *Israel*, is set down in the book of[8] *Genesis*; and therefore that book was not written entirely in the form now extant, before the reign of *Saul*. The writer set down the race of those Kings till his own time, and therefore wrote before *David* conquered *Edom*. The *Pentateuch* is composed of the Law and the history of God's people together; and the history hath been collected from several books, such as were the history of the Creation composed by *Moses*, *Gen.* ii. 4. the book of the generations of *Adam*, *Gen.* v. i. and the book of the wars of the Lord, *Num.* xxi. 14. This book of wars contained what was done at the Red-sea, and in the journeying of *Israel* thro' the Wilderness, and therefore was begun by *Moses*. And *Joshua* might carry it on to the conquest of *Canaan*. For *Joshua* wrote some things in the book of the Law of God, *Josh.* xxiv. 26 and therefore might write his own wars in the book of wars, those being the principal wars of God. These were publick books, and therefore not written without the authority of *Moses* and *Joshua*. And *Samuel* had leisure in the reign of *Saul*, to put them into the form of the books of *Moses* and *Joshua* now extant, inserting into the book of *Genesis*, the race of the Kings of *Edom*, until there reigned a King in *Israel*.

The book of the *Judges* is a continued history of the *Judges* down to the death of *Sampson*, and therefore was compiled after his death, out of the Acts of the *Judges*. Several things in this book are said to be done *when there was no King in* Israel, *Judg.* xvii. 6. xviii. 1. xix. 1. xxi. 25. and therefore this book was written after the beginning of the reign of *Saul*. When it was

---

[8] Gen. xxxvi. 31.

written, the *Jebusites* dwelt in *Jerusalem*, *Jud.* i. 21 and therefore it was written before the eighth year of *David*, 2 *Sam.* v. 8. and 1 *Chron.* xi. 6. The books of *Moses, Joshua,* and *Judges,* contain one continued history, down from the Creation to the death of *Sampson.* Where the *Pentateuch* ends, the book of *Joshua* begins; and where the book of *Joshua* ends, the book of *Judges* begins. Therefore all these books have been composed out of the writings of *Moses, Joshua,* and other records, by one and the same hand, after the beginning of the reign of *Saul,* and before the eighth year of *David.* And *Samuel* was a sacred writer, 1 *Sam.* x. 25. acquainted with the history of *Moses* and the *Judges,* 1 *Sam.* xii. 8, 9, 10, 11, 12. and had leisure in the reign of *Saul,* and sufficient authority to compose these books. He was a Prophet, and judged *Israel* all the days of his life, and was in the greatest esteem with the people; and the Law by which he was to judge the people was not to be published by less authority than his own, the Law-maker being not inferior to the judge. And the book of *Jasher,* which is quoted in the book of *Joshua, Josh.* x. 13. was in being at the death of *Saul,* 2 *Sam.* i. 18.

At the dedication of the Temple of *Solomon,* when the Ark was brought into the most holy place, there was nothing in it but the two tables, 1 *Kings* viii. 9. and therefore when the *Philistines* took the Ark, they took out of it the book of the Law, and the golden pot of Manna, and *Aaron*'s Rod. And this and other losses in the desolation of *Israel,* by the conquering *Philistines,* might give occasion to *Samuel,* after some respite from those enemies, to recollect the scattered writings of *Moses* and *Joshua,* and the records of the Patriarchs and Judges, and compose them in the form now extant.

The book of *Ruth* is a history of things done in the days of the *Judges,* and may be looked upon as an addition to the book of the *Judges,* written by the same author, and at the same time. For it was written after the birth of *David, Ruth* iv. 17, 22. and not long after, because the history of *Boaz* and *Ruth,* the great grandfather and great grandmother of *David,* and that of their contemporaries, could not well be remembered above two or three generations. And since this book derives the genealogy of *David* from *Boaz* and *Ruth,* and omits *David*'s elder brothers and his sons; it was written in honour of *David*, after he was anointed King by *Samuel*, and before he had children in *Hebron*, and by consequence in the reign of *Saul*. It proceeds not to the history of *David*, and therefore seems to have been written presently after he was anointed. They judge well therefore who ascribe to *Samuel* the books of *Joshua*, *Judges*, and *Ruth*.

Samuel is also reputed the author of the first book of *Samuel*, till the time of his death. The two books of *Samuel* cite no authors, and therefore seem to be originals. They begin with his genealogy, birth and education, and might be written partly in his lifetime by himself or his disciples the Prophets at *Naioth* in *Ramah*, 1 *Sam*. xix. 18, 19, 20. and partly after his death by the same disciples.

The books of the *Kings* cite other authors, as the book of the Acts of *Solomon*, the book of the *Chronicles* of the Kings of *Israel*, and the book of the *Chronicles* of the Kings of *Judah*. The books of the *Chronicles* cite the book of *Samuel* the Seer, the book of *Nathan* the Prophet, and the book of *Gad* the Seer, for the Acts of *David*; the book of *Nathan* the Prophet, the Prophecy of *Ahijah* the *Shilonite*, and the visions of *Iddo* the Seer, for the Acts of *Solomon*; the book of *Shemajah* the Prophet, and the book of *Iddo* the Seer concerning genealogies, for the Acts of *Rehoboam* and *Abijah*; the book of the Kings of *Judah* and *Israel* for the Acts of *Asa*, *Joash*, *Amaziah*, *Jotham*, *Ahaz*, *Hezekiah*, *Manasseh*, and *Josiah*; the book of *Hanani* the Seer, for the Acts of *Jehosaphat*; and the visions of *Isaiah* for the Acts of *Uzziah* and *Hezekiah*. These books were therefore collected out of the historical writings of the ancient Seers and Prophets. And because the books of the *Kings* and *Chronicles* quote one another, they were written at one and the same time. And this time was after the return from the *Babylonian* captivity, because they bring down the history of *Judah*, and the genealogies of the Kings of *Judah*, and of the High Priests, to that captivity. The book of *Ezra* was originally a part of the book of the *Chronicles*, and has been divided from it. For it begins with the two last verses of the books of *Chronicles*, and the first book of *Esdras* begins with the two last chapters thereof. *Ezra* was therefore the compiler of the books of *Kings* and *Chronicles*, and brought down the history to his own time. He was a ready Scribe in the Law of God; and for assisting him in this work *Nehemias* founded a library, and *gathered together the Acts of the Kings and the Prophets, and of* David, *and the Epistles of the Kings, concerning the holy gifts,* 2 *Maccab.* ii. 13. By the Acts of *David* I understand here the two books of *Samuel,* or at least the second book. Out of the Acts of the *Kings,* written from time to time by the Prophets, he composed the books of the Kings of *Judah* and *Israel,* the *Chronicles* of the Kings of *Judah,* and the *Chronicles* of the Kings of *Israel.* And in doing this he joined those Acts together, in due order of time, copying the very words of the authors, as is manifest from hence, that the books of the *Kings* and *Chronicles* frequently agree with one another in words for many sentences together. Where they agree in sense, there they agree in words also.

So the Prophecies of *Isaiah,* written at several times, he has collected into one body. And the like he did for those of *Jeremiah,* and the rest of the Prophets, down to the days of the second Temple. The book of *Jonah* is the history of *Jonah* written by another hand. The book of *Daniel* is a collection of papers written at several times. The six last chapters contain Prophecies written at several times by *Daniel* himself: the six first are a collection of historical papers written by others. The fourth chapter is a decree of *Nebuchadnezzar.* The first chapter was written after *Daniel*'s death: for the author saith, that *Daniel* continued to the first year of *Cyrus*; that is, to his first year over the *Persians* and *Medes,* and third year over *Babylon.* And, for the same reason, the fifth and sixth chapters were also written after his death. For they end with these words: *So this* Daniel *prospered in the reign of* Darius *and in the reign of* Cyrus *the* Persian. Yet these words might be added by the collector of the papers, whom I take to be *Ezra.*

The Psalms composed by *Moses, David,* and others, seem to have been also collected by *Ezra* into one volume. I reckon him the collector, because in this collection I meet with Psalms as late as the *Babylonian* captivity, but with none later.

After these things *Antiochus Epiphanes* spoiled the Temple, commanded the *Jews* to forsake the Law upon pain of death, and caused the sacred books to be burnt wherever they could be found: and in these troubles the book of the *Chronicles* of the Kings of *Israel* was entirely lost. But upon recovering from this oppression, *Judas Maccabæus* gathered together all those writings that were to be met with, 2 *Maccab.* ii. 14. and in reducing them into order, part of the Prophecies of *Isaiah*, or some other Prophet, have been added to the end of the Prophecies of *Zechariah*; and the book of *Ezra* has been separated from the book of *Chronicles*, and set together in two different orders; in one order in the book of *Ezra*, received into the Canon, and in another order in the first book of *Esdras*.

After the *Roman* captivity, the *Jews* for preserving their traditions, put them in writing in their *Talmud*, and for preserving their scriptures, agreed upon an Edition, and pointed it, and counted the letters of every sort in every book: and by preserving only this Edition, the antienter various lections, except what can be discovered by means of the *Septuagint* Version, are now lost; and such marginal notes, or other corruptions, as by the errors of the transcribers, before this Edition was made, had crept into the text, are now scarce to be corrected.

The *Jews* before the *Roman* captivity, distinguished the sacred books into the Law, the Prophets, and the *Hagiographa*, or holy writings; and read only the Law and the Prophets in their Synagogues. And Christ and his Apostles laid the stress of religion upon the Law and the Prophets, *Matt.* vii. 12. xxii. 4. *Luke* xvi. 16, 29, 31. xxiv. 44. *Acts* xxiv. 14. xxvi. 22. *Rom.* iii. 21. By the *Hagiographa* they meant the historical books called *Joshua, Judges, Ruth, Samuel, Kings, Chronicles, Ezra, Nehemiah,* and *Esther,* the book of *Job,* the *Psalms,* the books of *Solomon,* and the *Lamentations.* The Samaritans read only the *Pentateuch*: and when *Jehosaphat* sent men to teach in the cities, they had with them only the book of the Law; for the Prophecies now extant were not then written. And upon the return from the *Babylonian* captivity, *Ezra* read only the book of the Law to the people, from morning to noon on the first day of the seventh month; and from day to day in the feast of Tabernacles: for he had not yet collected the writings of the Prophets into the volume now extant; but instituted the reading of them after the collection was made. By reading the Law and the Prophets in the Synagogues, those books have been kept freer from corruption than the *Hagiographa.*

In the infancy of the nation of *Israel,* when God had given them a Law, and made a covenant with them to be their God if they would keep his commandments, he sent Prophets to reclaim them, as often as they revolted to the worship of other Gods: and upon their returning to him, they sometimes renewed the covenant which they had broken. These Prophets he continued to send, till the days of *Ezra:* but after their Prophecies were read in the Synagogues, those Prophecies were thought sufficient. For if the people would not hear *Moses* and the old Prophets, they would hear no new ones, no not *tho they should rise from the dead.* At length when a new truth was to be preached to the *Gentiles,* namely, *that Jesus was the Christ,* God sent new Prophets and Teachers: but after their writings were also received and read in the Synagogues of the Christians, Prophecy ceased a second time. We have *Moses,* the Prophets, and Apostles, and the words of Christ himself; and if we will not hear them, we shall be more inexcusable than the *Jews.* For the Prophets and Apostles have foretold, that as *Israel* often revolted and brake the covenant, and upon repentance renewed it; so there should be a falling away among the Christians, soon after the days of the Apostles; and that in the latter days God would destroy the impenitent revolters, and make a new covenant with his people. And the giving ear to the Prophets is a fundamental character of the true Church. For God has so ordered the Prophecies, that in the latter days *the wise may understand, but the wicked shall do wickedly, and none of the wicked shall understand,* Dan. xii. 9, 10. The authority of Emperors, Kings, and Princes, is human. The authority of Councils, Synods, Bishops, and Presbyters, is human. The authority of the Prophets is divine, and comprehends the sum of religion, reckoning *Moses* and the Apostles among the Prophets; and *if an Angel from Heaven preach any other gospel,* than what they have delivered, *let him be accursed.* Their writings contain the covenant between God and his people, with instructions for keeping this covenant; instances of God's judgments upon them that break it: and predictions of things to come. While the people of God keep the covenant, they continue to be his people: when they break it they cease to be his people or church, and become *the Synagogue of Satan, who say they are* Jews *and are not.* And no power on earth is authorized to alter this covenant.

The predictions of things to come relate to the state of the Church in all ages: and amongst the old Prophets, *Daniel* is most distinct in order of time, and easiest to be understood: and therefore in those things which relate to the last times, he must be made the key to the rest.

CHAP. II

Of the Prophetic Language

For understanding the Prophecies, we are, in the first place, to acquaint our-selves with the figurative language of the Prophets. This language is taken from the analogy between the world natural, and an empire or kingdom considered as a world politic.

Accordingly, the whole world natural consisting of heaven and earth, signifies the whole world politic, consisting of thrones and people, or so much of it as is considered in the Prophecy: and the things in that world signify the analogous things in this. For the heavens, and the things therein, signify thrones and dignities, and those who enjoy them; and the earth, with the things thereon, the inferior people; and the lowest parts of the earth, called *Hades* or Hell, the lowest or most miserable part of them. Whence ascending towards heaven, and descending to the earth, are put for rising and falling in power and honour: rising out of the earth, or waters, and falling into them, for the rising up to any dignity or dominion, out of the inferior state of the people, or falling down from the same into that inferior state; descending into the lower parts of the earth, for descending to a very low and unhappy estate; speaking with a faint voice out of the dust, for being in a weak and low condition; moving from one place to another, for translation from one office, dignity, or dominion, to another; great earthquakes, and the shaking of heaven and earth, for the shaking of kingdoms, so as to distract or overthrow them; the creating a new heaven and earth, and the passing away of an old one, or the beginning and end of the world, for the rise and ruin of the body politic signified thereby.

In the heavens, the Sun and Moon are, by interpreters of dreams, put for the persons of Kings and Queens; but in sacred

Prophecy, which regards not single persons, the Sun is put for the whole species and race of Kings, in the kingdom or kingdoms of the world politic, shining with regal power and glory; the Moon for the body of the common people, considered as the King's wife; the Stars for subordinate Princes and great men, or for Bishops and Rulers of the people of God, when the Sun is Christ; light for the glory, truth, and knowledge, wherewith great and good men shine and illuminate others; darkness for obscurity of condition, and for error, blindness and ignorance; darkning, smiting, or setting of the Sun, Moon, and Stars, for the ceasing of a kingdom, or for the desolation thereof, proportional to the darkness; darkning the Sun, turning the Moon into blood, and falling of the Stars, for the same; new Moons, for the return of a dispersed people into a body politic or ecclesiastic.

Fire and meteors refer to both heaven and earth, and signify as follows; burning any thing with fire, is put for the consuming thereof by war; a conflagration of the earth, or turning a country into a lake of fire, for the consumption of a kingdom by war; the being in a furnace, for the being in slavery under another nation; the ascending up of the smoke of any burning thing for ever and ever, for the continuation of a conquered people under the misery of perpetual subjection and slavery; the scorching heat of the sun, for vexatious wars, persecutions and troubles inflicted by the King; riding on the clouds, for reigning over much people; covering the sun with a cloud, or with smoke, for oppression of the King by the armies of an enemy; tempestuous winds, or the motion of clouds, for wars; thunder, or the voice of a cloud, for the voice of a multitude; a storm of thunder, lightning, hail, and overflowing rain, for a tempest of war descending from the heavens and clouds politic, on the heads of their enemies; rain, if not immoderate, and dew, and living water, for the graces and doctrines of the Spirit; and the defect of rain, for spiritual barrenness.

In the earth, the dry land and congregated waters, as a sea, a river, a flood, are put for the people of several regions, nations, and dominions; embittering of waters, for great affliction of the people by war and persecution; turning things into blood, for the mystical death of bodies politic, that is, for their dissolution; the overflowing of a sea or river, for the invasion of the earth politic, by the people of the waters; drying up of waters, for the conquest of their regions by the earth; fountains of waters for cities, the permanent heads of rivers politic; mountains and islands, for the cities of the earth and sea politic, with the territories and dominions belonging to those cities; dens and rocks of mountains, for the temples of cities; the hiding of men in those dens and rocks, for the shutting up of Idols in their temples; houses and ships, for families, assemblies, and towns, in the earth and sea politic; and a navy of ships of war, for an army of that kingdom that is signified by the sea.

Animals also and vegetables are put for the people of several regions and conditions; and particularly, trees, herbs, and land animals, for the people of the earth politic: flags, reeds, and fishes, for those of the waters politic; birds and insects, for those of the politic heaven and earth; a forest for a kingdom; and a wilderness for a desolate and thin people.

If the world politic, considered in prophecy, consists of many kingdoms, they are represented by as many parts of the world natural; as the noblest by the celestial frame, and then the Moon and Clouds are put for the common people; the less noble, by the earth, sea, and rivers, and by the animals or vegetables, or buildings therein; and then the greater and more powerful animals and taller trees, are put for Kings, Princes, and Nobles. And because the whole kingdom is the body politic of the King, therefore the Sun, or a Tree, or a Beast, or Bird, or a Man, whereby the King is represented, is put in a large signification for the whole kingdom; and several animals, as a Lion, a Bear, a Leopard, a Goat, according to their qualities, are put for several kingdoms and bodies politic; and sacrificing of beasts, for slaughtering and conquering of kingdoms; and friendship between beasts, for peace between kingdoms. Yet sometimes vegetables and animals are, by certain epithets or circumstances, extended to other significations; as a Tree, when called the *tree of life* or *of knowledge*; and a Beast, when called *the old serpent*, or worshipped.

When a Beast or Man is put for a kingdom, his parts and qualities are put for the analogous parts and qualities of the kingdom; as the head of a Beast, for the great men who precede and govern; the tail for the inferior people, who follow and are governed; the heads, if more than one, for the number of capital parts, or dynasties, or dominions in the kingdom, whether collateral or successive, with respect to the civil government; the horns on any head, for the number of kingdoms in that head, with respect to military power; seeing for understanding, and the eyes for men of understanding and policy, and in matters of religion for Επισκοποι, Bishops; speaking, for making laws; the mouth, for a law-giver, whether civil or sacred; the loudness of the voice, for might and power; the faintness thereof, for weakness; eating and drinking, for acquiring what is signified by the things eaten and drank; the hairs of a beast, or man, and the feathers of a bird, for people; the wings, for the number of kingdoms represented by the beast; the arm of a man, for his power, or for any people wherein his strength and power consists; his feet, for the lowest of the people, or for the latter end of the kingdom; the feet, nails, and teeth of beasts of prey, for armies and squadrons of armies; the bones, for strength, and for fortified places; the flesh, for riches and possessions; and the days of their acting, for years; and when a tree is put for a kingdom, its branches, leaves and fruit, signify as do the wings, feathers, and food of a bird or beast.

When a man is taken in a mystical sense, his qualities are often signified by his actions, and by the circumstances of things about him. So a Ruler is signified by his riding on a beast; a Warrior and Conqueror, by his having a sword and bow; a potent man, by his gigantic stature; a Judge, by weights and measures; a sentence of absolution, or condemnation, by a white or a black stone; a new dignity, by a new name; moral or civil qualifications, by garments; honour and glory, by splendid apparel; royal dignity, by purple or scarlet, or by a crown; righteousness, by white and clean robes; wickedness, by spotted and filthy garments; affliction, mourning, and humiliation, by clothing in sackcloth; dishonour, shame, and want of good works, by nakedness; error and misery, by drinking a cup of his or her wine that causeth it; propagating any religion for gain, by exercising traffick and merchandize with that people whose religion it is; worshipping or serving the false Gods of any nation, by committing adultery with their princes, or by worshipping them; a Council of a kingdom, by its image; idolatry, by blasphemy; overthrow in war, by a wound of man or beast; a durable plague of war, by a sore and pain; the affliction or persecution which a people suffers in labouring to bring forth a new kingdom, by the pain of a woman in labour to bring forth a man-child; the dissolution of a body politic or ecclesiastic, by the death of a man or beast; and the revival of a dissolved dominion, by the resurrection of the dead.

CHAP. III

Of the vision of the Image composed of four Metals.

T he Prophecies of *Daniel* are all of them related to one another, as if they were but several parts of one general Prophecy, given at several times. The first is the easiest to be understood, and every following Prophecy adds something new to the former. The first was given in a dream to *Nebuchadnezzar*, King of *Babylon*, in the second year of his reign; but the King forgetting his dream, it was given again to *Daniel* in a dream, and by him revealed to the King. And thereby, *Daniel* presently became famous for wisdom, and revealing of secrets: insomuch that *Ezekiel* his contemporary, in the nineteenth year of *Nebuchadnezzar*, spake thus of him to the King of *Tyre: Behold*, saith he, *thou art wiser than* Daniel, *there is no secret that they can hide from thee*, Ezek. xxviii. 3. And the same *Ezekiel*, in another place, joins *Daniel* with *Noah* and *Job*, as most high in the favour of God, *Ezek.* xiv. 14, 16, 18, 20. And in the last year of *Belshazzar*, the Queen-mother said of him to the King: *Behold there is a man in thy kingdom, in whom is the spirit of the holy gods; and in the days of thy father, light and understanding and wisdom, like the wisdom of the gods, was found in him; whom the king* Nebuchadnezzar *thy father, the king, I say, thy father made master of the magicians, astrologers,* Chaldeans *and soothsayers: forasmuch as an excellent spirit, and knowledge, and understanding, interpreting of dreams, and shewing of hard sentences, and dissolving of doubts, were found in the same* Daniel, *whom the king named* Belteshazzar, Dan. v. 11, 12. *Daniel* was in the greatest credit amongst the *Jews*, till the reign of the *Roman* Emperor *Hadrian*: and to reject his Prophecies, is to reject the Christian religion. For this religion is founded upon his Prophecy concerning the *Messiah*.

Now in this vision of the Image composed of four Metals, the foundation of all *Daniel's* Prophecies is laid. It represents a body of four great nations, which should reign over the earth successively, *viz.* the people of *Babylonia*, the *Persians*, the *Greeks*, and the *Romans*. And by a stone cut out without hands, which fell upon the feet of the Image, and brake all the four Metals to pieces, and *became a great mountain, and filled the whole earth*; it further represents that a new kingdom should arise, after the four, and conquer all those nations, and grow very great, and last to the end of all ages.

The head of the Image was of gold, and signifies the nations of *Babylonia*, who reigned first, as *Daniel* himself interprets. *Thou art this head of gold*, saith he to *Nebuchadnezzar*. These nations reigned till *Cyrus* conquered *Babylon*, and within a few months after that conquest revolted to the *Persians*, and set them up above the *Medes*. The breast and arms of the Image were of silver, and represent the *Persians* who reigned next. The belly and thighs of the Image were of brass, and represent the *Greeks*, who, under the dominion of *Alexander* the great, conquered the *Persians*, and reigned next after them. The legs were of iron, and represent the *Romans* who reigned next after the *Greeks*, and began to conquer them in the eighth year of *Antiochus Epiphanes*. For in that year they conquered *Perseus* King of *Macedon*, the fundamental kingdom of the *Greeks*; and from thence forward grew into a mighty empire, and reigned with great power till the days of *Theodosius* the great. Then by the incursion of many northern nations, they break into many smaller kingdoms, which are represented by the feet and toes of the Image, composed part of iron, and part of clay. For then, saith *Daniel*,[9] *the kingdom shall be divided, and there shall be in it of the strength of iron, but they shall not cleave one to another.*

And in the days of these Kings, saith *Daniel, shall the God of heaven set up a kingdom which shall never be destroyed: and the kingdom shall not be left to other people; but it shall break in pieces, and consume all these kingdoms, and it shall stand for ever. Forasmuch as thou sawest that the stone was cut out of the*

---

[9] Chap. ii. 41, &c.

mountains without hands, and that it brake in pieces the iron, the brass, the clay, the silver and the gold.

CHAP. IV

Of the vision of the four Beasts

I n the next vision, which is of the four Beasts, the Prophecy of the four Empires is repeated, with several new additions; such as are the two wings of the Lion, the three ribs in the mouth of the Bear, the four wings and four heads of the Leopard, the eleven horns of the fourth Beast, and the son of man coming in the clouds of Heaven, to the Antient of Days sitting in judgment.

The first Beast was like a lion, and had eagle's wings, to denote the kingdoms of *Babylonia* and *Media*, which overthrew the *Assyrian* Empire, and divided it between them, and thereby became considerable, and grew into great Empires. In the former Prophecy, the Empire of *Babylonia* was represented by the head of gold; in this both Empires are represented together by the two wings of the lion. *And I beheld,* saith[10] *Daniel, till the wings thereof were pluckt, and it was lifted up from the earth, and made to stand upon the feet as a man, and a man's heart was given to it*; that is, till it was humbled and subdued, and made to know its human state.

The second Beast was like a bear, and represents the Empire which reigned next after the *Babylonians*, that is, the Empire of the *Persians*. *Thy kingdom is divided*, or broken, saith *Daniel* to the last King of *Babylon, and given to the* Medes *and* Persians, *Dan.* v. 28. This Beast *raised itself up on one side*; the *Persians* being under the *Medes* at the fall of *Babylon*, but presently rising up above them.[11] *And it had three ribs in the mouth of it, between the teeth of it*, to signify the kingdoms of *Sardes, Babylon,* and *Egypt*, which were conquered by it, but did not belong to its

---

[10] Chap. vii. 4.
[11] Chap. vii. 5.

proper body. And it devoured much flesh, the riches of those three kingdoms.

The third Beast was the kingdom which succeeded the *Persian*; and this was the empire of the *Greeks, Dan.* viii. 6, 7, 20, 21. It was *like a Leopard*, to signify its fierceness; and had four heads and four wings, to signify that it should become divided into four kingdoms, *Dan.* viii 22. for it continued in a monarchical form during the reign of *Alexander* the great, and his brother *Aridæus*, and young sons *Alexander* and *Hercules*; and then brake into four kingdoms, by the governors of provinces putting crowns on their own heads, and by mutual consent reigning over their provinces. *Cassander* reigned over *Macedon*, *Greece*, and *Epirus*; *Lysimachus* over *Thrace* and *Bithynia*; *Ptolemy* over *Egypt*, *Lybia*, *Arabia*, *Cœlosyria*, and *Palestine*; and *Seleucus* over *Syria*.

The fourth Beast was the empire which succeeded that of the *Greeks*, and this was the *Roman*. This beast was exceeding dreadful and terrible, and had great iron teeth, and devoured and brake in pieces, and stamped the residue with its feet; and such was the *Roman* empire. It was larger, stronger, and more formidable and lasting than any of the former. It conquered the kingdom of *Macedon*, with *Illyricum* and *Epirus*, in the eighth year of *Antiochus Epiphanes, Anno Nabonass..* 580; and inherited that of *Pergamus, Anno Nabonass.* 615; and conquered that of *Syria, Anno Nabonass.* 679, and that of *Egypt, Anno Nabonass.* 718. And by these and other conquests it became greater and more terrible than any of the three former Beasts. This Empire continued in its greatness till the reign of *Theodosius* the great; and then brake into ten kingdoms, represented by the ten horns of this Beast; and continued in a broken form, till the Antient of days sat in a throne like fiery flame, and *the judgment was set, and the books were opened, and the Beast was slain and his body destroyed, and given to the burning flames; and one like the son of man came with the clouds of heaven, and came to the Antient of days*[12], and received dominion over all nations, and judgment

---

[12] Chap. vii. 13.

was given to the saints of the most high, and the time came that they possessed the kingdom.

I beheld, saith[13] *Daniel, till the Beast was slain, and his body destroyed, and given to the burning flames. As concerning the rest of the Beasts, they had their dominion taken away: yet their lives were prolonged for a season and a time.* And therefore all the four Beasts are still alive, tho the dominion of the three first be taken away. The nations of *Chaldea* and *Assyria* are still the first Beast. Those of *Media* and *Persia* are still the second Beast. Those of *Macedon, Greece* and *Thrace, Asia* minor, *Syria* and *Egypt,* are still the third. And those of *Europe,* on this side *Greece,* are still the fourth. Seeing therefore the body of the third Beast is confined to the nations on this side the river *Euphrates,* and the body of the fourth Beast is confined to the nations on this side *Greece;* we are to look for all the four heads of the third Beast, among the nations on this side of the river *Euphrates;* and for all the eleven horns of the fourth Beast, among the nations on this side of *Greece.* And therefore, at the breaking of the *Greek* empire into four kingdoms of the *Greeks,* we include no part of the *Chaldeans, Medes* and *Persians* in those kingdoms, because they belonged to the bodies of the two first Beasts. Nor do we reckon the *Greek* empire seated at *Constantinople,* among the horns of the fourth Beast, because it belonged to the body of the third.

---

[13] Chap. vii. 11, 12.

CHAP. V

Of the Kingdoms represented by the feet of the
Image composed of iron and clay.

*D*acia was a large country bounded on the south by the *Danube*, on the east by the *Euxine* sea, on the north by the river *Neister* and the mountain *Crapac*, and on the west by the river *Tibesis*, or *Teys*, which runs southward into the *Danube* a little above *Belgrade*. It comprehended the countries now called *Transylvania*, *Moldavia*, and *Wallachia*, and the eastern part of the upper *Hungary*. Its antient inhabitants were called *Getæ* by the *Greeks*, *Daci* by the *Latins*, and *Goths* by themselves. *Alexander* the great attacked them, and *Trajan* conquered them, and reduced their country into a Province of the *Roman* Empire: and thereby the propagation of the Gospel among them was much promoted. They were composed of several *Gothic* nations, called *Ostrogoths*, *Visigoths*, *Vandals*, *Gepides*, *Lombards*, *Burgundians*, *Alans*, &c. who all agreed in their manners, and spake the same language, as *Procopius* represents. While they lived under the *Romans*, the *Goths* or *Ostrogoths* were seated in the eastern parts of *Dacia*, the *Vandals* in the western part upon the river *Teys*, where the rivers *Maresh* and *Keresh* run into it. The *Visigoths* were between them. The *Gepides*, according to *Jornandes*, were upon the *Vistula*. The *Burgundians*, a *Vandalic* nation, were between the *Vistula* and the southern fountain of the *Boristhenes*, at some distance from the mountain *Crapac* northwards, where *Ptolemy* places them, by the names of *Phrugundiones* and *Burgiones*[14]. The *Alans*, another *Gothic* nation, were between the northern fountain of the *Boristhenes* and the mouth of the river *Tanais*, where *Ptolemy*

---

[14] Procop. l. 1. de Bello Vandalico.

placeth the mountain *Alanus*, and western side of the *Palus Mœotis*.

These nations continued under the dominion of the *Romans* till the second year of the Emperor *Philip*, and then for want of their military pay began to revolt; the *Ostrogoths* setting up a kingdom, which, under their Kings *Ostrogotha, Cniva, Araric, Geperic,* and *Hermanaric,* increased till the year of Christ 376; and then by an incursion of the *Huns* from beyond the *Tanais,* and the death of *Hermanaric,* brake into several smaller kingdoms. *Hunnimund,* the son of *Hermanaric,* became King over the *Ostrogoths; Fridigern* over the *Visigoths; Winithar,* or *Vinithar,* over a part of the *Goths* called *Gruthungi* by *Ammian, Gothunni* by *Claudian,* and *Sarmatæ* and *Scythians* by others: *Athanaric* reign'd over another part of the *Goths* in *Dacia,* called *Thervingi; Box* over the *Antes* in *Sarmatia;* and the *Gepides* had also their King. The *Vandals* fled over the *Danube* from *Geberic* in the latter end of the reign of *Constantine* the great, and had seats granted them in *Pannonia* by that Emperor, where they lived quietly forty years, *viz.* till the year 377, when several *Gothic* nations flying from the *Hunns* came over the *Danube,* and had seats granted them in *Mæsia* and *Thrace* by the *Greek* Emperor *Valens.* But the next year they revolted, called in some *Goths, Alans* and *Hunns,* from beyond the *Danube,* and routed the *Roman* army, slew the Emperor *Valens,* and spread themselves into *Greece* and *Pannonia* as far as the *Alps.* In the years 379 and 380 they were checkt by the arms of the Emperors *Gratian* and *Theodosius,* and made a submissive peace; the *Visigoths* and *Thervingi* returned to their seats in *Mæsia* and *Thrace,* the *Hunns* retired over the *Danube,* and the *Alans* and *Gruthingi* obtained seats in *Pannonia.*

About the year 373, or 374, the *Burgundians* rose from their seats upon the *Vistula,* with an army of eighty thousand men to invade *Gallia;* and being opposed, seated themselves upon the northern side of the *Rhine* over against *Mentz.* In the year 358, a body of the *Salian Franks,* with their King, coming from the river *Sala,* were received into the Empire by the Emperor *Julian,* and seated in *Gallia* between *Brabant* and the *Rhine:* and their King *Mellobaudes* was made *Comes domesticorum,* by the Emperor

Gratian. Richomer, another noble *Salian Frank,* was made *Comes domesticorum,* and *Magister utriusque Militiæ,* by *Theodosius*; and A.C. 384, was Consul with *Clearchus.* He was a great favourite of *Theodosius,* and accompanied him in his wars against *Eugenius,* but died in the expedition, and left a son called *Theudomir,* who afterwards became King of the *Salian Franks* in *Brabant.* In the time of this war some *Franks* from beyond the *Rhine* invaded *Gallia* under the conduct of *Genobald, Marcomir* and *Suno,* but were repulsed by *Stilico*; and *Marcomir* being slain, was succeeded in *Germany* by his son *Pharamond.*

While these nations remained quiet within the Empire, subject to the *Romans,* many others continued so beyond the *Danube* till the death of the Emperor *Theodosius,* and then rose up in arms. For *Paulus Diaconus* in his *Historia Miscell. lib.* xiv. speaking of the times next after the death of this Emperor, tells us: *Eodem tempore erant Gothi & aliæ gentes maximæ trans Danubium habitantes: ex quibus rationabiliores quatuor sunt, Gothi scilicet, Huisogothi, Gepides & Vandali; & nomen tantum & nihil aliud mutantes. Isti sub Arcadia & Honorio Danubium transeuntes, locati sunt in terra Romanorum: & Gepides quidem, ex quibus postea divisi sunt Longobardi & Avares, villas, quæ sunt circa Singidonum & Sirmium, habitavere:* and *Procopius* in the beginning of his *Historia Vandalica* writes to the same purpose. Hitherto the *Western Empire* continued entire, but now brake into many kingdoms.

Theodosius died A.C. 395; and then the *Visigoths,* under the conduct of *Alaric* the successor of *Fridigern,* rose from their seats in *Thrace* and wasted *Macedon, Thessaly, Achaia, Peloponnesus,* and *Epirus,* with fire and sword for five years together; when turning westward, they invaded *Dalmatia, Illyricum* and *Pannonia*; and from thence went into *Italy* A.C. 402; and the next year were so beaten at *Pollentia* and *Verona,* by *Stilico* the commander of the forces of the *Western Empire,* that *Claudian* calls the remainder of the forces of *Alaric, tanta ex gente reliquias breves,* and *Prudentius, Gentem deletam.* Thereupon *Alaric* made peace with the Emperor, being so far humbled, that *Orosius* saith, he did, *pro pace optima & quibuscunque sedibus suppliciter & simpliciter orare.* This peace was ratified by mutual hostages; *Ætius* was sent hostage to *Alaric*; and *Alaric* continued a free Prince in the seats now granted to him.

When *Alaric* took up arms, the nations beyond the *Danube* began to be in motion; and the next winter, between A.C. 395 and 396, a great body of *Hunns, Alans, Ostrogoths, Gepides,* and other northern nations, came over the frozen *Danube*, being invited by *Rufinus*: when their brethren, who had obtained seats within the Empire, took up arms also. *Jerome* calls this great multitude, *Hunns, Alans, Vandals, Goths, Sarmatians, Quades,* and *Marcomans*; and saith, that they invaded all places between *Constantinople* and the *Julian Alps*, wasting *Scythia, Thrace, Macedon, Dardania, Dacia, Thessaly, Achaia, Epirus, Dalmatia,* and all *Pannonia*. The *Suevians* also invaded *Rhœtia*: for when *Alaric* ravaged *Pannonia*, the *Romans* were defending *Rhœtia*; which gave *Alaric* an opportunity of invading *Italy*, as *Claudian* thus mentions.

> *Non nisi perfidiâ nacti penetrabile tempus,*
> *Irrupere Getæ, nostras dum Rhœtia vires*
> *Occupat, atque alio desudant Marte cohortes.*

And when *Alaric* went from those parts into *Italy*, some other barbarous nations invaded *Noricum* and *Vindelicia*, as the same Poet *Claudian* thus writes:

> *—Jam fœdera gentes*
> *Exuerant, Latiique auditâ clade feroces*
> *Vendelicos saltus & Norica rura tenebant.*

This was in the years 402 and 403. And among these nations I reckon the *Suevians, Quades,* and *Marcomans*; for they were all in arms at this time. The *Quades* and *Marcomans* were *Suevian* nations; and they and the *Suevians* came originally from *Bohemia*, and the river *Suevus* or *Sprake* in *Lusatia*; and were now united under one common King called *Ermeric*, who soon after led them into *Gallia*. The *Vandals* and *Alans* might also about this time extend themselves into *Noricum*. *Uldin* also with a great body of *Hunns* passed the *Danube* about the time of *Chrysostom*'s banishment, that is, A.C. 404, and wasted *Thrace* and *Mœsia*. *Radagaisus*, King of the *Gruthunni* and succesor of *Winithar*, inviting over more barbarians from beyond the *Danube*, invaded *Italy* with an army of above two hundred thousand *Goths*; and within a year or two, A.C. 405 or 406., was overcome by *Stilico*, and perished with his army. In this war *Stilico* was assisted with a great body of *Hunns* and *Ostrogoths*, under the conduct of *Uldin* and *Sarus*, who were hired by the Emperor *Honorius*. In all this confusion it was necessary for the *Lombards* in *Pannonia* to arm themselves in their own defence, and assert their liberty, the *Romans* being no longer able to protect them.

And now *Stilico* purposing to make himself Emperor, procured a military prefecture for *Alaric*, and sent him into the *East* in the service of *Honorius* the *Western* Emperor, committing some *Roman* troops to his conduct to strengthen his army of *Goths*, and promising to follow soon after with his own army. His pretence was to recover some regions of *Illyricum*, which the *Eastern* Emperor was accused to detain injuriously from the *Western*; but his secret design was to make himself Emperor, by the assistance of the *Vandals* and their allies: for he himself was a *Vandal*. For facilitating this design, he invited a great body of the barbarous nations to invade the *Western Empire*, while he and *Alaric* invaded the *Eastern*. And these nations under their several Kings, the *Vandals* under *Godegisilus*, the *Alans* in two bodies, the one under *Goar*, the other under *Resplendial*, and the *Suevians*, *Quades*, and *Marcomans*, under *Ermeric*, marched thro' *Rhœtia* to the side of the *Rhine*, leaving their seats in *Pannonia* to the *Hunns* and *Ostrogoths*, and joined the *Burgundians* under *Gundicar*, and ruffled the *Franks* in their further march. On the last of *December* A.C. 406, they passed the *Rhine* at *Ments*, and spread themselves into *Germania prima* and the adjacent regions; and amongst other actions the *Vandals* took *Triers*. Then they advanced into *Belgium*, and began to waste that country. Whereupon the *Salian Franks* in *Brabant* took up arms, and under the conduct of *Theudomir*, the son of *Ricimer*, or *Richomer*, abovementioned, made so stout a resistance, that they slew almost twenty thousand of the *Vandals*, with their King *Godegesilus*, in battel; the rest escaping only by a party of *Resplendial's Alans* which came timely to their assistance.

Then the *British* soldiers, alarm'd by the rumour of these things, revolted, and set up Tyrants there; first *Marcus*, whom they slew presently; then *Gratian*, whom they slew within four months; and lastly *Constantine*, under whom they invaded *Gallia* A.C. 408, being favoured by *Goar* and *Gundicar*. And *Constantine* having possessed a good part of *Gallia*, created his son *Constans Cæsar*, and sent him into *Spain* to order his affairs there, A.C. 409.

In the mean time *Resplendial*, seeing the aforesaid disaster of the *Vandals*, and that *Goar* was gone over to the *Romans*, led his army from the *Rhine*; and, together with the *Suevians* and residue of the *Vandals*, went towards *Spain*; the *Franks* in the mean time prosecuting their victory so far as to retake *Triers*, which after they had plundered they left to the *Romans*. The *Barbarians* were at first stopt by the *Pyrenean* mountains, which made them spread themselves into *Aquitain*: but the next year they had the passage betrayed by some soldiers of *Constans*; and entring *Spain* 4 Kal. *Octob.* A.C. 409, they conquered every one what he could; and at length, A.C. 411, divided their conquests by lot; the *Vandals* obtained *Bœtica*, and part of *Gallæcia*; the *Suevians* the rest of *Gallæcia*; and the *Alans Lusitania* and the *Carthaginian* Province: the Emperor for the sake of peace confirming them in those seats by grant A.C. 413.

The *Roman Franks* abovementioned, having made *Theudomir* their King, began strait after their conquest of the *Vandals* to invade their neighbours also. The first they set upon were the *Gauls* of *Brabant*[15] but meeting with notable resistance, they desired their alliance: and so those *Gauls* fell off from the *Romans*, and made an intimate league with the *Franks* to be as one people, marrying with one another, and conforming to one another's manners, till they became one without distinction. Thus by the access of these *Gauls*, and of the foreign *Franks* also, who

---

[15] Galli Arborici: *whence the region was named* Arboricbant, *and by contraction* Brabant.

afterwards came over the *Rhine*, the *Salian* kingdom soon grew very great and powerful.

Stilico's expedition against the *Greek* Emperor was stopt by the order of *Honorius*; and then *Alaric* came out of *Epirus* into *Noricum*, and requested a sum of money for his service. The Senate were inclined to deny him, but by *Stilico's* mediation granted it. But after some time *Stilico* being accused of a traiterous conspiracy with *Alaric*, and slain 10 Kal. *Sept.* A.C. 408; *Alaric* was thereby disappointed of his money, and reputed an enemy to the Empire; he then broke strait into *Italy* with the army he brought out of *Epirus*, and sent to his brother *Adolphus* to follow him with what forces he had in *Pannonia*, which were not great, but yet not to be despised. Thereupon *Honorius* fearing to be shut up in *Rome*, retired to *Ravenna* in *October* A.C. 408. And from that time *Ravenna* continued to be the seat of the *Western* Emperors. In those days the *Hunns* also invaded *Pannonia*; and seizing the deserted seats of the *Vandals*, *Alans*, and *Goths*, founded a new kingdom there. *Alaric* advancing to *Rome* besieged it, and 9 Kal. *Sept.* A.C. 410 took it: and afterwards attempting to pass into *Africa*, was shipwrackt. After which *Honorius* made peace with him, and got up an army to send against the Tyrant *Constantine*.

At the same time *Gerontius*, one of *Constantine's* captains, revolted from him, and set up *Maximus* Emperor in *Spain*. Whereupon *Constantine* sent *Edobec*, another of his captains, to draw to his assistance, the *Barbarians* under *Goar* and *Gundicar* in *Gallia*, and supplies of *Franks* and *Alemans* from beyond the *Rhine*; and committed the custody of *Vienne* in *Gallia Narbonensis* to his son *Constans*. *Gerontius* advancing, first slew *Constans* at *Vienne*, and then began to besiege *Constantine* at *Arles*. But *Honorius* at the same time sending *Constantius* with an army on the same errand, *Gerontius* fled, and *Constantius* continued the siege, strengthned by the access of the greatest part of the soldiers of *Gerontius*. After four months siege, *Edobec* having procured succours, the *Barbarian* Kings at *Ments*, *Goar* and *Gundicar*, constitute *Jovinus* Emperor, and together with him set forward to relieve *Arles*. At their approach *Constantius* retired. They pursued, and he beat them by surprize; but not prosecuting his victory, the *Barbarians* soon recovered themselves; yet not so as to hinder the fall of the tyrants *Constantine*, *Jovinus* and *Maximus*. *Britain* could not be recovered to the Empire, but remained ever after a distinct kingdom.

The next year, A.C. 412, the *Visigoths* being beaten in *Italy*, had *Aquitain* granted them to retire into: and they invaded it with much violence, causing the *Alans* and *Burgundians* to retreat, who were then depopulating of it. At the same time the *Burgundians* were brought to peace; and the Emperor granted them for inheritance a region upon the *Rhine* which they had invaded: and the same, I presume, he did with the *Alans*. But the *Franks* not long after retaking and burning *Triers*, *Castinus*, A.C. 415, was sent against them with an army, who routed them and slew *Theudomir* their King This was the second taking of *Triers* by the *Franks*. It was therefore taken four times, once by the *Vandals* and thrice by the *Franks*. *Theudomir* was succeeded by *Pharamond*, the Prince or King of the *Salian Franks* in *Germany*. From thence he brought new forces, reigned over the whole, and had seats granted to his people within the Empire near the *Rhine*.

And now the *Barbarians* were all quieted, and settled in several kingdoms within the Empire, not only by conquest, but also by the grants of the Emperor *Honorius*. For *Rutilius* in his *Itinerary*, written in Autumn, *Anno Urbis* 1169, that is, according to *Varro*'s computation then in use, A.C. 416, thus laments the wasted fields:

> *Illa quidem longis nimium deformia bellis*;
> And then adds,
> *Jam tempus laceris post longa incendia fundis*
> *Vel pastorales ædificare casas.*
> And a little after,
> *Æternum tibi Rhenus aret.*

And *Orosius* in the end of his history, which was finished A.C. 417, represents now a general pacification of the barbarous nations by the words *comprimere, coangustare, addicere gentes immanissimas*; terming them *imperio addictas*, because they had obtained seats in the Empire by league and compact; and *coangustatas*, because they did no longer invade all regions at pleasure, but by the same compact remained quiet in the seats then granted them. And these are the kingdoms, of which the feet of the Image were henceforward composed, and which are represented by iron and clay intermixed, which did not stick one to another, and were of different strength.

CHAP. VI

Of the ten Kingdoms represented by the ten horns
of the fourth Beast.

N
ow by the wars above described the *Western* Empire of the *Romans*, about the time that *Rome* was besieged and taken by the *Goths*, became broken into the following ten kingdoms.

1. The kingdom of the *Vandals* and *Alans* in *Spain* and *Africa*.
2. The kingdom of the *Suevians* in *Spain*.
3. The kingdom of the *Visigoths*.
4. The kingdom of the *Alans* in *Gallia*.
5. The kingdom of the *Burgundians*.
6. The kingdom of the *Franks*.
7. The kingdom of the *Britains*.
8. The kingdom of the *Hunns*.
9. The kingdom of the *Lombards*.
10. The kingdom of *Ravenna*.

Seven of these kingdoms are thus mentioned by *Sigonius*. [1]*Honorio regnante, in Pannoniam* [2]*Hunni, in Hispaniam* [3]*Vandali,* [4]*Alani,* [5]*Suevi* & [6]*Gothi, in Galliam* [4]*Alani* [7]*Burgundiones* & [6]*Gothi, certis sedibus permissis, accepti.* Add the *Franks, Britains,* and *Lombards,* and you have the ten: for these arose about the same time with the seven. But let us view them severally.

1. The Kings of the *Vandals* were, A.C. 407 *Godegesilus,* 407 *Gunderic,* 426 *Geiseric,* 477 *Hunneric,* 484 *Gundemund,* 496 *Thrasamund,* 513 *Geiseric,* 530 *Gelimer. Godegesilus* led them into *Gallia* A.C. 406, *Gunderic* into *Spain* A.C. 409, *Geiseric* into *Africa* A.C. 427; and *Gelimer* was conquered by *Belisarius* A.C. 533. Their kingdom lasted in *Gallia, Spain* and *Africa*

together 126 years; and in *Africa* they were very potent. The *Alans* had only two Kings of their own in *Spain*, *Resplendial*, and *Ataces*, *Utacus* or *Othacar*. Under *Resplendial* they went into *France* A.C. 407, and into *Spain* A.C. 409. *Ataces* was slain with almost all his army by *Vallia* King of the *Visigoths* A.C. 419. And then the remainder of these *Alans* subjected themselves to *Gunderic* King of the *Vandals* in *Bœtica*, and went afterwards with them into *Africa*, as I learn out of *Procopius*. Whence the Kings of the *Vandals* styled themselves Kings of the *Vandals* and *Alans*; as may be seen in the Edict of *Hunneric* recited by *Victor* in his *Vandalic* persecution. In conjunction with the *Chatti*, these *Alans* gave the name of *Cathalaunia*, or *Catth-Alania*, to the Province which is still so called. These *Alans* had also *Gepides* among them; and therefore the *Gepides* came into *Pannonia* before the *Alans* left it. There they became subject to the *Hunns* till the death of *Attila* A.C. 454, and at length were conquered by the *Ostrogoths*.

2. The Kings of the *Suevians* were, A.C. 407 *Ermeric*, 458 *Rechila*, 448 *Rechiarius*, 458 *Maldra*, 460 *Frumarius*, 463 *Regismund*. And after some other Kings who are unknown, reigned A.C. 558 *Theudomir*, 568 *Miro*, 582 *Euboricus*, and 583 *Andeca*. This kingdom, after it had been once seated in *Spain*, remained always in *Gallœcia* and *Lusitania*. *Ermeric* after the fall of the *Alan* kingdom, enlarged it into all *Gallœcia*, forcing the *Vandals* to retire into *Bœtica* and the *Carthaginian* Province. This kingdom lasted 177 years according to *Isidorus*, and then was subdued by *Leovigildus* King of the *Visigoths*, and made a Province of his kingdom A.C. 585.

3. The Kings of the *Visigoths* were, A.C. 400 *Alaric*, 410 *Athaulphus*, 415 *Sergeric* and *Vallia*, 419 *Theoderic*, 451 *Thorismund*, 452 *Theoderic*, 465 *Euric*, 482 *Alaric*, 505 *Gensalaric*, 526 *Amalaric*, 531 *Theudius*, 548 *Theudisclus*, &c. I date this kingdom from the time that *Alaric* left *Thrace* and *Greece* to invade the *Western Empire*. In the end of the reign of *Athaulphus* the *Goths* were humbled by the *Romans*, and attempted to pass out of *France* into *Spain*. *Sergeric* reigned but a few days. In the beginning of *Vallia*'s reign they assaulted the *Romans* afresh, but were again repulsed, and then made peace on

this condition, that they should on the behalf of the Empire invade the *Barbarian* kingdoms in *Spain*: and this they did, together with the *Romans*, in the years 417 and 418, overthrowing the *Alans* and part of the *Vandals*. Then they received *Aquitain* of the Emperor by a full donation, leaving their conquests in *Spain* to the Emperor: and thereby the seats of the conquered *Alans* came into the hands of the *Romans*. In the year 455, *Theoderic*, assisted by the *Burgundians*, invaded *Spain*, which was then almost all subject to the *Suevians*, and took a part of it from them. A.C. 506, the *Goths* were driven out of *Gallia* by the *Franks*. A.C. 585, they conquered the *Suevian* kingdom, and became Lords of all *Spain*. A.C. 713, the *Saracens* invaded them, but in time they recovered their dominions, and have reigned in *Spain* ever since.

4. The Kings of the *Alans* in *Gallia* were *Goar*, *Sambida*, *Eocharic*, *Sangibanus*, *Beurgus*, &c. Under *Goar* they invaded *Gallia* A.C. 407, and had seats given them near the *Rhine*, A.C. 412. Under *Sambida*, whom *Bucher* makes the successor, if not the son of *Goar*, they had the territories of *Valence* given them by *Ætius* the Emperor's General, A.C. 440. Under *Eocharic* they conquered a region of the rebelling *Galli Arborici*, given them also by *Ætius*. This region was from them named *Alenconium*, *quasi Alanorum conventus*. Under *Sangibanus* they were invaded, and their regal city *Orleans* was besieged by *Attila* King of the *Hunns*, with a vast army of 500000 men. *Ætius* and the *Barbarian* Kings of *Gallia* came to raise the siege, and beat the *Hunns* in a very memorable battle, A.C. 451, *in campis Catalaunicis*, so called from these *Alans* mixt with the *Chatti*. The region is now called *Campania* or *Champagne*. In that battle were slain on both sides 162000 men. A year or two after, *Attila* returned with an immense army to conquer this kingdom, but was again beaten by them and the *Visigoths* together in a battle of three days continuance, with a slaughter almost as great as the former. Under *Beurgus*, or *Biorgor*, they infested *Gallia* round about, till the reign of *Maximus* the Emperor; and then they passed the *Alps* in winter, and came into *Liguria*, but were there beaten, and *Beurgus* slain, by *Ricimer* commander of the Emperor's forces, A.C. 464. Afterwards they were again beaten,

by the joint force of *Odoacer* King of *Italy* and *Childeric* King of the *Franks*, about the year 480, and again by *Theudobert* King of the *Austrian Franks* about the year 511.

5. The Kings of the *Burgundians* were, A.C. 407 *Gundicar*, 436 *Gundioc*, 467 *Bilimer*, 473 *Gundobaldus* with his brothers, 510 *Sigismund*, 517 *Godomarus*. Under *Gundicar* they invaded *Gallia* A.C. 407, and had seats given them by the Emperor near the *Rhine* in *Gallia Belgica*, A.C. 412. They had *Saxons* among them, and were now so potent, that *Orosius* A.C. 417 wrote of them: '*Burgundionum esse prævalidam manum, Galliæ hodieque testes sunt, in quibus præsumpta possessione consistunt.* About the year 435 they received great overthrows by *Ætius*, and soon after by the *Hunns*: but five years after had *Savoy* granted them to be shared with the inhabitants; and from that time became again a potent kingdom, being bounded by the river *Rhodanus*, but afterwards extending much further into the heart of *Gallia*. *Gundobald* conquered the regions about the rivers *Araris* and *Rhodanus*, with the territories of *Marseilles*; and invading *Italy* in the time of the Emperor *Glycerius*, conquered all his brethren. *Godomarus* made *Orleans* his royal seat: whence the kingdom was called *Regnum Aurelianorum*. He was conquered by *Clotharius* and *Childebert*, Kings of the *Franks*, A.C. 526. From thenceforward this kingdom was sometimes united to the kingdom of the *Franks*, and sometimes divided from it, till the reign of *Charles* the great, who made his son *Carolottus* King of *Burgundy*. From that time, for about 300 years together, it enjoyed its proper Kings; and was then broken into the Dukedom of *Burgundy*, County of *Burgundy*, and County of *Savoy*; and afterwards those were broken into other lesser Counties.

6. The Kings of the *Franks* were, A.C. 407 *Theudomir*, 417 *Pharamond*, 428 *Clodio*, 448 *Merovæus*, 456 *Childeric*, 482 *Clodovæus*, &c. *Windeline* and *Bucher*, two of the most diligent searchers into the originals of this kingdom, make it begin the same year with the *Barbarian* invasions of *Gallia*, that is, A.C. 407. Of the first Kings there is in *Labbe's Bibliotheca M.S.* this record.

Historica quædam excerpta ex veteri stemmate genealogico Regum Franciæ.

Genobaldus, Marcomerus, Suno, Theodemeris. Isti duces vel reguli extiterunt à principio gentis Francorum diversis temporibus. Sed incertum relinquunt historici quali sibi procreations lineâ successerunt.

Pharamundus: sub hoc rege suo primo Franci legibus se subdunt, quas primores eorum tulerunt Wisogastus, Atrogastus, Salegastus.

Chlochilo. Iste, transito Rheno, Romanos in Carbonaria sylva devicit, Camaracum cepit & obtinuit, annis 20 regnavit. Sub hoc rege Franci usque Summam progressi sunt.

Merovechus. Sub hoc rege Franci Trevirim destruunt, Metim succendunt, usque Aurelianum perveniunt.

Now for *Genobaldus, Marcomer* and *Suno*, they were captains of the *Transrhenane Franks* in the reign of *Theodosius*, and concern us not. We are to begin with *Theudomir* the first King of the rebelling *Salii*, called *Didio* by *Ivo Carnotensis*, and *Thiedo* and *Theudemerus* by *Rhenanus*. His face is extant in a coin of gold found with this inscription, THEUDEMIR REX, published by *Petavius*, and still or lately extant, as *Windeline* testifies: which shews that he was a King, and that in *Gallia*; seeing that rude *Germany* understood not then the coining of money, nor used either *Latin* words or letters. He was the son of *Ricimer*, or *Richomer*, the favourite of the Emperor *Theodosius*; and so being a *Roman Frank*, and of the *Salian* royal blood, they therefore upon the rebellion made him King. The whole time of his reign you have stated in *Excerptis Gregorii Turonensis è Fredigario, cap.* 5, 6, 7, 8. where the making him King, the tyranny of *Jovinus*, the slaughter of the associates of *Jovinus*, the second taking of *Triers* by the *Franks*, and their war with *Castinus*, in which this King was slain, are as a series of successive things thus set down in order. *Extinctis Ducibus in Francis, denuo Reges creantur ex eadem stirpe qua prius fuerant. Eodem tempore Jovinus ornatus regios assumpsit. Constantinus fugam versus Italiam dirigit; missis a Jovino Principe percussoribus super Mentio flumine, capite truncatur. Multi nobilium jussu Jovini apud Avernis capti, & a ducibus Honorii crudeliter interempti sunt. Trevirorum civitas, factione unius ex senatoribus nomine Lucii, à Francis captà & incensa est.—*

Castinus Domesticorum Comes expeditionem accipit contra Francos, &c. Then returning to speak of *Theudomir*, he adds: *Franci electum à se regem, sicut prius fuerat, crinitum inquirentes diligenter ex genere Priami, Frigi & Francionis, super se crearunt nomine Theudemerum filium Richemeris, qui in hoc prælio quod supra memini, à Romanis interfectus est*; that is, in the battle with *Castinus*'s army. Of his death *Gregory Turonensis* makes this further mention: *In consularibus legimus Theodemerem regem Francorum filium Ricimeris quondam, & Ascilam matrem ejus, gladio interfectos.*

Upon this victory of the *Romans*, the *Franks* and rebelling *Gauls*, who in the time of *Theudomir* were at war with one another, united to strengthen themselves, as *Ordericus Vitalis*[16] thus mentions. *Cum Galli prius contra Romanos rebellâssent, Franci iis sociati sunt, & pariter juncti, Ferramundum Sunonis ducis filium, sibi regem præfecerunt. Prosper* sets down the time; *Anno 25 Honorii, Pharamundus regnat in Francia.* This, *Bucher* well observes, refers to the end of the year 416, or the beginning of the next year, dating the years of *Honorius* from the death of *Valentinian*; and argues well, that at this time *Pharamond* was not only King by the constitution of the *Franks*, but crowned also by the consent of *Honorius*, and had a part of *Gallia* assigned him by covenant. And this might be the cause that *Roman* writers reckoned him the first King: which some not understanding, have reputed him the founder of this kingdom by an army of the *Transrhenane Franks*. He might come with such an army, but he succeeded *Theudomir* by right of blood and consent of the people. For the above cited passage of *Fredigarius, Extinctis Ducibus, in Francis denuo Reges creantur ex eadem stirpe quâ prius fuerant*, implies that the kingdom continued to this new elected family during the reign of more Kings than one. If you date the years of *Honorius* from the death of his father, the reign of *Pharamond* might begin two years later than is assigned by *Bucher*. The *Salique* laws made in his reign, which are yet extant, shew by their name that it was the kingdom of the *Salii* over which he reigned; and, by the pecuniary mulcts in them, that the

---

[16] Apud Bucherum, l. 14. c. 9. n. 8.

place where he reigned abounded much with money, and consequently was within the Empire; rude *Germany* knowing not the use of money, till they mixed with the *Romans*. In the Preface also to the *Salique* laws, written and prefixed to them soon after the conversion of the *Franks* to the Christian religion, that is, in the end of the reign of *Merovæus*, or soon after, the original of this kingdom is thus described: *Hæc enim gens, quæ fortis dum esset & robore valida, Romanorum jugum durissimum de suis cervicibus excussit pugnando*, &c. This kingdom therefore was erected, not by invasion but by rebellion, as was described above. *Prosper* in registering their Kings in order, tells us: *Pharamundus regnat in Francia; Clodio regnat in Francia; Merovæus regnat in Francia*: and who can imagine but that in all these places he meant one and the same *Francia*? And yet 'tis certain that the *Francia* of *Merovæus* was in *Gallia*.

Yet the father of *Pharamond*, being king of a body of *Franks* in *Germany* in the reign of the Emperor *Theodosius*, as above, *Pharamond* might reign over the same *Franks* in *Germany* before he succeeded *Theudomir* in the kingdom of the *Salians* within the Empire, and even before *Theudomir* began his reign; suppose in the first year of *Honorius*, or when those *Franks* being repulsed by *Stilico*, lost their Kings *Marcomir* and *Suno*, one of which was the father of *Pharamond*: and the *Roman Franks*, after the death of *Theudomir*, might invite *Pharamond* with his people from beyond the *Rhine*. But we are not to regard the reign of *Pharamond* in *Germany*: we are to date this kingdom from its rise within the Empire, and to look upon it as strengthened by the access of other *Franks* coming from beyond the *Rhine*, whether in the reign of this King or in that of his successor *Clodio*. For in the last year of *Pharamond*'s reign, *Ætius* took from him a part of his possession in *Gallia*: but his successor *Clodio*, whom *Fredigarius* represents as the son of *Theudomir*, and some call *Clogio, Cloio*, and *Claudius*, inviting from beyond the *Rhine* a great body of *Franks*, recovered all, and carried on their conquests as far as the river *Soame*. Then those *Franks* dividing conquests with him, erected certain new kingdoms at *Cologn* and *Cambray*, and some other cities: all which were afterwards conquered by *Clodovæus*, who also drove the *Goths* out of

Gallia, and fix'd his seat at *Paris*, where it has continued ever since. And this was the original of the present kingdom of *France*.

7. The Kings of *Britain* were, A.C. 407 or 408, *Marcus*, *Gratian*, and *Constantine* successively; A.C. 425 *Vortigern*, 466 *Aurelius Ambrosius*, 498 *Uther Pendraco*, 508 *Arthur*, 542 *Constantinus*, 545 *Aurelius Cunanus*, 578 *Vortiporeus*, 581 *Malgo*, 586 *Careticus*, 613 *Cadwan*, 635 *Cadwalin*, 676 *Cadwallader*. The three first were *Roman* Tyrants, who revolted from the Empire. *Orosius*, *Prosper* and *Zosimus* connect their revolt with the irruptions of the *Barbarians* into *Gallia*, as consequent thereunto. *Prosper*, with whom *Zosimus* agrees, puts it in the year which began the day after that irruption. The just time I thus collect: *Marcus* reigned not many days, *Gratian* four months, and *Constantine* three years. He was slain the year after the taking of *Rome*, that is A.C. 411, 14 Kal. *Octob.* Whence the revolt was in Spring A.C. 408. *Sozomen* joins *Constantine*'s expedition into *Gallia* with *Arcadius*'s death, or the times a little after; and *Arcadius* died A.C. 408 *May* the 1st. Now tho the reign of these Tyrants was but short, yet they gave a beginning to the kingdom of *Britain*, and so may be reckoned the three first Kings, especially since the posterity of *Constantine*, *viz.* his sons *Aurelius Ambrosius*, and *Uther Pendraco*, and his grandson *Arthur*, reigned afterwards. For from the time of the revolt of these Tyrants *Britain* continued a distict kingdom absolved from subjection to the Empire, the Emperor not being able to spare soldiers to be sent thither to receive and keep the Island, and therefore neglecting it; as we learn by unquestionable records. For *Prosper* tells us; *A.C.* 410, *Variane Cos. Hac tempestate præ valetudine Romanorum, vires funditùs attenuatæ Britanniæ.* And *Sigebert*, conjoining this with the siege of *Rome*, saith: *Britannorum vires attenuatæ, & substrahunt se à Romanorum dominatione.* And *Zosimus lib.* 6. *The* Transrhenane Barbarians *invading all places, reduced the inhabitants of the island of* Britain, *and also certain* Celtic *nations to that pass, that they fell off from the* Roman *Empire; and being no longer obedient to the* Roman *laws*, κατ' 'εαυτον βιατευειν, *they lived in separate bodies after their own pleasure. The* Britons *therefore taking up*

arms, and hazarding themselves for their own safety, freed their cities from the imminent Barbarians. *In like manner all* Brabant *and some other Provinces of the* Gauls *imitating the* Britons, *freed themselves also, ejecting the* Roman *Presidents, and forming themselves into a sort of commonwealth according to their own pleasure. This rebellion of* Britain *and the* Celtic *nations happened when* Constantine *usurped the kingdom.* So also *Procopius, lib.* 1. *Vandal.* speaking of the same *Constantine,* saith: Constantine *being overcome in battle, was slain with his children:* Βρεταννιαν μεν τοι Ρωμαιοι ανασωσασθαι ουκετι εχον· αλλ' ουσα 'υπο τυραννους απ' αυτου εμενε. *Yet the* Romans *could not recover* Britain *any more, but from that time it remained under Tyrants.* And *Beda, l.* 1. *c.* 11. *Fracta est Roma à Gothis anno 1164 suæ conditionis; ex quo tempore Romani in Britannia regnare cessaverunt.* And *Ethelwaldus: A tempore Romæ à Gothis expugnatæ, cessavit imperium Romanorum à Britannia insula, & ab aliis; quas sub jugo servitutis tenebant, multis terris.* And *Theodoret, serm.* 9. *de curand. Græc. affect.* about the year 424, reckons the *Britons* among the nations which were not then in subjection to the *Roman* Empire. Thus *Sigonius: ad annum 411, Imperium Romanorum post excessum Constantini in Britannia nullum fuit.*

Between the death of *Constantine* and the reign of *Vortigern* was an interregnum of about 14 years, in which the *Britons* had wars with the *Picts* and *Scots,* and twice obtained the assistance of a *Roman* Legion, who drove out the enemy, but told them positively at their departure that they would come no more. Of *Vortigern's* beginning to reign there is this record in an old Chronicle in *Nennius,* quoted by *Camden* and others: *Guortigernus tenuit imperium in Britannia, Theodosio & Valentiniano Coss.* [*viz.* A.C. 425.] *& in quarto anno regni sui Saxones ad Britanniam venerunt, Felice & Tauro Coss.* [*viz.* A.C. 428.] This coming of the *Saxons, Sigebert* refers to the 4th year of *Valentinian,* which falls in with the year 428 assigned by this Chronicle: and two years after, the *Saxons* together with the *Picts* were beaten by the *Britons.* Afterwards in the reign of *Martian* the Emperor, that is, between the years 450 and 456, the *Saxons* under *Hengist* were called in by the *Britons,* but six years after revolted from them, made war upon them with various success, and by degrees succeeded them. Yet the *Britons* continued a flourishing kingdom till the reign of *Careticus*; and the war between the two nations continued till the pontificate of *Sergius* A.C. 688.[17]

8. The Kings of the *Hunns* were, A.C. 406 *Octar* and *Rugila*, 433 *Bleda* and *Attila*. *Octar* and *Rugila* were the brothers of *Munzuc* King of the *Hunns* in *Gothia* beyond the *Danube*; and *Bleda* and *Attila* were his sons, and *Munzuc* was the son of *Balamir*. The two first, as *Jornandes* tells us, were Kings of the *Hunns*, but not of them all; and had the two last for their successors. I date the reign of the *Hunns* in *Pannonia* from the time that the *Vandals* and *Alans* relinquished *Pannonia* to them, A.C. 407. *Sigonius* from the time that the *Visigoths* relinquished *Pannonia* A. C. 408. *Constat*, saith he, *quod Gothis ex Illyrico profectis, Hunni successerunt, atque imprimis Pannoniam tenuerunt. Neque enim Honorius viribus ad resistendum in tantis difficultatibus destitutus, prorsus eos prohibere potuit, sed meliore consilio, animo ad pacem converso, fœdus cum eis, datis acceptisque obsidibus fecit; ex quibus qui dati sunt, Ætius, qui etiam Alarico tributus fuerat, præcipue memoratur.* How *Ætius* was hostage to the *Goths* and *Hunns* is related by *Frigeridus*, who when he had mentioned that *Theodosius* Emperor of the *East* had sent grievous commands to *John*, who after the death of *Honorius* had usurped the crown of the *Western Empire*, he subjoins: *Iis permotus Johannes, Ætium id tempus curam palatii gerentem cum ingenti auri pondere ad Chunnos transmisit, notos sibi obsidiatûs sui tempore & familiari amicitiâ devinctos*—And a little after: *Ætius tribus annis Alarici obses, dehinc Chunnorum, postea Carpilionis gener ex Comite domesticorum & Joannis curopalatæ.* Now *Bucher* shews that *Ætius* was hostage to *Alaric* till the year 410, when *Alaric* died, and to the *Hunns* between the years 411 and 415, and son-in-law to *Carpilio* about the year 417 or 418, and *Curopalates* to *John* about the end of the year 423. Whence 'tis probable that he became hostage to the *Hunns* about the year 412 or 413, when *Honorius* made

---

[17] Rolevinc's Antiqua Saxon. l. 1. c. 6.

leagues with almost all the barbarous nations, and granted them seats: but I had rather say with *Sigonius*, that *Ætius* became hostage to *Alaric* A.C. 403. It is further manifest out of *Prosper*, that the *Hunns* were in quiet possession of *Pannonia* in the year 432. For in the first book of *Eusebius*'s Chronicle *Prosper* writes: *Anno decimo post obitum Honorii, cum ad Chunnorum gentem cui tunc Rugila præerat, post prælium cum Bonifacio se Ætius contulisset, impetrato auxilio ad Romanorum solum regreditur.* And in the second book: *Ætio & Valerio Coss. Ætius depositâ potestate profugus ad Hunnos in Pannonia pervenit, quorum amicitiâ auxilioque usus, pacem principum interpellatæ potestatis obtinuit.* Hereby it appears that at this time *Rugila*, or as *Maximus* calls him, *Rechilla*, reigned over the *Hunns* in *Pannonia*; and that *Pannonia* was not now so much as accounted within the soil of the Empire, being formerly granted away to the *Hunns*; and that these were the very same body of *Hunns* with which *Ætius* had, in the time of his being an hostage, contracted friendship: by virtue of which, as he sollicited them before to the aid of *John* the Tyrant A.C. 424, so now he procured their intercession for himself with the Emperor. *Octar* died A.C. 430; for *Socrates* tells us, that about that time the *Burgundians* having been newly vext by the *Hunns*, upon intelligence of *Octar*'s death, seeing them without a leader, set upon them suddenly with so much vigour, that 3000 *Burgundians* slew 10000 *Hunns*. Of *Rugila*'s being now King in *Pannonia* you have heard already. He died A.C. 433, and was succeeded by *Bleda*, as *Prosper* and *Maximus* inform us. This *Bleda* with his brother *Attila* were before this time Kings of the *Hunns* beyond the *Danube*, their father *Munzuc*'s kingdom being divided between them; and now they united the kingdom *Pannonia* to their own. Whence *Paulus Diaconus* saith, they did *regnum intra Pannoniam Daciamque gerere.* In the year 441, they began to invade the Empire afresh, adding to the *Pannonian* forces new and great armies from *Scythia*. But this war was presently composed, and then *Attila*, seeing *Bleda* inclined to peace, slew him, A.C. 444, inherited his dominions, and invaded the Empire again. At length, after various great wars with the *Romans*, *Attila* perished A.C. 454; and his sons quarrelling about his dominions, gave occasion to the *Gepides*, *Ostrogoths* and other nations who were their subjects, to rebel and make war upon them. The same year the *Ostrogoths* had seats granted them in *Pannonia* by the Emperors *Marcian* and *Valentinian*; and with the *Romans* ejected the *Hunns* out of *Pannonia*, soon after the death of *Attila*, as all historians agree. This ejection was in the reign of *Avitus*, as is mentioned in the *Chronicum Boiorum*, and in *Sidonius, Carm. 7 in Avitum*, which speaks thus of that Emperor.

> —*Cujus solum amissas post sæcula multa*
> *Pannonias revocavit iter, jam credere promptum est.*
> *Quid faciet bellis.*

The Poet means, that by the coming of *Avitus* the *Hunns* yielded more easily to the *Goths*. This was written by *Sidonius* in the beginning of the reign of *Avitus*: and his reign began in the end of the year 455, and lasted not one full year.

Jornandes tells us: *Duodecimo anno regni Valiæ, quando & Hunni post pene quinquaginta annos invasa Pannonia, à Romanis & Gothis expulsi sunt.* And *Marcellinus*: *Hierio & Ardaburio Coss. Pannoniæ, quæ per quinquaginta annos ab Hunnis retinebantur, à Romanis receptæ sunt*: whence it should seem that the *Hunns* invaded and held *Pannonia* from the year 378 or 379 to the year 427, and then were driven out of it. But this is a plain mistake: for it is certain that the Emperor *Theodosius* left the Empire entire; and we have shewed out of *Prosper*, that the *Hunns* were in quiet possession of *Pannonia* in the year 432. The *Visigoths* in those days had nothing to do with *Pannonia*, and the *Ostrogoths* continued subject to the *Hunns* till the death of *Attila*, A.C. 454; and *Valia* King of the *Visigoths* did not reign twelve years. He began his reign in the end of the year 415, reigned three years, and was slain A.C. 419, as *Idacius*, *Isidorus*, and the *Spanish* manuscript Chronicles seen by *Grotius* testify. And *Olympiodorus*, who carries his history only to the year 425, sets down therein the death of *Valia* King of the *Visigoths*, and conjoins it with that of *Constantius* which happened A.C. 420. Wherefore the *Valia* of *Jornandes*, who reigned at the least twelve years, is some other King. And I suspect that this name hath been put by mistake for *Valamir* King of the *Ostrogoths*: for the action recorded was of the *Romans* and *Ostrogoths* driving the *Hunns* out of *Pannonia* after the death of *Attila*; and it is not likely that the historian would refer the history of the *Ostrogoths* to the years of the *Visigothic* Kings. This action happened in the end of the year 455, which I take to be the twelfth year of *Valamir* in *Pannonia*, and which was almost fifty years after the year 406, in which the *Hunns* succeeded the *Vandals* and *Alans* in *Pannonia*. Upon the ceasing of the line of *Hunnimund* the son of *Hermaneric*, the *Ostrogoths* lived without Kings of their own nation about forty years together, being subject to the *Hunns*. And when *Alaric* began to make war upon the *Romans*, which was in the year 444, he made *Valamir*, with his brothers *Theodomir* and *Videmir* the grandsons of *Vinethar*, captains or kings of these *Ostrogoths* under him. In the twelfth year of *Valamir*'s reign dated from thence, the *Hunns* were driven out of *Pannonia*.

Yet the *Hunns* were not so ejected, but that they had further contests with the *Romans*, till the head of *Denfix* the son of *Attila*, was carried to *Constantinople*, A.C. 469, in the Consulship of *Zeno* and *Marcian*, as *Marcellinus* relates. Nor were they yet totally ejected the Empire: for besides their reliques in *Pannonia*, *Sigonius* tells us, that when the Emperors *Marcian* and *Valentinian* granted *Pannonia* to the *Goths*, which was in the year 454, they granted part of *Illyricum* to some of the *Hunns* and *Sarmatians*. And in the year 526, when the *Lombards* removing into *Pannonia* made war there with the *Gepides*, the *Avares*, a part of the *Hunns*, who had taken the name of *Avares* from one of their Kings, assisted the *Lombards* in that war; and the *Lombards* afterwards, when they went into *Italy*, left their seats in *Pannonia* to the *Avares* in recompence of their friendship. From that time the *Hunns* grew again very powerful; their Kings, whom they called *Chagan*, troubling the Empire much in the reigns of the Emperors *Mauritius*, *Phocas*, and *Heraclius*: and this is the original of the present kingdom of *Hungary*, which from these *Avares* and other *Hunns* mixed together, took the name of *Hun-Avaria*, and by contraction *Hungary*.

9. The *Lombards*, before they came over the *Danube*, were commanded by two captains, *Ibor* and *Ayon*: after whose death they had Kings, *Agilmund, Lamisso, Lechu, Hildehoc, Gudehoc, Classo, Tato, Wacho, Walter, Audoin, Alboin, Cleophis*, &c. *Agilmund* was the son of *Ayon*, who became their King, according to *Prosper*, in the Consulship of *Honorius* and *Theodosius* A.C. 389, reigned thirty three years, according to *Paulus Warnefridus*, and was slain in battle by the *Bulgarians*. *Prosper* places his death in the Consulship of *Marinianus* and *Asclepiodorus*, A.C. 413. *Lamisso* routed the *Bulgarians*, and reigned three years, and *Lechu* almost forty. *Gudehoc* was contemporary to *Odoacer* King of the *Heruli* in *Italy*, and led his people from *Pannonia* into *Rugia*, a country on the north side of *Noricum* next beyond the *Danube*; from whence *Odoacer* then carried his people into *Italy*. *Tato* overthrew the kingdom of the *Heruli* beyond the *Danube*. *Wacho* conquered the *Suevians*, a kingdom then bounded on the east by *Bavaria*, on the west by *France*, and on the south by the *Burgundians*. *Audoin* returned into *Pannonia* A.C. 526, and there overcame the *Gepides*. *Alboin* A.C. 551 overthrew the kingdom of the *Gepides*, and slew their King *Chunnimund*: A.C. 563 he assisted the *Greek* Emperor against *Totila* King of the *Ostrogoths* in *Italy*; and A.C. 568 led his people out of *Pannonia* into *Lombardy*, where they reigned till the year 774.

According to *Paulus Diaconus*, the *Lombards* with many other *Gothic* nations came into the Empire from beyond the *Danube* in the reign of *Arcadius* and *Honorius*, that is, between the years 395 and 408. But they might come in a little earlier: for we are told that the *Lombards*, under their captains *Ibor* and *Ayon*, beat the *Vandals* in battle; and *Prosper* placeth this victory in the Consulship of *Ausonius* and *Olybrius*, that is, A.C. 379. Before this war the *Vandals* had remained quiet forty years in the seats granted them in *Pannonia* by *Constantine* the great. And therefore if these were the same *Vandals*, this war must have been in *Pannonia*; and might be occasioned by the coming of the *Lombards* over the *Danube* into *Pannonia*, a year or two before the battle; and so have put an end to that quiet which had lasted forty years. After *Gratian* and *Theodosius* had quieted the

Barbarians, they might either retire over the *Danube*, or continue quiet under the *Romans* till the death of *Theodosius*; and then either invade the Empire anew, or throw off all subjection to it. By their wars, first with the *Vandals*, and then with the *Bulgarians*, a *Scythian* nation so called from the river *Volga* whence they came; it appears that even in those days they were a kingdom not contemptible.

10. These nine kingdoms being rent away, we are next to consider the residue of the *Western Empire*. While this Empire continued entire, it was the Beast itself: but the residue thereof is only a part of it. Now if this part be considered as a horn, the reign of this horn may be dated from the translation of the imperial seat from *Rome* to *Ravenna*, which was in *October* A.C. 408. For then the Emperor *Honorius*, fearing that *Alaric* would besiege him in *Rome*, if he staid there, retired to *Millain*, and thence to *Ravenna*: and the ensuing siege and sacking of *Rome* confirmed his residence there, so that he and his successors ever after made it their home. Accordingly *Macchiavel* in his *Florentine* history writes, that *Valentinian* having left *Rome*, translated the seat of the Empire to *Ravenna*.

Rhætia belonged to the *Western* Emperors, so long as that Empire stood; and then it descended, with *Italy* and the *Roman* Senate, to *Odoacer* King of the *Heruli* in *Italy*, and after him to *Theoderic* King of the *Ostrogoths* and his successors, by the grant of the *Greek* Emperors. Upon the death of *Valentinian* the second, the *Alemans* and *Suevians* invaded *Rhætia* A.C. 455. But I do not find they erected any settled kingdom there: for in the year 457, while they were yet depopulating *Rhætia*, they were attacked and beaten by *Burto* Master of the horse to the Emperor *Majoranus*; and I hear nothing more of their invading *Rhætia*. *Clodovæus* King of *France*, in or about the year 496, conquered a kingdom of the *Alemans*, and slew their last King *Ermeric*. But this kingdom was seated in *Germany*, and only bordered upon *Rhætia*: for its people fled from *Clodovæus* into the neighbouring kingdom of the *Ostrogoths* under *Theoderic*, who received them as friends, and wrote a friendly letter to *Clodovæus* in their behalf: and by this means they became inhabitants of *Rhætia*, as subjects under the dominion of the *Ostrogoths*.

When the *Greek* Emperor conquered the *Ostrogoths*, he succeeded them in the kingdom of *Ravenna*, not only by right of conquest but also by right of inheritance, the *Roman* Senate still going along with this kingdom. Therefore we may reckon that this kingdom continued in the Exarchate of *Ravenna* and Senate of *Rome*: for the remainder of the *Western Empire* went along with the Senate of *Rome*, by reason of the right which this Senate still retained, and at length exerted, of chusing a new *Western* Emperor.

I have now enumerated the ten kingdoms, into which the *Western Empire* became divided at its first breaking, that is, at the time of *Rome*'s being besieged and taken by the *Goths*. Some of these kingdoms at length fell, and new ones arose: but whatever was their number afterwards, they are still called the *Ten Kings* from their first number.

CHAP. VII

Of the eleventh horn of Daniel*'s fourth Beast.*

[18]*Now Daniel, considered the horns, and behold there came up among them another horn, before whom there were three of the first horns pluckt up by the roots; and behold in this horn were eyes like the eyes of a man, and a mouth speaking great things,—and*[19] his *look was more stout than his fellows,—and the same horn made war with the saints, and prevailed against them:* and one who stood by, and made *Daniel* know the interpretation of these things, told him, that[20] *the ten horns were ten kings that should arise, and another should arise after them, and be diverse from the first, and he should subdue three kings,*[21] *and speak great words against the most High, and wear out the saints, and think to change times and laws: and that they should be given into his hands until a time and times and half a time.* Kings are put for kingdoms, as above; and therefore the little horn is a little kingdom. It was a horn of the fourth Beast, and rooted up three of his first horns; and therefore we are to look for it among the nations of the *Latin* Empire, after the rise of the ten horns. But it was a kingdom of a different kind from the other ten kingdoms, having a life or soul peculiar to itself, with eyes and a mouth. By its eyes it was a Seer; and by its mouth speaking great things and changing times and laws, it was a Prophet as well as a King. And such a Seer, a Prophet and a King, is the Church of *Rome*.

A Seer, Επισκοπος, is a Bishop in the literal sense of the word; and this Church claims the universal Bishoprick.

---

[18] Chap. vii. 8.
[19] Ver. 20, 21.
[20] Ver. 24.
[21] Ver. 25.

With his mouth he gives laws to kings and nations as an Oracle; and pretends to Infallibility, and that his dictates are binding to the whole world; which is to be a Prophet in the highest degree.

In the eighth century, by rooting up and subduing the Exarchate of *Ravenna*, the kingdom of the *Lombards*, and the Senate and Dukedom of *Rome*, he acquired *Peter*'s Patrimony out of their dominions; and thereby rose up as a temporal Prince or King, or horn of the fourth Beast.

In a small book printed at *Paris* A.C. 1689, entitled, *An historical dissertation upon some coins of* Charles *the great*, Ludovicus Pius, Lotharius, *and their successors stamped at* Rome, it is recorded, that in the days of Pope *Leo* X, there was remaining in the *Vatican*, and till those days exposed to public view, an inscription in honour of *Pipin* the father of *Charles* the great, in these words: *Pipinum pium, primum fuisse qui amplificandæ Ecclesiæ Romanæ viam aperuerit, Exarchatu Ravennate, & plurimis aliis oblatis*; "That *Pipin* the pious was the first who opened a way to the grandeur of the Church of *Rome*, conferring upon her the Exarchate of *Ravenna* and many other oblations." In and before the reign of the Emperors *Gratian* and *Theodosius*, the Bishop of *Rome* lived splendidly; but this was by the oblations of the *Roman* Ladies, as *Ammianus* describes. After those reigns *Italy* was invaded by foreign nations, and did not get rid of her troubles before the fall of the kingdom of *Lombardy*. It was certainly by the victory of the see of *Rome* over the *Greek* Emperor, the King of *Lombardy*, and the Senate of *Rome*, that she acquired *Peter*'s Patrimony, and rose up to her greatness. The donation of *Constantine* the Great is a fiction, and so is the donation of the *Alpes Cottiæ* to the Pope by *Aripert* King of the *Lombards*: for the *Alpes Cottiæ* were a part of the Exarchate, and in the days of *Aripert* belonged to the *Greek* Emperor.

The invocation of the dead, and veneration of their images, being gradually introduced in the 4th, 5th, 6th and 7th centuries, the *Greek* Emperor *Philippicus* declared against the latter, A.C. 711 or 712. And[22] the Emperor *Leo Isaurus*, to put a stop to it,

---

[22] Sigonius de Regno Italiæ, ad Ann. 726.

called a meeting of Counsellors and Bishops in his Palace, A.C. 726; and by their advice put out an Edict against that worship, and wrote to Pope *Gregory* II. that a general Council might be called. But the Pope thereupon called a Council at *Rome*, confirmed the worship of Images, excommunicated the *Greek* Emperor, absolved the people from their allegiance, and forbad them to pay tribute, or otherwise be obedient to him. Then the people of *Rome*, *Campania*, *Ravenna* and *Pentapolis*, with the cities under them, revolted and laid violent hands upon their magistrates, killing the Exarch *Paul* at *Ravenna*, and laying aside *Peter* Duke of *Rome* who was become blind: and when *Exhileratus* Duke of *Campania* incited the people against the Pope, the *Romans* invaded *Campania*, and slew him with his son *Hadrian*. Then a new Exarch, *Eutychius*, coming to *Naples*, sent some secretly to take away the lives of the Pope and the Nobles of *Rome*: but the plot being discovered, the *Romans* revolted absolutely from the *Greek* Emperor, and took an oath to preserve the life of the Pope, to defend his state, and be obedient to his authority in all things. Thus *Rome* with its Duchy, including part of *Tuscany* and part of *Campania*, revolted in the year 726, and became a free state under the government of the Senate of this city. The authority of the Senate in civil affairs was henceforward absolute, the authority of the Pope extending hitherto no farther than to the affairs of the Church only.

At that time[23] the *Lombards* also being zealous for the worship of images, and pretending to favour the cause of the Pope, invaded the cities of the Exarchate: and at length, *viz.* A.C. 752, took *Ravenna*, and put an end to the Exarchate. And this was the first of the three kingdoms which fell before the little horn.

In the year 751[24] Pope *Zechary* deposed *Childeric*, a slothful and useless King of *France*, and the last of the race of *Merovæus*; and absolving his subjects from their oath of allegiance, gave the kingdom to *Pipin* the major of the Palace; and thereby made a new and potent friend. His successor[25] Pope *Stephen* III, knowing

---

[23] Sigonius ib. ad Ann. 726, 752.

[24] Sigon. ib. Ann. 750.

[25] Sigon. ib. Ann. 753, 754, 755.

better how to deal with the *Greek* Emperor than with the *Lombards*, went the next year to the King of the *Lombards*, to persuade him to return the Exarchate to the Emperor. But this not succeeding, he went into *France*, and persuaded *Pipin* to take the Exarchate and *Pentapolis* from the *Lombards*, and give it to St. *Peter*. Accordingly *Pipin* A.C. 754 came with an army into *Italy*, and made *Aistulphus* King of the *Lombards* promise the surrender: but the next year *Aistulphus*, on the contrary, to revenge himself on the Pope, besieged the city of *Rome*. Whereupon the Pope sent letters to *Pipin*, wherein he told him that if he came not speedily against the *Lombards*, *pro data sibi potentia, alienandum fore à regno Dei & vita æterna*, he should be excommunicated. *Pipin* therefore, fearing a revolt of his subjects, and being indebted to the Church of *Rome*, came speedily with an army into *Italy*, raised the siege, besieged the *Lombards* in *Pavia*, and forced them to surrender the Exarchate and region of *Pentapolis* to the Pope for a perpetual possession. Thus the Pope became Lord of *Ravenna*, and the Exarchate, some few cities excepted; and the keys were sent to *Rome*, and laid upon the confession of St. *Peter*, that is, upon his tomb at the high Altar, *in signum veri perpetuique dominii, sed pietate Regis gratuita*, as the inscription of a coin of *Pipin* hath it. This was in the year of Christ 755. And henceforward the Popes being temporal Princes, left off in their Epistles and Bulls to note the years of the *Greek* Emperors, as they had hitherto done.

After this[26] the *Lombards* invading the Pope's countries, Pope *Adrian* sent to *Charles* the great, the son and successor of *Pipin*, to come to his assistance. Accordingly *Charles* entered *Italy* with an army, invaded the *Lombards*, overthrew their kingdom, became master of their countries, and restored to the Pope, not only what they had taken from him, but also the rest of the Exarchate which they had promised *Pipin* to surrender to him, but had hitherto detained; and also gave him some cities of the *Lombards*, and was in return himself made *Patricius* by the *Romans*, and had the authority of confirming the elections of the Popes conferred upon him. These things were done in the years

---

[26] Sigon. ib. Ann. 773.

773 and 774. This kingdom of the *Lombards* was the second kingdom which fell before the little horn. But *Rome*, which was to be the seat of his kingdom, was not yet his own.

In the year 796,[27] *Leo* III being made Pope, notified his election to *Charles* the great by his Legates, sending to him for a present, the golden keys of the Confession of *Peter*, and the Banner of the city of *Rome*: the first as an acknowledgment of the Pope's holding the cities of the Exarchate and *Lombardy* by the grant of *Charles*; the other as a signification that *Charles* should come and subdue the Senate and people of *Rome*, as he had done the Exarchate and the kingdom of the *Lombards*. For the Pope at the same time desired *Charles* to send some of his Princes to *Rome*, who might subject the *Roman* people to him, and bind them by oath *in fide & subjectione*, in fealty and subjection, as his words are recited by *Sigonius*. An anonymous Poet, publish'd by *Boeclerus* at *Strasburg*, expresseth it thus:

> *Admonuitque piis precibus, qui mittere vellet*
> *Ex propriis aliquos primoribus, ac sibi plebem*
> *Subdere Romanam, servandaque foedera cogens*
> *Hanc fidei sacramentis promittere magnis.*

Hence arose a misunderstanding between the Pope and the city: and the *Romans* about two or three years after, by assistance of some of the Clergy, raised such tumults against him, as gave occasion to a new state of things in all the *West*. For two of the Clergy accused him of crimes, and the *Romans* with an armed force, seized him, stript him of his sacerdotal habit, and imprisoned him in a monastery. But by assistance of his friends he made his escape, and fled into *Germany* to *Charles* the great, to whom he complained of the *Romans* for acting against him out of a design to throw off all authority of the Church, and to recover their antient freedom. In his absence his accusers with their forces ravaged the possessions of the Church, and sent the accusations to *Charles*; who before the end of the year sent the Pope back to *Rome* with a large retinue. The Nobles and Bishops

---

[27] Sigon. de Regno Ital. ad Ann. 796.

of *France* who accompanied him, examined the chief of his accusers at *Rome*, and sent them into *France* in custody. This was in the year 799. The next year *Charles* himself went to *Rome*, and upon a day appointed presided in a Council of *Italian* and *French* Bishops to hear both parties. But when the Pope's adversaries expected to be heard, the Council declared[28] that he who was the supreme judge of all men, was above being judged by any other than himself: whereupon he made a solemn declaration of his innocence before all the people, and by doing so was looked upon as acquitted.

Soon after, upon *Christmas*-day, the people of *Rome*, who had hitherto elected their Bishop, and reckoned that they and their Senate inherited the rights of the antient Senate and people of *Rome*, voted *Charles* their Emperor, and subjected themselves to him in such manner as the old *Roman* Empire and their Senate were subjected to the old *Roman* Emperors. The Pope crowned him, and anointed him with holy oil, and worshipped him on his knees after the manner of adoring the old *Roman* Emperors; as the aforesaid Poet thus relates:

Post laudes igitur dictas & summus eundem
Præsul adoravit, sicut mos debitus olim
Principibus fuit antiquis.

The Emperor, on the other hand, took the following oath to the Pope: *In nomine Christi spondeo atque polliceor, Ego Carolus Imperator coram Deo & beato Petro Apostolo, me protectorem ac defensorem fore hujus sanctæ Romanæ Ecclesiæ in omnibus utilitatibus, quatenùs divino fultus fuero adjutorio, prout sciero poteroque.* The Emperor was also made Consul of *Rome*, and his son *Pipin* crowned King of *Italy*: and henceforward the Emperor stiled himself: *Carolus serenissimus, Augustus, à Deo coronatus, magnus, pacificus, Romæ gubernans imperium*, or *Imperator Romanorum*; and was prayed for in the Churches of *Rome*. His image was henceforward put upon the coins of *Rome*: while the enemies of the Pope, to the number of

---

[28] Vide Anastasium.

three hundred *Romans* and two or three of the Clergy, were sentenced to death. The three hundred *Romans* were beheaded in one day in the *Lateran* fields: but the Clergymen at the intercession of the Pope were pardoned, and banished into *France*. And thus the title of *Roman* Emperor, which had hitherto been in the *Greek* Emperors, was by this act transferred in the *West* to the Kings of *France*.

After these things[29] *Charles* gave the City and Duchy of *Rome* to the Pope, subordinately to himself as Emperor of the *Romans*; spent the winter in ordering the affairs of *Rome*, and those of the Apostolic see, and of all *Italy*, both civil and ecclesiastical, and in making new laws for them; and returned the next summer into *France*: leaving the city under its Senate, and both under the Pope and himself. But hearing that his new laws were not observed by the judges in dictating the law, nor by the people in hearing it; and that the great men took servants from free men, and from the Churches and Monasteries, to labour in their vineyards, fields, pastures and houses, and continued to exact cattle and wine of them, and to oppress those that served the Churches: he wrote to his son *Pipin* to remedy these abuses, to take care of the Church, and see his laws executed.

Now the Senate and people and principality of *Rome* I take to be the third King the little horn overcame, and even the chief of the three. For this people elected the Pope and the Emperor; and now, by electing the Emperor and making him Consul, was acknowledged to retain the authority of the old *Roman* Senate and people. This city was the Metropolis of the old *Roman* Empire, represented in *Daniel* by the fourth Beast; and by subduing the Senate and people and Duchy, it became the Metropolis of the little horn of that Beast, and completed *Peter*'s Patrimony, which was the kingdom of that horn. Besides, this victory was attended with greater consequences than those over the other two Kings. For it set up the *Western Empire*, which continues to this day. It set up the Pope above the judicature of the *Roman* Senate, and above that of a Council of *Italian* and *French* Bishops, and even above all human judicature; and gave

---

[29] Sigon. de Regno Ital.

him the supremacy over the *Western* Churches and their Councils in a high degree. It gave him *a look more stout than his fellows*; so that when this new religion began to be established in the minds of men, he grappled not only with Kings, but even with the *Western* Emperor himself. It is observable also, that the custom of kissing the Pope's feet, an honour superior to that of Kings and Emperors, began about this time. There are some instances of it in the ninth century: *Platina* tells us, that the feet of Pope *Leo* IV were kissed, according to antient custom, by all who came to him: and some say that *Leo* III began this custom, pretending that his hand was infected by the kiss of a woman. The Popes began also about this time to canonize saints, and to grant indulgences and pardons: and some represent that *Leo* III was the first author of all these things. It is further observable, that *Charles* the great, between the years 775 and 796, conquered all *Germany* from the *Rhine* and *Danube* northward to the *Baltic* sea, and eastward to the river *Teis*; extending his conquests also into *Spain* as far as the river *Ebro*: and by these conquests he laid the foundation of the new Empire; and at the same time propagated the *Roman* Catholic religion into all his conquests, obliging the *Saxons* and *Hunns* who were heathens, to receive the *Roman* faith, and distributing his northern conquests into Bishopricks, granting tithes to the Clergy and *Peter-pence* to the Pope: by all which the Church of *Rome* was highly enlarged, enriched, exalted, and established.

In the forementioned *dissertation upon some coins of* Charles *the great,* Ludovicus Pius, Lotharius, *and their successors, stamped at* Rome, there is a draught of a piece of *Mosaic* work which Pope *Leo* III. caused to be made in his Palace near the Church of *John Lateran*, in memory of his sending the standard or banner of the city of *Rome* curiously wrought, to *Charles* the great; and which still remained there at the publishing of the said book. In the *Mosaic* work there appeared *Peter* with three keys in his lap, reaching the *Pallium* to the Pope with his right hand, and the banner of the city to *Charles* the great with his left. By the Pope was this inscription, SCISSIMUS D.N. LEO PP; by the King this, D.N. CARVLO REGI; and under the feet of *Peter* this, BEATE PETRE, DONA VITAM LEONI PP,

ET BICTORIAM CARVLO REGI DONA. This Monument gives the title of King to *Charles*, and therefore was erected before he was Emperor. It was erected when *Peter* was reaching the *Pallium* to the Pope, and the Pope was sending the banner of the city to *Charles*, that is, A.C. 796. The words above, *Sanctissimus Dominus noster Leo Papa Domino nostro Carolo Regi*, relate to the message; and the words below, *Beate Petre, dona vitam Leoni Papæ & victoriam Carolo regi dona*, are a prayer that in this undertaking God would preserve the life of the Pope, and give victory to the King over the *Romans*. The three keys in the lap of *Peter* signify the keys of the three parts of his Patrimony, that of *Rome* with its Duchy, which the Pope claimed and was conquering, those of *Ravenna* with the Exarchate, and of the territories taken from the *Lombards*; both which he had newly conquered. These were the three dominions, whose keys were in the lap of St. *Peter*, and whose Crowns are now worn by the Pope, and by the conquest of which he became the little horn of the fourth Beast. By *Peter*'s giving the *Pallium* to the Pope with his right hand, and the banner of the city to the King with his left, and by naming the Pope before the King in the inscription, may be understood that the Pope was then reckoned superior in dignity to the Kings of the earth.

After the death of *Charles* the great, his son and successor *Ludovicus Pius*, at the request of the Pope,[30] confirmed the donations of his grandfather and father to the see of *Rome*. And in the confirmation he names first *Rome* with its Duchy extending into *Tuscany* and *Campania*; then the Exarchate of *Ravenna*, with *Pentapolis*; and in the third place, the territories taken from the *Lombards*. These are his three conquests, and he was to hold them of the Emperor for the use of the Church *sub integritate*, entirely, without the Emperor's medling therewith, or with the jurisdiction or power of the Pope therein, unless called thereto in certain cases. This ratification the Emperor *Ludovicus* made under an oath: and as the King of the *Ostrogoths*, for acknowledging that he held his kingdom of *Italy* of the *Greek* Emperor, stamped the effigies of the Emperor on one side of his

---

[30] Confirmationem recitat Sigonius, lib. 4. de Regno Italiæ, ad An. 817.

coins and his own on the reverse; so the Pope made the like acknowledgment to the *Western* Emperor. For the Pope began now to coin money, and the coins of *Rome* are henceforward found with the heads of the Emperors, *Charles, Ludovicus Pius, Lotharius,* and their successors, on the one side, and the Pope's inscription on the reverse, for many years.

CHAP. VIII

Of the power of the eleventh horn of Daniel*'s fourth Beast,*
to change times and laws.

In the reign of the *Greek* Emperor *Justinian*, and again in the
reign of *Phocas*, the Bishop of *Rome* obtained some
dominion over the *Greek* Churches, but of no long
continuance. His standing dominion was only over the nations of
the *Western Empire*, represented by *Daniel*'s fourth Beast. And
this jurisdiction was set up by the following Edict of the
Emperors *Gratian* and *Valentinian.*—[1] *Volumus ut quicunque*
judicio Damasi, quod ille cum Concilio quinque vel septem
habuerit Episcoporum, vel eorum qui Catholici sunt judicio vel
Concilio condemnatus fuerit, si juste voluerit Ecclesiam
retentare, ut qui ad sacerdotale judicium per contumeliam non
ivisset: ut ab illustribus viris Præfectis Prætorio Galliæ atque
Italiæ, authoritate adhibitâ, ad Episcopale judicium remittatur,
sive à Consularibus vel Vicariis, ut ad Urbem Romam sub
prosecutione perveniat. Aut si in longinquioribus partibus
alicujus ferocitas talis emerserit, omnis ejus causæ edictio ad
Metropolitæ in eadem Provincia Episcopi deduceretur examen.
Vel si ipse Metropolitanus est, Romam necessariò, vel ad eos
quos Romanus Episcopus judices dederit, sine delatione
contendat.——*Quod si vel Metropolitani Episcopi vel*
cujuscunque sacerdotis iniquitas est suspecta, aut gratia; ad
Romanum Episcopum, vel ad Concilium quindecim finitimorum
Episcoporum accersitum liceat provocare; modo ne post examen
habitum, quod definitum fuerit, integretur. This Edict wanting the
name of both *Valens* and *Theodosius* in the Title, was made in the
time between their reigns, that is, in the end of the year 378, or
the beginning of 379. It was directed to the *Præfecti Prætorio*
Italiæ & Galliæ, and therefore was general. For the *Præfectus*
Prætorio Italiæ governed *Italy, Illyricum occidentale* and *Africa*;

and the *Præfectus Prætorio Galliæ* governed *Gallia*, *Spain*, and *Britain*.

The granting of this jurisdiction to the Pope gave several Bishops occasion to write to him for his resolutions upon doubtful cases, whereupon he answered by decretal Epistles; and henceforward he gave laws to the *Western* Churches by such Epistles. *Himerius* Bishop of *Tarraco*, the head city of a province in *Spain*, writing to Pope *Damasus* for his direction about certain Ecclesiastical matters, and the Letter not arriving at *Rome* till after the death of *Damasus*, A.C. 384; his successor *Siricius* answered the same with a legislative authority, telling him of one thing: *Cum hoc fieri—missa ad Provincias à venerandæ memoriæ prædecessore meo Liberio generalia decreta, prohibeant.* Of another: *Noverint se ab omni ecclesiastico honore, quo indignè usi sunt, Apostolicæ Sedis auctoritate, dejectos.* Of another: *Scituri posthac omnium Provinciarum summi Antistites, quod si ultrò ad sacros ordines quenquam de talibus esse assumendum, & de suo & de aliorum statu, quos contra Canones & interdicta nostra provexerint, congruam ab Apostolica Sede promendam esse sententiam.* And the Epistle he concludes thus: *Explicuimus, ut arbitror, frater charissime, universa quæ digesta sunt in querelam; & ad singulas causas, de quibus ad Romanam Ecclesiam, utpote ad caput tui corporis, retulisti; sufficientia, quantum opinor, responsa reddidimus. Nunc fraternitatis tuæ animum ad servandos canones, & tenenda decretalia constituta, magis ac magis incitamus: ad hæc quæ ad tua consulta rescripsimus in omnium Coepiscoporum perferri facias notionem; & non solum corum, qui in tua sunt diœcesi constituti, sed etiam ad universos Carthaginenses ac Bœticos, Lusitanos atque [2] Gallicos, vel eos qui vicinis tibi collimitant hinc inde Provinciis, hæc quæ a nobis sunt salubri ordinatione disposita, sub literarum tuarum prosecutione mittantur. Et quanquam statuta sedis Apostolicæ vel Canonum venerabilia definita, nulli Sacerdotum Domini ignorare sit liberum: utilius tamen, atque pro antiquitate sacerdotii tui, dilectioni tuæ esse admodùm poterit gloriosum, si ea quæ ad te speciali nomine generaliter scripta sunt, per unanimitatis tuæ sollicitudinem in universorum fratrum nostrorum notitiam perferantur; quatenus*

& quæ à nobis non inconsultè sed providè sub nimia cautela & deliberatione sunt salubriter constituta, intemerata permaneant, & omnibus in posterum excusationibus aditus, qui jam nulli apud nos patere poterit, obstruatur. Dat. 3 Id. Febr. Arcadio & Bautone viris clarissimis Consulibus, A.C. 385. Pope *Liberius* in the reign of *Jovian* or *Valentinian* I. sent general Decrees to the Provinces, ordering that the *Arians* should not be rebaptized: and this he did in favour of the Council of *Alexandria*, that nothing more should be required of them than to renounce their opinions. Pope *Damasus* is said to have decreed in a *Roman* Council, that *Tithes* and *Tenths* should be paid upon pain of an *Anathema*; and that *Glory be to the Father*, &c. should be said or sung at the end of the *Psalms*. But the first decretal Epistle now extant is this of *Siricius* to *Himerius*; by which the Pope made *Himerius* his Vicar over all *Spain* for promulging his Decrees, and seeing them observed. The Bishop of *Sevill* was also the Pope's Vicar sometimes; for *Simplicius* wrote thus to *Zeno* Bishop of that place: *Talibus idcirco gloriantes indiciis, congruum duximus vicariâ Sedis nostræ te auctoritate fulciri: cujus vigore munitus, Apostolicæ institutionis Decreta, vel sanctorum terminos Patrum, nullatenus transcendi permittas.* And Pope *Hormisda* [3] made the Bishop of *Sevill* his Vicar over *Bœtica* and *Lusitania*, and the Bishop of *Tarraco* his Vicar over all the rest of *Spain*, as appears by his Epistles to them.

Pope *Innocent* the first, in his decretal Epistle to *Victricius* Bishop of *Rouen* in *France*, A.C. 404, in pursuance of the Edict of *Gratian*, made this Decree: *Si quæ autem causæ vel contentiones inter Clericos tam superioris ordinis quam etiam inferioris fuerint exortæ; ut secundum Synodum Nicenam congregatis ejusdem Provinciæ Episcopis jurgium terminetur: nec alicui liceat,* [4] *Romanæ Ecclesiæ, cujus in omnibus causis debet reverentia custodiri, relictis his sacerdotibus, qui in eadem Provincia Dei Ecclesiam nutu Divino gubernant, ad alias convolare Provincias. Quod siquis fortè præsumpserit; & ab officio Clericatûs summotus, & injuriarum reus judicetur. Si autem majores causæ in medium fuerint devolutæ, ad Sedem Apostolicam sicut Synodus statuit, & beata consuetudo exigit, post judicium Episcopale referantur.* By these Letters it seems to me that *Gallia* was now subject to the Pope, and had been so for some time, and that the Bishop of *Rouen* was then his Vicar or one of them: for the Pope directs him to refer the greater causes to the See of *Rome*, according to custom. But the Bishop of *Arles* soon after became the Pope's Vicar over all *Gallia*: for Pope *Zosimus*, A.C. 417, ordaining that none should have access to him without the credentials of his Vicars, conferred upon *Patroclus* the Bishop of *Arles* this authority over all *Gallia*, by the following Decree.

Zosimus universis Episcopis per Gallias & septem Provincias constitutis.

Placuit Apostolicæ Sedi, ut siquis ex qualibet Galliarum parte sub quolibet ecclesiastico gradu ad nos Romæ venire contendit, vel aliò terrarum ire disponit, non aliter proficiscatur nisi Metropolitani Episcopi Formatas acceperit, quibus sacerdotium suum vel locum ecclesiasticum quem habet, scriptorum ejus adstipulatione perdoceat: quod ex gratia statuimus quia plures episcopi sive presbyteri sive ecclesiastici simulantes, quia nullum documentum Formatarum extat per quod valeant confutari, in nomen venerationis irrepunt, & indebitam reverentiam promerentur. Quisquis igitur, fratres charissimi, prætermissà supradicti Formatâ sive episcopus, sive presbyter, sive diaconus, aut deinceps inferiori gradu sit, ad nos venerit: sciat se omnino suscipi non posse. Quam auctoritatem ubique nos misisse manifestum est, ut cunctis regionibus innotescat id quod statuimus omnimodis esse servandum. Siquis autem hæc salubriter constituta temerare tentaverit sponte suâ, se a nostra noverit communione discretum. Hoc autem privilegium Formatarum sancto Patroclo fratri & coepiscopo nostro, meritorum ejus speciali contemplatione, concessimus. And that the Bishop of *Arles* was sometimes the Pope's Vicar over all *France*, is affirmed also by all the Bishops of the Diocess of *Arles* in their Letter to Pope *Leo* I. *Cui id etiam honoris dignitatisque collatum est,* say they, *ut non tantum has Provincias potestate propriâ gubernaret; verum etiam omnes Gallias sibi Apostolicæ Sedis vice mandatas, sub omni ecclesiastica regula contineret.* And Pope *Pelagius* I. A.C. 556, in his Epistle to *Sapaudus* Bishop of *Arles*: *Majorum nostrorum, operante Dei misericordiâ, cupientes inhærere vestigiis & eorum actus divino examine in omnibus imitari: Charitati tuæ per universam Galliam, sanctæ Sedis Apostolicæ, cui divinâ gratiâ præsidemus, vices injungimus.*

By the influence of the same imperial Edict, not only *Spain* and *Gallia*, but also *Illyricum* became subject to the Pope. *Damasus* made *Ascholius*, or *Acholius*, Bishop of *Thessalonica* the Metropolis of *Oriental Illyricum*, his Vicar for hearing of causes; and in the year 382, *Acholius* being summoned by Pope *Damasus*, came to a Council at *Rome*. Pope *Siricius* the successor of *Damasus*, decreed that no Bishop should be ordained in *Illyricum* without the consent of *Anysius* the successor of *Acholius*. And the following Popes gave *Rufus* the successor of *Anysius*, a power of calling Provincial Councils: for in the Collections of *Holstenius* there is an account of a Council of *Rome* convened under Pope *Boniface* II. in which were produced Letters of *Damasus, Syricius, Innocent* I. *Boniface* I. and *Cælestine* Bishops of *Rome*, to *Ascholius, Anysius* and *Rufus*, Bishops of *Thessalonica*: in which Letters they commend to them the hearing of causes in *Illyricum*, granted by the Lord and the holy Canons to the Apostolic See thro'out that Province. And Pope *Siricius* saith in his Epistle to *Anysius*: *Etiam dudum, frater charissime, per Candidianum Episcopum, qui nos præcessit ad Dominum, hujusmodi literas dederamus, ut nulla licentia esset, sine consensu tuo in Illyrico Episcopos ordinare præsumere, quæ utrum ad te pervenerint scire non potui. Multa enim gesta sunt per contentionem ab Episcopis in ordinationibus faciendis, quod tua melius caritas novit.* And a little after: *Ad omnem enim hujusmodi audaciam comprimendam vigilare debet instantia tua, Spiritu in te Sancto fervente: ut vel ipse, si potes, vel quos judicaveris Episcopos idoneos, cum literis dirigas, dato consensu qui possit, in ejus locum qui defunctus vel depositus fuerit, Catholicum Episcopum vitâ & moribus probatum, secundum Nicænæ Synodi statuta vel Ecclesiæ Romanæ, Clericum de Clero meritum ordinare.* And Pope *Innocent* I. saith in his Epistle to *Anysius*: *Cui* [Anysio] *etiam anteriores tanti ac tales viri prædecessores mei Episcopi, id est, sanctæ memoriæ Damasus, Siricius, atque supra memoratus vir ita detulerunt; ut omnia quæ in omnibus illis partibus gererentur, Sanctitati tuæ, quæ plena justitiæ est, traderent cognoscenda.* And in his Epistle to *Rufus* the successor of *Anysius*: *Ita longis intervallis disterminatis à me ecclesiis discat consulendum; ut prudentiæ gravitatique tuæ committendam curam causasque, siquæ exoriantur, per Achaiæ, Thessaliæ, Epiri veteris, Epiri novæ, & Cretæ, Daciæ mediterraneæ, Daciæ ripensis, Mœsiæ, Dardaniæ, & Prævali ecclesias, Christo Domino annuente, censeam. Verè enim ejus sacratissimis monitis lectissimæ sinceritatis tuæ providentiæ & virtuti hanc injungimus sollicitudinem: non primitùs hæc statuentes, sed Præcessores nostros Apostolicos imitati, qui beatissimis Acholio & Anysio injungi pro meritis ista voluerunt.* And *Boniface* I. in his decretal Epistle to *Rufus* and the rest of the Bishops in *Illyricum*: *Nullus, ut frequenter dixi, alicujus ordinationem citra ejus* [Episcopi Thessalonicensis] *conscientiam celebrare præsumat: cui, ut supra dictum est, vice nostrâ cuncta committimus.* And Pope *Cælestine*, in his decretal Epistle to the Bishops thro'out *Illyricum*, saith: *Vicem nostram per vestram Provinciam noveritis* [Rufo] *esse commissam, ita ut ad eum, fratres carissimi, quicquid de causis agitur, referatur. Sine ejus consilio nullus ordinetur. Nullus usurpet, eodem inconscio, commissam illi Provinciam; colligere nisi cum ejus voluntate Episcopus non præsumat.* And in the cause of *Perigenes*, in the title of his Epistle, he thus enumerates the Provinces under this Bishop: *Rufo & cæteris Episcopis per Macedoniam, Achaiam, Thessaliam, Epirum veterem, Epirum novam, Prævalin, & Daciam constitutis.* And Pope *Xistus* in a decretal Epistle to the same Bishops: *Illyricanæ omnes Ecclesiæ, ut à decessoribus nostris recepimus, & nos quoque fecimus, ad curam nunc pertinent Thessalonicensis Antistitis, ut suâ sollicitudine, siquæ inter fratres nascantur, ut assolent, actiones distinguat atque definiat; & ad eum, quicquid à singulis sacerdotibus agitur, referatur. Sit Concilium, quotiens causæ fuerint, quotiens ille pro necessitatum emergentium ratione decreverit.* And Pope *Leo* I. in his decretal Epistle to *Anastasius* Bishop of *Thessalonica*: *Singulis autem Metropolitanis sicut potestas ista committitur, ut in suis Provinciis jus habeant ordinandi; ita eos Metropolitanos à te volumus ordinari; maturo tamen & decocto judicio.*

Occidental Illyricum comprehended *Pannonia prima* and *secunda, Savia, Dalmatia, Noricum mediterraneum*, and *Noricum ripense*; and its Metropolis was *Sirmium*, till *Attila* destroyed this city. Afterwards *Laureacum* became the Metropolis of *Noricum* and both *Pannonias*, and *Salona* the Metropolis of *Dalmatia*. Now [5] the Bishops of *Laureacum* and *Salona* received the *Pallium* from the Pope: and *Zosimus*, in his decretal Epistle to *Hesychius* Bishop of *Salona*, directed him to denounce the Apostolic decrees as well to the Bishops of his own, as to those of the neighbouring Provinces. The subjection of these Provinces to the See of *Rome* seems to have begun in *Anemius*, who was ordained Bishop of *Sirmium* by *Ambrose* Bishop of *Millain*, and who in the Council of *Aquileia* under Pope *Damasus*, A.C. 381, declared his sentence in these words: *Caput Illyrici non nisi civitas Sirmiensis: Ego igitur illius civitatis Episcopus sum. Eum qui non confitetur filium Dei æternum, & coeternum patri, qui est sempiternus, anathema dico.* The next year *Anemius* and *Ambrose*, with *Valerian* Bishop of *Aquileia, Acholias* Bishop of *Thessalonica*, and many others, went to the Council of *Rome*, which met for overruling the *Greek* Church by majority of votes, and exalting the authority of the Apostolic See, as was attempted before in the Council of *Sardica*.

Aquileia was the second city of the *Western Empire*, and by some called the second *Rome*. It was the Metropolis of *Istria, Forum Julium*, and *Venetia*; and its subjection to the See of *Rome* is manifest by the decretal Epistle of *Leo* I. directed to *Nicetas* Bishop of this city; for the Pope begins his Epistle thus: *Regressus ad nos filius meus Adeodatus Diaconus Sedis nostræ, dilectionem tuam poposcisse memorat, ut de his à nobis authoritatem Apostolicæ Sedis acciperes, quæ quidem magnam difficultatem dijudicationis videntur afferre.* Then he sets down an answer to the questions proposed by *Nicetas*, and concludes thus: *Hanc autem Epistolam nostram, quam ad consultationem tuæ fraternitatis emisimus, ad omnes fratres & comprovinciales tuos Episcopos facies pervenire, ut in omnium observantia, data profit authoritas. Data 1-2 Kal. Apr. Majorano Aug. Cos.* A.C. 458. *Gregory* the great A.C. 591, [6] cited *Severus* Bishop of *Aquileia* to appear before him in judgment in a Council at *Rome*.

The Bishops of *Aquileia* and *Millain* created one another, and therefore were of equal authority, and alike subject to the See of *Rome*. Pope *Pelagius* about the year 557, testified this in the following words: [7] *Mos antiquus fuit*, saith he, *ut quia pro longinquitate vel difficultate itineris, ab Apostolico illis onerosum fuerit ordinari, ipsi se invicem Mediolanensis & Aquileiensis ordinare Episcopos debuissent.* These words imply that the ordination of these two Bishops belonged to the See of *Rome*. When *Laurentius* Bishop of *Millain* had excommunicated *Magnus*, one of his Presbyters, and was dead, [8] *Gregory* the great absolved *Magnus*, and sent the *Pallium* to the new elected Bishop *Constantius*; whom the next year [9] he reprehended of partiality in judging *Fortunatus*, and commanded him to send *Fortunatus* to *Rome* to be judged there: four years after [10] he appointed the Bishops of *Millain* and *Ravenna* to hear the cause of one *Maximus*; and two years after, *viz.* A.C. 601, when *Constantius* was dead, and the people of *Millain* had elected *Deusdedit* his successor, and the *Lombards* had elected another, [11] *Gregory* wrote to the Notary, Clergy, and People of *Millain*, that by the authority of his Letters *Deusdedit* should be ordained, and that he whom the *Lombards* had ordained was an unworthy successor of *Ambrose*: whence I gather, that the Church of *Millain* had continued in this state of subordination to the See of *Rome* ever since the days of *Ambrose*; for *Ambrose* himself acknowledged the authority of that See. *Ecclesia Romana*, [12] saith he, *hanc consuetudinem non habet, cujus typum in omnibus sequimur, & formam.* And a little after: *In omnibus cupio sequi Ecclesiam Romanam.* And in his Commentary upon 1 *Tim.* iii. *Cum totus mundus Dei sit, tamen domus ejus Ecclesia dicitur, cujus hodie rector est Damasus.* In his Oration on the death of his brother *Satyrus*, he relates how his brother coming to a certain city of *Sardinia, advocavit Episcopum loci, percontatusque est ex eo utrum cum Episcopis Catholicis hoc est cum Romana Ecclesia conveniret?* And in conjunction with the Synod of *Aquileia* A.C. 381, in a synodical Epistle to the Emperor *Gratian*, he saith: *Totius orbis Romani caput Romanam Ecclesiam, atque illam sacrosanctam Apostolorum fidem, ne turbari sineret, obsecranda fuit clementia vestra; inde enim in omnes venerandœ communionis jura dimanant.* The Churches therefore of *Aquileia* and *Millain* were subject to the See of *Rome* from the days of the Emperor *Gratian. Auxentius* the predecessor of *Ambrose* was not subject to the see of *Rome*, and consequently the subjection of the Church of *Millain* began in *Ambrose.* This Diocese of *Millain* contained *Liguria* with *Insubria*, the *Alpes Cottiœ* and *Rhœtia*; and was divided from the Diocese of *Aquileia* by the river *Addua.* In the year 844, the Bishop of *Millain* broke off from the See of *Rome*, and continued in this separation about 200 years, as is thus related by [13] *Sigonius: Eodem anno Angilbertus Mediolanensis Archiepiscopus ab Ecclesia Romana parum comperta de causa descivit, tantumque exemplo in posterum valuit, ut non nisi post ducentos annos Ecclesia Mediolanensis ad Romanœ obedientiam auctoritatemque redierit.*

The Bishop of *Ravenna*, the Metropolis of *Flaminia* and *Æmilia*, was also subject to the Pope: for *Zosimus*, A.C. 417, excommunicated some of the Presbyters of that Church, and wrote a commonitory Epistle about them to the Clergy of that Church as a branch of the *Roman* Church: *In sua*, saith he, *hoc est, in Ecclesia nostra Romana.* When those of *Ravenna*, having elected a new Bishop, gave notice thereof to Pope *Sixtus*, the Pope set him aside, and [14] ordained *Peter Chrysologus* in his room. *Chrysologus* in his Epistle to *Eutyches*, extant in the Acts of the Council of *Chalcedon*, wrote thus: *Nos pro studio pacis & fidei, extra consensum Romanœ civitatis Episcopi, causas fidei audire non possumus.* Pope *Leo* I. being consulted by *Leo* Bishop of *Ravenna* about some questions, answered him by a decretal Epistle A.C. 451. And Pope *Gregory* the great, [15] reprehending *John* Bishop of *Ravenna* about the use of the *Pallium*, tells him of a Precept of one of his Predecessors, Pope *John*, commanding that all the Privileges formerly granted to the Bishop and Church of *Ravenna* should be kept: to this *John* returned a submissive answer; and after his death Pope *Gregory* ordered a visitation of the Church of *Ravenna*, confirmed the privileges heretofore granted them, and sent his *Pallium*, as of antient custom, to their new Bishop *Marinian.* Yet this Church revolted sometimes from the Church of *Rome*, but returned again to its obedience.

The rest of *Italy*, with the Islands adjacent, containing the *suburbicarian* regions, or ten Provinces under the temporal Vicar of *Rome, viz.* [1]*Campania*, [2]*Tuscia* and *Umbria*, [3]*Picenum suburbicarium*, [4]*Sicily*, [5]*Apulia* and *Calabria*, [6]*Brutii* and *Lucania*, [7]*Samnium*, [8]*Sardinia*, [9]*Corsica*, and [10]*Valeria*, constituted the proper Province of the Bishop of *Rome*. For the Council of *Nice* in their fifth Canon ordained that Councils should be held every spring and autumn in every Province; and according to this Canon, the Bishops of this Province met at *Rome* every half year. In this sense Pope *Leo* I. applied this Canon to *Rome*, in a decretal Epistle to the Bishops of *Sicily*, written *Alippio & Ardabure Coss.* A.C. 447. *Quia saluberrime,* saith he, *à sanctis patribus constitutum est, binos in annis singulis Episcoporum debere esse conventus, terni semper ex vobis ad diem tertium Kalendarum Octobrium Romam æterno concilio sociandi occurrant. Et indissimulanter à vobis hæc consuetudo servetur, quoniam adjuvante Dei gratiâ, faciliùs poterit provideri, ut in Ecclesiis Christi nulla scandala, nulli nascantur errores; cum coram Apostolo Petro semper in communione tractatum fuerit, ut omnia Canonum Decreta apud omnes Domini sacerdotes inviolata permaneant.* The Province of *Rome* therefore comprehended *Sicily*, with so much of *Italy* and the neighbouring Islands as sent Bishops to the annual Councils of *Rome*; but extended not into the Provinces of *Ravenna*, *Aquileia, Millain, Arles,* &c. those Provinces having Councils of their own. The Bishops in every Province of the *Roman* Empire were convened in Council by the Metropolitan or Bishop of the head city of the Province, and this Bishop presided in that Council: but the Bishop of *Rome* did not only preside in his own Council of the Bishops of the *suburbicarian* regions, but also gave Orders to the Metropolitans of all the other Provinces in the *Western Empire*, as their universal governor; as may be further perceived by the following instances.

Pope *Zosimus* A.C. 417, cited *Proculus* Bishop of *Marseilles* to appear before a Council at *Rome* for illegitimate Ordinations; and condemned him, as he mentions in several of his Epistles. Pope *Boniface* I. A.C. 419, upon a complaint of the Clergy of *Valentia* against *Maximus* a Bishop, summoned the Bishops of all

Gallia and the seven Provinces to convene in a Council against him; and saith in his Epistle, that his Predecessors had done the like. Pope *Leo* I. called a general Council of all the Provinces of *Spain* to meet in *Gallæcia* against the *Manichees* and *Priscillianists*, as he says in his decretal Epistle to *Turribius* a *Spanish* Bishop. And in one of his decretal Epistles to *Nicetas* Bishop of *Aquileia*, he commands him to call a Council of the Bishops of that Province against the *Pelagians*, which might ratify all the Synodal Decrees which had been already ratified by the See of *Rome* against this heresy. And in his decretal Epistle to *Anastasius* Bishop of *Thessalonica*, he ordained that Bishop should hold two Provincial Councils every year, and refer the harder causes to the See of *Rome*: and if upon any extraordinary occasion it should be necessary to call a Council, he should not be troublesom to the Bishops under him, but content himself with two Bishops out of every Province, and not detain them above fifteen days. In the same Epistle he describes the form of Church-Government then set up, to consist in a subordination of all the Churches to the See of *Rome*: *De qua forma*, saith he, *Episcoporum quoque est orta distinctio, & magna dispositione provisum est ne omnes sibi omnia vindicarent, sed essent in singulis Provinciis singuli quorum inter fratres haberetur prima sententia, & rursus quidam in majoribus urbibus constituti sollicitudinem sumerent ampliorem, per quos ad unam Petri Sedem universalis Ecclesiæ cura conflueret, & nihil usque à suo capite dissideret. Qui ergo scit se quibusdam esse præpositum, non moleste ferat aliquem sibi esse præpositum; sed obedientiam quam exigit etiam ipse dependat; et sicut non vult gravis oneris sarcinam ferre, ita non audeat aliis importabile pondus imponere.* These words sufficiently shew the monarchical form of government then set up in the Churches of the *Western Empire* under the Bishop of *Rome*, by means of the imperial Decree of *Gratian*, and the appeals and decretal Epistles grounded thereupon.

The same Pope *Leo*, having in a Council at *Rome* passed sentence upon *Hilary* Bishop of *Arles*, for what he had done by a Provincial Council in *Gallia*, took occasion from thence to procure the following Edict from the *Western* Emperor

Valentinian III. for the more absolute establishing the authority of his See over all the Churches of the *Western Empire.*

Impp. Theodosius & Valentinianus AA. Aetio Viro illustri, Comiti & Magistro utriusque militiæ & Patricio.

Certum est & nobis & imperio nostro unicum esse præsidium in supernæ Divinitatis favore, ad quem promerendum præcipue Christiana fides & veneranda nobis religio suffragatur. Cum igitur Sedis Apostolicæ Primatum sancti Petri meritum, qui princeps est Episcopalis coronæ & Romanæ dignitas civitatis, sacræ etiam Synodi firmavit auctoritas: ne quid præter auctoritatem Sedis istius illicitum præsumptio attemperare nitatur: tunc enim demum Ecclesiarum pax ubique servabitur, si Rectorem suum agnoscat Universitas. Hæc cum hactenus inviolabiliter suerint custodita, Hilarius Arelatensis, sicut venerabilis viri Leonis Romani Papæ fideli relatione comperimus, contumaci ausu illicita quædam præsumenda tentavit, & ideo Transalpinas Ecclesias abominabilis tumultus invasit, quod recens maximè testatur exemplum. Hilarius enim qui Episcopus Arelatensis vocatur, Ecclesiæ Romanæ urbis inconsulto Pontifice indebitas sibi ordinationes Episcoporum solâ temeritate usurpans invasit. Nam alios incompetenter removit; indecenter alios, invitis & repugnantibus civibus, ordinavit. Qui quidem, quoniam non facile ab his qui non elegerant, recipiebantur, manum sibi contrahebat armatam, & claustra murorum in hostilem morem vel obsidione cingebat, vel aggressione reserabat, & ad sedem quietis pacem prædicaturus per bella ducebat: His talibus contra Imperii majestatem, & contra reverentiam Apostolicæ Sedis admissis, per ordinem religiosi viri Urbis Papæ cognitione discussis, certa in eum, ex his quos malè ordinaverat, lata sententia est. Erat quidem ipsa sententia per Gallias etiam sine Imperiali Sanctione valitura: quid enim Pontificis auctoritate non liceret? Sed nostram quoque præceptionem hæc ratio provocavit. Nec ulterius vel Hilario, quem adhuc Episcopum nuncupare sola mansueta Præsulis permittit humanitas, nec cuiquam alteri ecclesiasticis rebus arma miscere, aut præceptis Romani Antistitis liceat obviare: ausibus enim talibus fides & reverentia nostri violatur Imperii. Nec hoc solum, quod est maximi criminis, submovemus: verum ne levis saltem inter Ecclesias turba nascatur, vel in aliquo minui religionis disciplina videatur, hoc perenni sanctione discernimus; nequid tam Episcopis Gallicanis quam aliarum Provinciarum contra consuetudinem veterem liceat, sine viri venerabilis Papæ Urbis æternæ auctoritate, tentare. Sed illis omnibusque pro lege sit, quicquid sanxit vel sanxerit Apostolicæ Sedis auctoritas: ita ut quisquis Episcoporum ad judicium Romani Antistitis evocatus venire neglexerit, per Moderatorem ejusdem Provinciæ adesse cogatur, per omnia servatis quæ Divi parentes nostri Romanæ Ecclesiæ detulerunt, Aetî pater carissime Augusti. Unde illustris & præclara magnificentia tua præsentis Edictalis Legis auctoritate faciet quæ sunt superius statuta servari, decem librarum auri multa protinus exigenda ab unoquoque Judice qui passus fuerit præcepta nostra violari. Divinitas te servet per multos annos, parens carissime. Dat. viii. *Id. Jun. Romæ, Valentiniano A.* vi. *Consule,* A.C. 445. By this Edict the Emperor *Valentinian* enjoined an absolute obedience to the will of the Bishop of *Rome* thro'out all the Churches of his Empire; and declares, that for the Bishops to attempt any thing without the Pope's authority is contrary to antient custom, and that the Bishops summoned to appear before his judicature must be carried thither by the Governor of the Province; and he ascribes these privileges of the See of *Rome* to the concessions of his dead Ancestors, that is, to the Edict of *Gratian* and *Valentinian* II. as above: by which reckoning this dominion of the Church of *Rome* was now of 66 years standing: and if in all this time it had not been sufficiently established, this new Edict was enough to settle it beyond all question thro'out the *Western Empire.*

Hence all the Bishops of the Province of *Arles* in their Letter to Pope *Leo,* A.C. 450, petitioning for a restitution of the privileges of their Metropolitan, say: *Per beatum Petrum Apostolorum principem, sacrosancta Ecclesia Romana tenebat supra omnes totius mundi Ecclesias principatum.* And *Ceratius, Salonius* and *Veranus,* three Bishops of *Gallia,* say, in their Epistle to the same Pope: *Magna præterea & ineffabili quadam nos peculiares tui gratulatione succrescimus, quod illa specialis doctrinæ vestræ pagina ita per omnium Ecclesiarum conventicula celebratur, ut vere consona omnium sententia declaretur; merito illic principatum Sedis Apostolicæ constitutum, unde adhuc Apostolici spiritus oracula reserentur.* And *Leo* himself, in [16] his Epistle to the metropolitan Bishops thro'out *Illyricum*: *Quia per omnes Ecclesias cura nostra distenditur, exigente hoc à nobis Domino, qui Apostolicæ dignitatis beatissimo Apostolo Petro primatum, fidei sui remuneratione commisit, universalem Ecclesiam in fundamenti ipsius soliditate constituens.*

While this Ecclesiastical Dominion was rising up, the northern barbarous nations invaded the *Western Empire*, and founded several kingdoms therein, of different religions from the Church of *Rome*. But these kingdoms by degrees embraced the *Roman* faith, and at the same time submitted to the Pope's authority. The *Franks* in *Gaul* submitted in the end of the fifth Century, the *Goths* in *Spain* in the end of the sixth; and the *Lombards* in *Italy* were conquered by *Charles* the great A.C. 774. Between the years 775 and 794, the same *Charles* extended the Pope's authority over all *Germany* and *Hungary* as far as the river *Theysse* and the *Baltic* sea; he then set him above all human judicature, and at the same time assisted him in subduing the City and Duchy of *Rome*. By the conversion of the ten kingdoms to the *Roman* religion, the Pope only enlarged his spiritual dominion, but did not yet rise up as a horn of the Beast. It was his temporal dominion which made him one of the horns: and this dominion he acquired in the latter half of the eighth century, by subduing three of the former horns as above. And now being arrived at a temporal dominion, and a power above all human judicature, he reigned [17] *with a look more stout than his fellows,* and [18] *times and laws were* henceforward *given into his hands, for a time times and half a time,* or three times and an half; that is, for 1260 solar years, reckoning a time for a Calendar year of 360 days, and a day for a solar year. After which [19] *the judgment is to sit, and they shall take away his dominion,* not at once, but by degrees, *to consume, and to destroy it unto the end.* [20] *And the kingdom and dominion, and greatness of the kingdom under the whole heaven shall,* by degrees, *be given unto the people of the saints of the most High, whose kingdom is an everlasting kingdom, and all dominions shall serve and obey him.*

Notes to Chap. VIII

[1] *See the Annals of* Baronius, Anno 381. Sect. 6.

[2] Populos Galliciæ.

[3] Hormisd. Epist. 24. 26.

[4] *The words,* sine auctoritate, *seem wanting.*

[5] Vide Caroli a S. Paulo Geographiam sacram, p. 72, 73.

[6] Greg. M. lib. 1. Indic. 9. Epist. 16.

[7] Apud Gratianum de Mediolanensi & Aquileiensi Episcopis.

[8] Greg. M. lib. 3. Epist. 26. & lib. 4. Epist. 1.

[9] Greg. lib. 5. Epist. 4.

[10] Greg. lib. 9. Epist. 10 & 67.

[11] Greg. lib. 11. Epist. 3, 4.

[12] Ambros l. 3. de sacramentis, c. 1.

[13] Sigonius de Regno Italiæ, lib. 5.

[14] *See* Baronius, Anno 433. Sect. 24.

[15] Greg. M. lib. 3. Epist. 56, 57. & lib. 5. Epist. 25, 26, 56.

[16] Epist. 25. apud Holstenium.

[17] Dan. vii. 20.

[18] Ver. 25.

[19] Ver. 26.

[20] Ver. 27.

CHAP. IX

Of the kingdoms represented in Daniel
by the Ram and He-Goat.

T he second and third Empires, represented by the Bear and Leopard, are again represented by the Ram and He-Goat; but with this difference, that the Ram represents the kingdoms of the *Medes* and *Persians* from the beginning of the four Empires, and the Goat represents the kingdom of the *Greeks* to the end of them. By this means, under the type of the Ram and He-Goat, the times of all the four Empires are again described: *I lifted up mine eyes*, saith [1] *Daniel, and saw, and behold there stood before the river* [Ulai] *a Ram which had two horns, and the two horns were high, but one was higher than the other, and the higher came up last.—And the Ram having two horns, are the kings of* Media *and* Persia: not two persons but two kingdoms, the kingdoms of *Media* and *Persia*; and the kingdom of *Persia* was the higher horn and came up last. The kingdom of *Persia* rose up, when *Cyrus* having newly conquered *Babylon*, revolted from *Darius* King of the *Medes*, and beat him at *Pasargadæ*, and set up the *Persians* above the *Medes*. This was the horn which came up last. And the horn which came up first was the kingdom of the *Medes*, from the time that *Cyaxares* and *Nebuchadnezzar* overthrew *Nineveh*, and shared the Empire of the *Assyrians* between them. The Empires of *Media* and *Babylon* were contemporary, and rose up together by the fall of the *Assyrian* Empire; and the Prophecy of the four Beasts begins with one of them, and that of the Ram and He-Goat with the other. As the Ram represents the kingdom of *Media* and *Persia* from the beginning of the four Empires; so the He-Goat represents the Empire of the *Greeks* to the end of those Monarchies. In the reign of his great horn, and of the four horns which succeeded it, he represents this Empire during the reign of the Leopard: and in the reign of his little horn, which stood up in the latter time of the kingdom of the four, and after their fall became mighty but not by his own power, he represents it during the reign of the fourth Beast.

The rough Goat, saith *Daniel, is the King of* Grecia, that is, the kingdom; *and the great horn between his eyes is the first King*: not the first Monarch, but the first kingdom, that which lasted during the reign of *Alexander* the great, and his brother *Aridæus* and two young sons, *Alexander* and *Hercules.* [2] *Now that* [horn] *being broken off, whereas four* [horns] *stood up for it, four kingdoms shall stand up out of the nation* [of the *Greeks*], *but not in his* [the first horn's] *power.* The four horns are therefore four kingdoms; and by consequence, the first great horn which they succeeded is the first great kingdom of the *Greeks*, that which was founded by *Alexander* the great, *An. Nabonass.* 414, and lasted till the death of his son *Hercules*, *An. Nabonass.* 441. And the four are those of *Cassander, Lysimachus, Antigonus*, and *Ptolemy*, as above.

[3] *And in the latter time of their kingdom, when the transgressors are come to the full, a King* [or new kingdom] *of fierce countenance, and understanding dark sentences, shall stand up: and his power shall be mighty, but not by his own power.* This King was the last horn of the Goat, the little horn which came up out of one of the four horns, and waxed exceeding great. The latter time of their kingdom was when the *Romans* began to conquer them, that is, when they conquered *Perseus* King of *Macedonia*, the fundamental kingdom of the *Greeks*. And at that time the transgressors came to the full: for then the High-priesthood was exposed to sale, the Vessels of the Temple were sold to pay for the purchase; and the High-priest, with some of the *Jews*, procured a licence from *Antiochus Epiphanes* to do after the ordinances of the heathen, and set up a school at *Jerusalem* for teaching those ordinances. Then *Antiochus* took *Jerusalem* with an armed force, slew 4000 *Jews*, took as many prisoners and sold them, spoiled the Temple, interdicted the worship, commanded the Law of *Moses* to be burnt, and set up the worship of the heathen Gods in all *Judea*. In the very same year, *An. Nabonass.* 580, the *Romans* conquered

Macedonia, the chief of the four horns. Hitherto the Goat was mighty by its own power, but henceforward began to be under the *Romans*. *Daniel* distinguishes the times, by describing very particularly the actions of the Kings of the north and south, those two of the four horns which bordered upon *Judea*, until the *Romans* conquered *Macedonia*; and thenceforward only touching upon the main revolutions which happened within the compass of the nations represented by the Goat. In this latter period of time the little horn was to stand up and grow mighty, but not by his own power.

The three first of *Daniel's* Beasts had their dominions taken away, each of them at the rise of the next Beast; but their lives were prolonged, and they are all of them still alive. The third Beast, or Leopard, reigned in his four heads, till the rise of the fourth Beast, or Empire of the *Latins*; and his life was prolonged under their power. This Leopard reigning in his four heads, signifies the same thing with the He-Goat reigning in his four horns: and therefore the He-Goat reigned in his four horns till the rise of *Daniel's* fourth Beast, or Empire of the *Latins*: then its dominion was taken away by the *Latins*, but its life was prolonged under their power. The *Latins* are not comprehended among the nations represented by the He-Goat in this Prophecy: their power over the *Greeks* is only named in it, to distinguish the times in which the He-Goat was mighty by his own power, from the times in which he was mighty but not by his own power. He was mighty by his own power till his dominion was taken away by the *Latins*; after that, his life was prolonged under their dominion, and this prolonging of his life was in the days of his last horn: for in the days of this horn the Goat became mighty, but not by his own power.

Now because this horn was a horn of the Goat, we are to look for it among the nations which composed the body of the Goat. Among those nations he was to rise up and grow mighty: he grew mighty [4] *towards the south, and towards the east, and towards the pleasant land*; and therefore he was to rise up in the north-west parts of those nations, and extend his dominion towards *Egypt*, *Syria* and *Judea*. In the latter time of the kingdom of the four horns, it was to rise up out of one of them and subdue the rest, but not by its own power. It was to be assisted by a foreign power, a power superior to itself, the power which took away the dominion of the third Beast, the power of the fourth Beast. And such a little horn was the kingdom of *Macedonia*, from the time that it became subject to the *Romans*. This kingdom, by the victory of the *Romans* over *Persius* King of *Macedonia*, *Anno Nabonass.* 580, ceased to be one of the four horns of the Goat, and became a dominion of a new sort: not a horn of the fourth Beast, for *Macedonia* belonged to the body of the third; but a horn of the third Beast of a new sort, a horn of the Goat which grew mighty but not by his own power, a horn which rose up and grew potent under a foreign power, the power of the *Romans*.

The *Romans*, by the legacy of *Attalus* the last King of *Pergamus*, *An. Nabonass.* 615, inherited that kingdom, including all *Asia Minor* on this side mount *Taurus*. *An. Nabonass.* 684 and 685 they conquered *Armenia*, *Syria* and *Judea*; *An. Nabonass.* 718, they subdued *Egypt*. And by these conquests the little horn [5] *waxed exceeding great towards the south, and towards the east, and towards the pleasant land. And it waxed great even to the host of heaven; and cast down some of the host and of the stars to the ground, and stamped upon them,* that is, upon the people and great men of the *Jews*. [6] *Yea, he magnified himself even to the Prince of the Host,* the *Messiah*, the Prince of the *Jews,* whom he put to death, *An. Nabonass.* 780. *And by him the daily sacrifice was taken away, and the place of his sanctuary was cast down, viz.* in the wars which the armies of the *Eastern* nations under the conduct of the *Romans* made against *Judea,* when *Nero* and *Vespasian* were Emperors, *An. Nabonass.* 816, 817, 818. [7] *And an host was given him against the daily sacrifice by reason of transgression, and it cast down the truth to the ground, and it practised and prospered.* This transgression is in the next words called *the transgression of desolation;* and in *Dan.* xi. 31. *the abomination which maketh desolate;* and in *Matth.* xxiv. 15. *the abomination of desolation, spoken of by* Daniel *the prophet, standing in the holy place.* It may relate chiefly to the worship of *Jupiter Olympius* in his Temple built by the Emperor *Hadrian*, in the place of the Temple of the *Jews*, and to the revolt of the *Jews* under *Barchochab* occasioned thereby, and to the desolation of *Judea* which followed thereupon; all the *Jews*, being thenceforward banished *Judea* upon pain of death. *Then I heard*, saith [8] *Daniel, one saint speaking, and another saint said unto that certain saint which spake, How long shall be the vision concerning the daily sacrifice, and the transgression of desolation, to give both the sanctuary and the host to be trodden under foot? And he said unto me, Unto two thousand and three hundred days; then shall the sanctuary be cleansed. Daniel's* days are years; and these years may perhaps be reckoned either from the destruction of the Temple by the *Romans* in the reign of *Vespasian*, or from the pollution of the Sanctuary by the worship of *Jupiter Olympius*, or from the desolation of *Judea* made in the end of the *Jewish* war by the banishment of all the *Jews* out of their own country, or from some other period which time will discover. Henceforward the last horn of the Goat continued mighty under the *Romans*, till the reign of *Constantine* the great and his sons: and then by the division of the *Roman* Empire between the *Greek* and *Latin* Emperors, it separated from the *Latins*, and became the *Greek* Empire alone, but yet under the dominion of a *Roman* family; and at present it is mighty under the dominion of the *Turks*.

This last horn is by some taken for *Antiochus Epiphanes*, but not very judiciously. A horn of a Beast is never taken for a single person: it always signifies a new kingdom, and the kingdom of *Antiochus* was an old one. *Antiochus* reigned over one of the four horns, and the little horn was a fifth under its proper kings. This horn was at first a little one, and waxed exceeding great, but so did not *Antiochus*. It is described great above all the former horns, and so was not *Antiochus*. His kingdom on the contrary was weak, and tributary to the *Romans*, and he did not enlarge it. The horn was a *King of fierce countenance, and destroyed wonderfully, and prospered and practised*; that is, he prospered in his practises against the holy people: but *Antiochus* was frighted out of *Egypt* by a mere message of the *Romans*, and afterwards routed and baffled by the *Jews*. The horn was mighty by another's power, *Antiochus* acted by his own. The horn stood up against the Prince of the Host of heaven, the Prince of Princes;

and this is the character not of *Antiochus* but of *Antichrist*. The horn cast down the Sanctuary to the ground, and so did not *Antiochus*; he left it standing. The Sanctuary and Host were trampled under foot 2300 days; and in *Daniel*'s Prophecies days are put for years: but the profanation of the Temple in the reign of *Antiochus* did not last so many natural days. These were to last till the time of the end, till the last end of the indignation against the *Jews*; and this indignation is not yet at an end. They were to last till the Sanctuary which had been cast down should be cleansed, and the Sanctuary is not yet cleansed.

This Prophecy of the Ram and He-Goat is repeated in the last Prophecy of *Daniel*. There the Angel tells *Daniel*, that [9] *he stood up to strengthen* Darius *the* Mede, *and that there should stand up yet three kings in* Persia, [*Cyrus, Cambyses,* and *Darius Hystaspis*] *and the fourth* [*Xerxes*] *should be far richer than they all; and by his wealth thro' his riches he should stir up all against the realm of* Grecia. This relates to the Ram, whose two horns were the kingdoms of *Media* and *Persia*. Then he goes on to describe the horns of the Goat by the [10] *standing up of a mighty king, which should rule with great dominion, and do according to his will*; and by the breaking of his kingdom into four smaller kingdoms, and not descending to his own posterity. Then he describes the actions of two of those kingdoms which bordered on *Judea, viz. Egypt* and *Syria,* calling them the Kings of the *South* and *North,* that is, in respect of *Judea*; and he carries on the description till the latter end of the kingdoms of the four, and till the reign of *Antiochus Epiphanes,* when transgressors were come to the full. In the eighth year of *Antiochus,* the year in which he profaned the Temple and set up the heathen Gods in all *Judea,* and the *Romans* conquered the kingdom of *Macedon*; the prophetic Angel leaves off describing the affairs of the kings of the *South* and *North,* and begins to describe those of the *Greeks* under the dominion of the *Romans,* in these words: [11] *And after him Arms* [the *Romans*] *shall stand up, and they shall pollute the sanctuary of strength.* As ךלמם signifies *after the king,* Dan. xi. 8; so here ונמם may signify *after him*: and so תחאה־ןמ may signify *after one of them,* Dan. viii. 9. Arms are every where in these Prophecies of *Daniel* put for the military power of a kingdom, and they stand up when they conquer and grow powerful. The *Romans* conquered *Illyricum, Epirus* and *Macedonia*, in the year of *Nabonassar* 580; and thirty five years after, by the last will and testament of *Attalus* the last King of *Pergamus*, they inherited that rich and flourishing kingdom, that is, all *Asia* on this side mount *Taurus*: and sixty nine years after, they conquered the kingdom of *Syria*, and reduced it into a Province: and thirty four years after they did the like to *Egypt*. By all these steps the *Roman* arms stood up over the *Greeks*. And after 95 years more, by making war upon the *Jews, they polluted the sanctuary of strength, and took away the daily sacrifice, and*, in its room soon after, *placed the abomination which made* the Land *desolate*: for this abomination was placed after the days of Christ, *Matth.* xxiv. 15. In the 16th year of the Emperor *Hadrian*, A. C. 132, they placed this abomination by building a Temple to *Jupiter Capitolinus*, where the Temple of God in *Jerusalem* had stood. Thereupon the *Jews* under the conduct of *Barchochab* rose up in arms against the *Romans*, and in that war had 50 cities demolished, 985 of their best towns destroyed, and 580000 men slain by the sword: and in the end of the war, A.C. 136, they were all banished *Judea* upon pain or death; and that time the land hath remained desolate of its old inhabitants.

Now that the prophetic Angel passes in this manner from the four kingdoms of the *Greeks* to the *Romans* reigning over the *Greeks*, is confirmed from hence, that in the next place he describes the affairs of the *Christians* unto the time of the end, in these words: [12] *And they that understand among the people shall instruct many, yet they shall fall by the sword and by flame, by captivity and by spoil many days. Now when they shall fall they shall be holpen with a little help*, viz. in the reign of *Constantine* the great; *but many shall cleave to them with dissimulation. And some of them of understanding there shall fall to try them, and to purge* them from the dissemblers; *and to make them white even to the time of the end.* And a little after, the time of the end is said to be *a time, times, and half a time*: which is the duration of the reign of the last horn of *Daniel*'s fourth Beast, and of the *Woman* and her *Beast* in the *Apocalypse*.

Notes to Chap. IX

[1] Chap. viii. 3.
[2] Ver. 22.
[3] Ver. 23.
[4] Chap. viii. 9.
[5] Chap. viii. 9, 10.
[6] Ver. 11.
[7] Ver. 12.
[8] Ver. 13, 14.
[9] Dan. xi. 1, 2.
[10] Ver. 3.
[11] Dan xi. 31.
[12] Chap. xi. 33, &c.

CHAP. X

Of the Prophecy of the Seventy Weeks

The Vision of the Image composed of four Metals was given first to *Nebuchadnezzar*, and then to *Daniel* in a dream: and *Daniel* began then to be celebrated for revealing of secrets, *Ezek.* xxviii. 3. The Vision of the four Beasts, and of *the Son of man* coming in the clouds of heaven, was also given to *Daniel* in a dream. That of the Ram and the He-Goat appeared to him in the day time, when he was by the bank of the river *Ulay*; and was explained to him by the prophetic Angel *Gabriel*. It concerns the *Prince of the host*, and the *Prince of Princes*: and now in the first year of *Darius* the *Mede* over *Babylon*, the same prophetic Angel appears to *Daniel* again, and explains to him what is meant by the *Son of man*, by the *Prince of the host*, and the *Prince of Princes*. The Prophecy of the *Son of man* coming in the clouds of heaven relates to the second coming of *Christ*; that of the *Prince of the host* relates to his first coming: and this Prophecy of the *Messiah*, in explaining them, relates to both comings, and assigns the times thereof.

This Prophecy, like all the rest of *Daniel's*, consists of two parts, an introductory Prophecy and an explanation thereof; the whole I thus translate and interpret.

[1] '*Seventy weeks are* [2] *cut out upon thy people, and upon thy holy city, to finish transgression, and* [3] *to make an end of sins, to expiate iniquity, and to bring in everlasting righteousness, to consummate the Vision and* [4] *the Prophet, and to anoint the most Holy.*

'*Know also and understand, that from the going forth of the commandment to cause to return and to build* Jerusalem, *unto* [5] *the Anointed the Prince, shall be seven weeks.*

'*Yet threescore and two weeks shall* [6] *it return, and the street be built and the wall; but in troublesome times: and after the threescore and two weeks, the Anointed shall be cut off, and [6] it shall not be his; but the people of a Prince to come shall destroy the city and the sanctuary: and the end thereof shall be with a flood, and unto the end of the war, desolations are determined.*

'*Yet shall he confirm the covenant with many for one week: and in half a week he shall cause the sacrifice and oblation to cease: and upon a wing of abominations he shall make it desolate, even until the consummation, and that which is determined be poured upon the desolate.*'

Seventy weeks are cut out upon thy people, and upon thy holy city, to finish transgression, &c. Here, by putting a week for seven years, are reckoned 490 years from the time that the dispersed *Jews* should be re-incorporated into [7] a people and a holy city, until the death and resurrection of *Christ*; whereby *transgression should be finished, and sins ended, iniquity be expiated, and everlasting righteousness brought in, and this Vision be accomplished, and the Prophet consummated,* that Prophet whom the *Jews* expected; and whereby *the most Holy* should be *anointed,* he who is therefore in the next words called the *Anointed,* that is, the *Messiah,* or the *Christ.* For by joining the accomplishment of the vision with the expiation of sins, the 490 years are ended with the death of *Christ.* Now the dispersed *Jews* became a people and city when they first returned into a polity or body politick; and this was in the seventh year of *Artaxerxes Longimanus,* when *Ezra* returned with a body of *Jews* from captivity, and revived the *Jewish* worship; and by the King's commission created Magistrates in all the land, to judge and govern the people according to the laws of God and the King, *Ezra* vii. 25. There were but two returns from captivity, *Zerubbabel*'s and *Ezra*'s; in *Zerubbabel*'s they had only commission to build the Temple, in *Ezra*'s they first became a polity or city by a government of their own. Now the years of this *Artaxerxes* began about two or three months after the summer solstice, and his seventh year fell in with the third year of the eightieth *Olympiad*; and the latter part thereof, wherein *Ezra* went up to *Jerusalem,* was in the year of the *Julian Period* 4257. Count the time from thence to the death of *Christ,* and you will find it just 490 years. If you count in *Judaic* years commencing in autumn, and date the reckoning from the first autumn after *Ezra's* coming to *Jerusalem*, when he put the King's decree in execution; the death of *Christ* will fall on the year of the *Julian Period* 4747, *Anno Domini* 34; and the weeks will be *Judaic* weeks, ending with sabbatical years; and this I take to be the truth: but if you had rather place the death of *Christ* in the year before, as is commonly done, you may take the year of *Ezra's* journey into the reckoning.

Know also and understand, that from the going forth of the commandment to cause to return and to build Jerusalem, *unto the Anointed the Prince, shall be seven weeks.* The former part of the Prophecy related to the first coming of *Christ*, being dated to his coming as a Prophet; this being dated to his coming to be Prince or King, seems to relate to his second coming. There, the Prophet was consummate, and the most holy anointed: here, he that was anointed comes to be Prince and to reign. For *Daniel's* Prophecies reach to the end of the world; and there is scarce a Prophecy in the Old Testament concerning *Christ*, which doth not in something or other relate to his second coming. If divers of the antients, as [8] *Irenæus*, [9] *Julius Africanus, Hippolytus* the martyr, and *Apollinaris* Bishop of *Laodicea*, applied the half week to the times of *Antichrist*; why may not we, by the same liberty of interpretation, apply the seven weeks to the time when *Antichrist* shall be destroyed by the brightness of *Christ's* coming?

The *Israelites* in the days of the antient Prophets, when the ten Tribes were led into captivity, expected a double return; and that at the first the *Jews* should build a new Temple inferior to *Solomon's*, until the time of that age should be fulfilled; and afterwards they should return from all places of their captivity, and build *Jerusalem* and the Temple gloriously, *Tobit* xiv. 4, 5, 6: and to express the glory and excellence of this city, it is figuratively said to be built of precious stones, *Tobit* xiii. 16, 17, 18. *Isa.* liv. 11, 12. *Rev.* xi. and called the *New Jerusalem*, the *Heavenly Jerusalem*, the *Holy City*, the *Lamb's Wife*, the *City of the Great King*, the *City into which the Kings of the earth do bring their glory and honour. Now* while such a return from captivity was the expectation of *Israel*, even before the times of *Daniel*, I know not why *Daniel* should omit it in his Prophecy. This part of the Prophecy being therefore not yet fulfilled, I shall not attempt a particular interpretation of it, but content myself with observing, that as the *seventy* and the *sixty two weeks* were *Jewish* weeks, ending with sabbatical years; so the *seven weeks* are the compass of a *Jubilee*, and begin and end with actions proper for a *Jubilee*, and of the highest nature for which a *Jubilee* can be kept: and that since *the commandment to return and to build* Jerusalem, precedes the *Messiah the Prince* 49 years; it may perhaps come forth not from the *Jews* themselves, but from some other kingdom friendly to them, and precede their return from captivity, and give occasion to it; and lastly, that this rebuilding of *Jerusalem* and the waste places of *Judah* is predicted in *Micah* vii. 11. *Amos* ix. 11, 14. *Ezek.* xxxvi. 33, 35, 36, 38. *Isa.* liv. 3, 11, 12. lv. 12. lxi. 4. lxv. 18, 21,22. and *Tobit* xiv. 5. and that the return from captivity and coming of the *Messiah* and his kingdom are described in *Daniel* vii. *Rev.* xix. *Acts* i. *Mat.* xxiv. *Joel* iii. *Ezek.* xxxvi. xxxvii. *Isa.* lx. lxii. lxiii. lxv. and lxvi. and many other places of scripture. The manner I know not. Let time be the Interpreter.

Yet threescore and two weeks shall it return, and the street be built and the wall, but in troublesome times: and after the threescore and two weeks the Messiah *shall be cut off, and it shall not be his; but the people of a Prince to come shall destroy the city and the sanctuary,* &c. Having foretold both comings of *Christ*, and dated the last from their returning and building *Jerusalem*; to prevent the applying that to the building *Jerusalem* by *Nehemiah*, he distinguishes this from that, by saying that from this period to the *Anointed* shall be, not seven weeks, but threescore and two weeks, and this not in prosperous but in troublesome times; and at the end of these Weeks the *Messiah* shall not be the Prince of the *Jews*, but be cut off; and *Jerusalem* not be his, but the city and sanctuary be destroyed. Now *Nehemiah* came to *Jerusalem* in the 20th year of this same *Artaxerxes*, while *Ezra* still continued there, *Nehem.* xii. 36, and found the city lying waste, and the houses and wall unbuilt, *Nehem.* ii. 17. vii. 4, and finished the wall the 25th day of the month *Elul, Nehem.* vi. 15, in the 28th year of the King, that is, in *September* in the year of the *Julian Period* 4278. Count now from this year threescore and two weeks of years, that is 434 years, and the reckoning will end in *September* in the year of the *Julian Period* 4712 which is the year in which *Christ* was born, according to *Clemens Alexandrinus, Irenæus, Eusebius, Epiphanius, Jerome, Orosius, Cassiodorus,* and other antients; and this was the general opinion, till *Dionysius Exiguus* invented the vulgar account, in which *Christ's* birth is placed two years later. If with some you reckon that *Christ* was born three or four years before the vulgar account, yet his birth will fall in the latter part of the last week, which is enough. How after these weeks *Christ* was cut off and the city and sanctuary destroyed by the *Romans,* is well known.

Yet shall he confirm the covenant with many for one week. He kept it, notwithstanding his death, till the rejection of the *Jews,* and calling of *Cornelius* and the *Gentiles* in the seventh year after his passion.

And in half a week he shall cause the sacrifice and oblation to cease; that is, by the war of the *Romans* upon the *Jews*: which war, after some commotions, began in the 13th year of *Nero,* A.D. 67, in the spring, when *Vespasian* with an army invaded them; and ended in the second year of *Vespasian,* A.D. 70, in autumn, *Sept.* 7, when *Titus* took the city, having burnt the Temple 27 days before: so that it lasted three years and an half.

And upon a wing of abominations he shall cause desolation, even until the consummation, and that which is determined be poured upon the desolate. The Prophets, in representing kingdoms by Beasts and Birds, put their wings stretcht out over any country for their armies sent out to invade and rule over that country. Hence a wing of abominations is an army of false Gods: for an abomination is often put in scripture for a false God; as where *Chemosh* is called [10] the abomination of *Moab,* and *Molech* the abomination of *Ammon.* The meaning therefore is, that the people of a Prince to come shall destroy the sanctuary, and abolish the daily worship of the true God, and overspread the land with an army of false gods; and by setting up their dominion and worship, cause desolation to the *Jews,* until the times of the

Gentiles be fulfilled. For *Christ* tells us, that the abomination of desolation spoken of by *Daniel* was to be set up in the times of the *Roman Empire, Matth.* xxiv. 15.

Thus have we in this short Prophecy, a prediction of all the main periods relating to the coming of the *Messiah*; the time of his birth, that of his death, that of the rejection of the *Jews*, the duration of the *Jewish* war whereby he caused the city and sanctuary to be destroyed, and the time of his second coming: and so the interpretation here given is more full and complete and adequate to the design, than if we should restrain it to his first coming only, as Interpreters usually do. We avoid also the doing violence to the language of *Daniel*, by taking the *seven weeks* and *sixty two weeks* for one number. Had that been *Daniel's* meaning, he would have said *sixty and nine weeks*, and not *seven weeks* and *sixty two weeks*, a way of numbring used by no nation. In our way the years are *Jewish Luni-solar years*, [11] as they ought to be; and the *seventy weeks of years* are *Jewish weeks* ending with *sabbatical years*, which is very remarkable. For they end either with the year of the birth of *Christ*, two years before the vulgar account, or with the year of his death, or with the seventh year after it: all which are *sabbatical years*. Others either count by Lunar years, or by weeks not *Judaic*: and, which is worst, they ground their interpretations on erroneous Chronology, excepting the opinion of *Funccius* about the *seventy weeks*, which is the same with ours. For they place *Ezra* and *Nehemiah* in the reign of *Artaxerxes Mnemon*, and the building of the Temple in the reign of *Darius Nothus*, and date the weeks of *Daniel* from those two reigns.

The grounds of the Chronology here followed, I will now set down as briefly as I can.

The *Peloponnesian* war began in spring *An.* 1 *Olymp.* 87, as *Diodorus, Eusebius*, and all other authors agree. It began two months before *Pythodorus* ceased to be *Archon, Thucyd. l.* 2. that is, in *April*, two months before the end of the *Olympic* year. Now the years of this war are most certainly determined by the 50 years distance of its first year from the transit of *Xerxes* inclusively, *Thucyd. l.* 2. or 48 years exclusively, *Eratosth. apud Clem. Alex.* by the 69 years distance of its end, or 27th year, from the beginning of *Alexander*'s reign in *Greece*; by the acting of the *Olympic* games in its 4th and 12th years, *Thucyd. l.* 5; and by three eclipses of the sun, and one of the moon, mentioned by *Thucydides* and *Xenophon*. Now *Thucydides*, an unquestionable witness, tells us, that the news of the death of *Artaxerxes Longimanus* was brought to *Ephesus*, and from thence by some *Athenians* to *Athens*, in the 7th year of this *Peloponnesian* war, when the winter half year was running; and therefore he died *An.* 4 *Olymp.* 88, in the end of *An. J.P.* 4289, suppose a month or two before midwinter; for so long the news would be in coming. Now *Artaxerxes Longimanus* reigned 40 years, by the consent of *Diodorus, Eusebius, Jerome, Sulpitius*; or 41, according to *Ptol. in can. Clem. Alexand. l.* 1. *Strom. Chron. Alexandr. Abulpharagius, Nicephorus*, including therein the reign of his successors *Xerxes* and *Sogdian*, as *Abulpharagius* informs us. After *Artaxerxes* reigned his son *Xerxes* two months, and *Sogdian* seven months; but their reign is not reckoned apart in summing up the years of the Kings, but is included in the 40 or 41 years reign of *Artaxerxes*: omit these nine months, and the precise reign of *Artaxerxes* will be thirty nine years and three months. And therefore since his reign ended in the beginning of winter *An. J.P.* 4289, it began between midsummer and autumn, *An. J.P.* 4250.

The same thing I gather also thus. *Cambyses* began his reign in spring *An. J.P.* 4185, and reigned eight years, including the five months of *Smerdes*; and then *Darius Hystaspis* began in spring *An. J.P.* 4193, and reigned thirty six years, by the unanimous consent of all Chronologers. The reigns of these two Kings are determined by three eclipses of the moon observed at *Babylon*, and recorded by *Ptolemy*; so that it cannot be disputed. One was in the seventh year of *Cambyses, An. J.P.* 4191, *Jul.* 16, at 11 at night; another in the 20th year of *Darius, An. J.P.* 4212, *Nov.* 19, at $11^{h.}$ 45' at night; a third in the 31st year of *Darius, An. J.P.* 4223, *Apr.* 25, at $11^{h.}$ 30 at night. By these eclipses, and the Prophecies of *Haggai* and *Zechary* compared together, it is manifest that his years began after the 24th day of the 11th *Jewish* month, and before the 25th day of *April*, and by consequence about *March*. *Xerxes* therefore began in spring *An. J.P.* 4229: for *Darius* died in the fifth year after the battle at

Marathon, as *Herodotus*, *lib.* 7, and *Plutarch* mention; and that battle was in *October An. J.P.* 4224, ten years before the battle at *Salamis*. *Xerxes* therefore began within less than a year after *October An. J.P.* 4228, suppose in the spring following: for he spent his first five years, and something more, in preparations for his expedition against the *Greeks*; and this expedition was in the time of the *Olympic* games, *An.* 1 *Olymp.* 75, *Calliade Athenis Archonte*, 28 years after the *Regifuge*, and Consulship of the first Consul *Junius Brutus*, *Anno Urbis conditæ* 273, *Fabio & Furio Coss.* The passage of *Xerxes*'s army over the *Hellespont* began in the end of the fourth year of the 74th *Olympiad*, that is, in *June An. J.P.* 4234, and took up one month: and in autumn, three months after, on the full moon, the 16th day of the month *Munychion*, was the battle at *Salamis*, and a little after that an eclipse of the sun, which by the calculation fell on *Octob.* 2. His sixth year therefore began a little before *June*, suppose in spring *An. J.P.* 4234, and his first year consequently in spring *An. J.P.* 4229, as above. Now he reigned almost twenty one years, by the consent of all writers. Add the 7 months of *Artabanus*, and the sum will be 21 years and about four or five months, which end between midsummer and autumn *An. J.P.* 4250. At this time therefore began the reign of his successor *Artaxerxes*, as was to be proved.

The same thing is also confirmed by *Julius Africanus*, who informs us out of former writers, that the 20th year of this *Artaxerxes* was the 115th year from the beginning of the reign of *Cyrus* in *Persia,* and fell in with *An.* 4 *Olymp.* 83. It began therefore with the *Olympic* year, soon after the summer Solstice, *An. J.P.* 4269. Subduct nineteen years, and his first year will begin at the same time of the year *An. J.P.* 4250, as above.

His 7th year therefore began after midsummer *An. J.P.* 4256; and the Journey of *Ezra* to *Jerusalem* in the spring following fell on the beginning of *An. J.P.* 4257, as above.

Notes to Chap. X

[1] Chap. ix. 24, 25, 26, 27.

[2] *Cut upon.* A phrase in *Hebrew*, taken from the practise of numbring by cutting notches.

[3] Heb. *to seal*, i.e. to finish or consummate: a metaphor taken from sealing what is finished. So the *Jews* compute, *ad obsignatum Misna, ad obsignatum Talmud*, that is, *ad absolutum.*

[4] Heb. *the Prophet*, not the Prophecy.

[5] Heb. *the Messiah*, that is, in *Greek, the Christ*; in *English, the Anointed.* I use the *English* word, that the relation of this clause to the former may appear.

[6] *Jerusalem.*

[7] See *Isa.* xxiii. 13.

[8] Iren. l. 5. Hær. c. 25.

[9] Apud Hieron. in h. l.

[10] 1 Kings xi. 7.

[11] The antient solar years of the eastern nations consisted of 12 months, and every month of 30 days: and hence came the division of a circle into 360 degrees. This year seems to be used by *Moses* in his history of the Flood, and by *John* in the *Apocalypse*, where a time, times and half a time, 42 months and 1260 days, are put equipollent. But in reckoning by many of these years together, an account is to be kept of the odd days which were added to the end of these years. For the *Egyptians* added five days to the end of this year; and so did the *Chaldeans* long before the times of *Daniel*, as appears by the *Æra*, of *Nabonassar*: and the *Persian* Magi used the same year of 365 days, till the Empire of the *Arabians*. The antient *Greeks* also used the same solar year of 12 equal months, or 360 days; but every other year added an intercalary month, consisting of 10 and 11 days alternately.

The year of the *Jews*, even from their coming out of *Egypt*, was Luni-solar. It was solar, for the harvest always followed the Passover, and the fruits of the land were always gathered before the feast of Tabernacles, *Levit.* xxiii. But the months were lunar, for the people were commanded by *Moses* in the beginning of every month to blow with trumpets, and offer burnt offerings with their drink offerings, *Num.* x. 10. xxviii. 11, 14. and this solemnity was kept on the new moons, *Psal.* lxxxi. 3,4,5. 1 *Chron.* xxiii. 31. These months were called by *Moses* the first, second, third, fourth month, *&c.* and the first month was also called *Abib*, the second *Zif*, the seventh *Ethanim*, the eighth *Bull, Exod.* xiii. 4. 1 *Kings* vi. 37, 38. viii. 2. But in the *Babylonian* captivity the *Jews* used the names of the *Chaldean* months, and by those names understood the months of their own year; so that the *Jewish* months then lost their old names, and are now called by those of the *Chaldeans*.

The *Jews* began their civil year from the autumnal Equinox, and their sacred year from the vernal: and the first day of the first month was on the visible new moon, which was nearest the Equinox.

Whether *Daniel* used the *Chaldaick* or *Jewish* year, is not very material; the difference being but six hours in a year, and 4 months in 480 years. But I take his months to be *Jewish*: first, because *Daniel* was a *Jew*, and the *Jews* even by the names of the *Chaldean* months understood the months of their own year: secondly, because this Prophecy is grounded on *Jeremiah*'s concerning the 70 years captivity, and therefore must be understood of the same sort of years with the seventy; and those are *Jewish*, since that Prophecy was given in *Judea* before the captivity: and lastly, because *Daniel* reckons by weeks of years, which is a way of reckoning peculiar to the *Jewish* years. For as their days ran by sevens, and the last day of every seven was a sabbath; so their years ran by sevens, and the last year of every seven was a sabbatical year, and seven such weeks of years made a *Jubilee*.

CHAP. XI

Of the Times of the Birth and Passion of Christ

The times of the Birth and Passion of *Christ*, with such like niceties, being not material to religion, were little regarded by the *Christians* of the first age. They who began first to celebrate them, placed them in the cardinal periods of the year; as the annunciation of the Virgin *Mary*, on the 25th of *March*, which when *Julius Cæsar* corrected the Calendar was the vernal Equinox; the feast of *John* Baptist on the 24th of *June*, which was the summer Solstice; the feast of St. *Michael* on *Sept.* 29, which was the autumnal Equinox; and the birth of *Christ* on the winter Solstice, *Decemb.* 25, with the feasts of St. *Stephen*, St. *John* and the *Innocents*, as near it as they could place them. And because the Solstice in time removed from the 25th of *December* to the 24th, the 23d, the 22d, and so on backwards, hence some in the following centuries placed the birth of *Christ* on *Decemb.* 23, and at length on *Decemb.* 20: and for the same reason they seem to have set the feast of St. *Thomas* on *Decemb.* 21, and that of St. *Matthew* on *Sept.* 21. So also at the entrance of the Sun into all the signs in the *Julian* Calendar, they placed the days of other Saints; as the conversion of *Paul* on *Jan.* 25, when the Sun entred ♒; St. *Matthias* on *Feb.* 25, when he entred ♓; St. *Mark* on *Apr.* 25, when he entred ♉; *Corpus Christi* on *May* 26, when he entred ♊; St. *James* on *July* 25, when he entred ♋; St. *Bartholomew* on *Aug.* 24, when he entred ♍; *Simon* and *Jude* on *Octob.* 28, when he entred ♏: and if there were any other remarkable days in the *Julian* Calendar, they placed the Saints upon them, as St. *Barnabas* on *June* 11, where *Ovid* seems to place the feast of *Vesta* and *Fortuna*, and the goddess *Matuta*; and St. *Philip* and *James* on the first of *May*, a day dedicated both to the *Bona Dea*, or *Magna Mater*, and to the goddess *Flora*, and still celebrated with her rites. All which shews that these days were fixed in the first *Christian* Calendars by Mathematicians at pleasure, without any ground in tradition; and that the *Christians* afterwards took up with what they found in the Calendars.

Neither was there any certain tradition about the years of *Christ*. For the *Christians* who first began to enquire into these things, as *Clemens Alexandrinus, Origen, Tertullian, Julius Africanus, Lactantius, Jerome*, St. *Austin, Sulpicius Severus, Prosper*, and as many as place the death of *Christ* in the 15th or 16th year of *Tiberius*, make *Christ* to have preached but one year, or at most but two. At length *Eusebius* discovered four successive Passovers in the Gospel of *John*, and thereupon set on foot an opinion that he preacht three years and an half; and so died in the 19th year of *Tiberius*. Others afterwards, finding the opinion that he died in the Equinox *Mar.* 25, more consonant to the times of the *Jewish* Passover, in the 17th and 20th years, have placed his death in one of those two years. Neither is there any greater certainty in the opinions about the time of his birth. The first *Christians* placed his baptism near the beginning of the 15th year of *Tiberius*; and thence reckoning thirty years backwards, placed his birth in the 43d *Julian* year, the 42d of *Augustus* and 28th of the *Actiac* victory. This was the opinion which obtained in the first ages, till *Dionysius Exiguus*, placing the baptism of *Christ* in the 16th year of *Tiberius*, and misinterpreting the text of *Luke*, iii. 23. as if *Jesus* was only beginning to be 30 years old when he was baptized, invented the vulgar account, in which his birth is placed two years later than before. As therefore relating to these things there is no tradition worth considering; let us lay aside all and examine what prejudices can be gathered from records of good account.

The fifteenth year of *Tiberius* began *Aug.* 28, *An. J.P.* 4727. So soon as the winter was over, and the weather became warm enough, we may reckon that *John* began to baptize; and that before next winter his fame went abroad, and all the people came to his baptism, and *Jesus* among the rest. Whence the first Passover after his baptism mentioned *John* ii. 13. was in the 16th year of *Tiberius*. After this feast *Jesus* came into the land of *Judea*, and staid there baptizing, whilst *John* was baptizing in

Ænon, John iii. 22, 23. But when he heard that *John* was cast into prison, he departed into *Galilee, Mat.* iii. 12. being afraid, because the Pharisees had heard that he baptized more disciples than *John, John* iv. 1. and in his journey he passed thro' *Samaria* four months before the harvest, *John* iv. 35. that is, about the time of the winter Solstice. For their harvest was between *Easter* and *Whitsunday*, and began about a month after the vernal Equinox. *Say not ye*, saith he, *there are yet four months, and then cometh harvest? Behold I say unto you, lift up your eyes, and look on the fields, for they are white already to harvest*; meaning, that the people in the fields were ready for the Gospel, as his next words shew[1]. *John* therefore was imprisoned about *November*, in the 17th year of *Tiberius*; and *Christ* thereupon went from *Judea* to *Cana* of *Galilee* in *December*, and was received there of the *Galileans*, who had seen all he did at *Jerusalem* at the Passover: and when a Nobleman of *Capernaum* heard he was returned into *Galilee*, and went to him and desired him to come and cure his son, he went not thither yet, but only said, *Go thy way, thy son liveth; and the Nobleman returned and found it so, and believed, he and his house*, John iv. This is the beginning of his miracles in *Galilee*; and thus far *John* is full and distinct in relating the actions of his first year, omitted by the other Evangelists. The rest of his history is from this time related more fully by the other Evangelists than by *John*; for what they relate he omits.

From this time therefore *Jesus* taught in the Synagogues of *Galilee* on the sabbath-days, being glorified of all: and coming to his own city *Nazareth*, and preaching in their Synagogue, they were offended, and thrust him out of the city, and led him to the brow of the hill on which the city was built to cast him headlong; but he passing thro' the midst of them, went his way, and came and dwelt at *Capernaum, Luke* iv. And by this time we may reckon the second Passover was either past or at hand.

All this time *Matthew* passeth over in few words, and here begins to relate the preaching and miracles of *Christ. When* Jesus, saith he, *had heard that* John *was cast into prison, he departed into* Galilee; *and leaving* Nazareth, *he came and dwelt at* Capernaum, *and from that time began to preach and say, Repent, for the kingdom of heaven is at hand*, Matth. iv. 12. Afterwards he called his disciples *Peter, Andrew, James* and *John*; and then *went about all* Galilee, *teaching in the Synagogues,—and healing all manner of sickness:—and his fame went thro'out all* Syria; *and they brought unto him all sick people,—and there followed him great multitudes of people from* Galilee, *and from* Decapolis, *and from* Jerusalem, *and from* Judea, *and from beyond* Jordan, Matth, iv. 18, 25. All this was done before the sermon in the mount: and therefore we may certainly reckon that the second Passover was past before the preaching of that sermon. The multitudes that followed him from *Jerusalem* and *Judea*, shew that he had lately been there at the feast. The sermon in the mount was made when great multitudes came to him from all places, and followed him in the open fields; which is an argument of the summer-season: and in this sermon he pointed at the lilies of the field then in the flower before the eyes of his auditors. *Consider,* saith he, *the lilies of the field, how they grow; they toil not, neither do they spin; and yet* Solomon *in all his glory was not arayed like one of these. Wherefore if God so clothe the grass of the field, which to day is and to morrow is cast into the oven,* &c. *Matth.* vi. 28. So therefore the grass of the field was now in the flower, and by consequence the month of *March* with the Passover was past.

Let us see therefore how the rest of the feasts follow in order in *Matthew*'s Gospel: for he was an eye-witness of what he relates, and so tells all things in due order of time, which *Mark* and *Luke* do not.

Some time after the sermon in the mount, when the time came that he should be received, that is, when the time of a feast came that he should be received by the *Jews*, he set his face to go to *Jerusalem*: and as he went with his disciples in the way, when the *Samaritans* in his passage thro' *Samaria* had denied him lodgings, and a certain Scribe said unto him, *Master, I will follow thee whithersoever thou goest,* Jesus *said unto him, The foxes have holes, and the birds of the air have nests, but the Son of man hath not where to lay his head,* Matth. viii. 19. Luke ix. 51, 57. The Scribe told *Christ* he would bear him company in his journey, and *Christ* replied that he wanted a lodging. Now this feast I take to be the feast of Tabernacles, because soon after I find *Christ* and his Apostles on the sea of *Tiberias* in a storm so great, that the ship was covered with water and in danger of sinking, till *Christ rebuked the winds and the sea*, Matth. viii. 23. For this storm shews that winter was now come on.

After this *Christ* did many miracles, and *went about all the cities and villages of* Galilee, *teaching in their Synagogues, and preaching the gospel of the kingdom, and healing every sickness, and every disease among the people*, Matth. ix. he then sent forth the twelve to do the like, *Matth.* x. and at length when he had received a message from *John*, and answered it, he said to the multitudes, *From the days of* John *the Baptist until now the kingdom of heaven suffereth violence*; and upbraided the cities, *Chorazin*, *Bethsaida*, and *Capernaum*, wherein most of his mighty works were done, because they repented not, *Matth.* xi. Which several passages shew, that from the imprisonment of *John* till now there had been a considerable length of time: the winter was now past, and the next Passover was at hand; for immediately after this, *Matthew*, in chap. xii. subjoins, that *Jesus went on the sabbath-day thro' the corn, and his disciples were an hungred, and began to pluck the ears of corn and to eat,— rubbing them*, saith *Luke, in their hands*: the corn therefore was not only in the ear, but ripe; and consequently the Passover, in which the first-fruits were always offered before the harvest, was now come or past. *Luke* calls this sabbath δευτεροπρωτον, the second prime sabbath, that is, the second of the two great feasts of the Passover. As we call *Easter* day high *Easter*, and its *octave* low *Easter* or *Lowsunday*: so *Luke* calls the feast on the seventh day of the unlevened bread, the second of the two prime sabbaths.

In one of the sabbaths following he went into a Synagogue, and healed a man with a withered hand, *Matth.* xii. 9. *Luke* vi. 6. And when the Pharisees took counsel to destroy him, *he withdrew himself from thence, and great multitudes followed him; and he healed them all, and charged them that they should not make him known*, Matth. xii. 14. Afterwards being in a ship, and the multitude standing on the shore, he spake to them three parables together, taken from the seeds-men sowing the fields, *Matth.* xiii. by which we may know that it was now seed-time, and by consequence that the feast of Tabernacles was past. After this he went *into his own country, and taught them in their Synagogue,* but *did not many mighty works there because of their unbelief.* Then the twelve having been abroad a year, returned, and told *Jesus* all that they had done: and at the same time *Herod* beheaded *John* in prison, and his disciples came and told *Jesus*; and when *Jesus* heard it, he took the twelve and departed thence privately by ship into a desert place belonging to *Bethsaida*: and the people when they knew it, followed him on foot out of the cities, the winter being now past; and he healed their sick, and in the desert fed them to the number of five thousand men, besides women and children, with only five loaves and two fishes, *Matth.* xiv. *Luke* ix. at the doing of which miracle the Passover of the *Jews* was nigh, *John* vi. 4. But *Jesus* went not up to this feast; but *after these things walked in* Galilee*, because the* Jews at the Passover before had taken counsel to destroy him, and still *sought to kill him,* John vii. i. Henceforward therefore he is found first in the coast of *Tyre* and *Sidon,* then by the sea of *Galilee,* afterwards in the coast of *Cæsarea Philippi*; and lastly at *Capernaum, Matth.* xv. 21, 29. xvi. 13. xvii. 34.

Afterwards when the feast of Tabernacles was at hand, his brethren upbraided him for walking secretly, and urged him to go up to the feast. But he went not till they were gone, and then went up privately, *John* vii. 2. and when the *Jews* sought to stone him, he escaped, *John* viii. 59. After this he was at the feast of the Dedication in winter, *John* x. 22. and when they sought again to take him, he fled beyond *Jordan, John* x. 39, 40. *Matth.* xix. 1. where he stayed till the death of *Lazarus,* and then came to *Bethany* near *Jerusalem,* and raised him, *John* xi. 7, 18. whereupon the *Jews* took counsel from that time to kill him: and *therefore* he *walked no more openly among the* Jews*, but went thence into a country near to the wilderness, into a city called* Ephraim*; and there continued with his disciples* till the last Passover, in which the *Jews* put him to death, *John* xi. 53, 54.

Thus have we, in the Gospels of *Matthew* and *John* compared together, the history of *Christ*'s actions in continual order during five Passovers. *John* is more distinct in the beginning and end; *Matthew* in the middle: what either omits, the other supplies. The first Passover was between the baptism of *Christ* and the imprisonment of *John, John* ii. 13. the second within four months after the imprisonment of *John*, and *Christ's* beginning to preach in *Galilee, John* iv. 35. and therefore it was either that feast to which *Jesus* went up, when the Scribe desired to follow him, *Matth.* viii. 19. *Luke* ix. 51, 57. or the feast before it. The third was the next feast after it, when the corn was eared and ripe, *Matth,* xii. 1. *Luke* vi. 1. The fourth was that which was nigh at hand when *Christ* wrought the miracle of the five loaves, *Matth.* xiv. 15. *John* vi. 4, 5. and the fifth was that in which *Christ* suffered, *Matth.* xx. 17. *John* xii. 1.

Between the first and second Passover *John* and *Christ* baptized together, till the imprisonment of *John*, which was four months before the second. Then *Christ* began to preach, and call his disciples; and after he had instructed them a year, lent them to preach in the cities of the *Jews*: at the same time *John* hearing of the fame of *Christ*, sent to him to know who he was. At the third, the chief Priests began to consult about the death of *Christ*. A little before the fourth, the twelve after they had preached a year in all the cities, returned to *Christ*; and at the same time *Herod* beheaded *John* in prison, after he had been in prison two years and a quarter: and thereupon *Christ* fled into the desart for fear of *Herod*. The fourth *Christ* went not up to *Jerusalem* for fear of the *Jews*, who at the Passover before had consulted his death, and because his time was not yet come. Thenceforward therefore till the feast of Tabernacles he walked in *Galilee*, and that secretly for fear of *Herod*: and after the feast of Tabernacles he returned no more into *Galilee*, but sometimes was at *Jerusalem*, and sometimes retired beyond *Jordan*, or to the city *Ephraim* by the wilderness, till the Passover in which he was betrayed, apprehended, and crucified.

John therefore baptized two summers, and *Christ* preached three. The first summer *John* preached to make himself known, in order to give testimony to *Christ*. Then, after *Christ* came to his baptism and was made known to him, he baptized another summer, to make *Christ* known by his testimony; and *Christ* also baptized the same summer, to make himself the more known: and by reason of *John's* testimony there came more to *Christ's* baptism than to *John*'s. The winter following *John* was imprisoned; and now his course being at an end, *Christ* entered upon his proper office of preaching in the cities. In the beginning of his preaching he completed the number of the twelve Apostles, and instructed them all the first year in order to send them abroad. Before the end of this year, his fame by his preaching and miracles was so far spread abroad, that the *Jews* at the Passover following consulted how to kill him. In the second year of his preaching, it being no longer safe for him to converse openly in *Judea*, he sent the twelve to preach in all their cities: and in the end of the year they returned to him, and told him all they had done. All the last year the twelve continued with him to be instructed more perfectly, in order to their preaching to all nations after his death. And upon the news of *John*'s death, being afraid of *Herod* as well as of the *Jews*, he walked this year more secretly than before; frequenting desarts, and spending the last half of the year in *Judea*, without the dominions of *Herod*.

Thus have we in the Gospels of *Matthew* and *John* all things told in due order, from the beginning of *John*'s preaching to the death of *Christ*, and the years distinguished from one another by such essential characters that they cannot be mistaken. The second Passover is distinguished from the first, by the interposition of *John*'s imprisonment. The third is distinguished from the second, by a double character: first, by the interposition of the feast to which *Christ* went up, *Mat.* viii. 19. *Luke* ix. 57. and secondly, by the distance of time from the beginning of *Christ*'s preaching: for the second was in the beginning of his preaching, and the third so long after, that before it came *Christ* said, *from the days of* John *the Baptist until now*, &c. and upbraided the cities of *Galilee* for their not repenting at his preaching, and mighty works done in all that time. The fourth is distinguished from the third, by the mission of the twelve from *Christ* to preach in the cities of *Judea* in all the interval. The fifth is distinguished from all the former by the twelve's being returned from preaching, and continuing with *Christ* during all the interval, between the fourth and fifth, and by the passion and other infallible characters.

Now since the first summer of *John*'s baptizing fell in the fifteenth year of the Emperor *Tiberius*, and by consequence the first of these five Passovers in his sixteenth year; the last of them, in which *Jesus* suffered, will fall on the twentieth year of the same Emperor; and by consequence in the Consulship of *Fabius* and *Vitellius*, in the 79th *Julian* year, and year of *Christ* 34, which was the sabbatical year of the *Jews*. And that it did so, I further confirm by these arguments.

I take it for granted that the passion was on friday the 14th day of the month *Nisan*, the great feast of the Passover on saturday the 15th day of *Nisan*, and the resurrection on the day following. Now the 14th day of *Nisan* always fell on the full moon next after the vernal Equinox; and the month began at the new moon before, not at the true conjunction, but at the first appearance of the new moon: for the *Jews* referred all the time of the silent moon, as they phrased it, that is, of the moon's disappearing, to the old moon; and because the first appearance might usually be about 18 hours after the true conjunction, they therefore began their month from the sixth hour at evening, that is, at sun set, next after the eighteenth hour from the conjunction. And this rule they called הי *Jah*, designing by the letters י and ה the number 18.

I know that *Epiphanius* tells us, if some interpret his words rightly, that the *Jews* used a vicious cycle, and thereby anticipated the legal new moons by two days. But this surely he spake not as a witness, for he neither understood *Astronomy* nor *Rabbinical* learning, but as arguing from his erroneous hypothesis about the time of the passion. For the *Jews* did not anticipate, but postpone their months: they thought it lawful to begin their months a day later than the first appearance of the new moon, because the new moon continued for more days than one; but not a day sooner, lest they should celebrate the new moon before there was any. And the *Jews* still keep a tradition in their books, that the *Sanhedrim* used diligently to define the new moons by sight: sending witnesses into mountainous places, and examining them about the moon's appearing, and translating the new moon from the day they had agreed on to the day before, as often as witnesses came from distant regions, who had seen it a day sooner than it was seen at *Jerusalem*. Accordingly *Josephus*, one of the *Jewish* Priests who ministred in the temple, tells us [2] that the Passover was kept *on the 14th day of* Nisan, κατα σεληνην *according to the moon, when the sun was in* Aries. This is confirmed also by two instances, recorded by him, which totally overthrow the hypothesis of the *Jews* using a vicious cycle. For that year in which *Jerusalem* was taken and destroyed, he saith, the Passover was on the 14th day of the month *Xanticus*, which according to *Josephus* is our *April*; and that five years before, it fell on the 8th day of the same month. Which two instances agree with the course of the moon.

Computing therefore the new moons of the first month according to the course of the moon and the rule *Jah*, and thence counting 14 days, I find that the 14th day of this month in the year of *Christ* 31, fell on tuesday *March* 27; in the year 32, on sunday *Apr.* 13; in the year 33, on friday *Apr.* 3; in the year 34, on wednesday *March* 24, or rather, for avoiding the Equinox which fell on the same day, and for having a fitter time for harvest, on thursday *Apr.* 22. also in the year 35, on tuesday *Apr.* 12. and in the year 36, on saturday *March* 31.

But because the 15th and 21st days of *Nisan*, and a day or two of *Pentecost*, and the 10th, 15th, and 22d of *Tisri*, were always sabbatical days or days of rest, and it was inconvenient on two sabbaths together to be prohibited burying their dead and making ready fresh meat, for in that hot region their meat would be apt in two days to corrupt: to avoid these and such like inconveniences, the *Jews* postponed their months a day, as often as the first day of the month *Tisri*, or, which is all one, the third of the month *Nisan*, was sunday, wednesday or friday: and this rule they called אדו *Adu*, by the letters ו , ד , א signifying the numbers 1, 4, 6; that is, the 1st, 4th, and 6th days of the week; which days we call sunday, wednesday and friday. Postponing therefore by this rule the months found above; the 14th day of the month *Nisan* will fall in the year of *Christ* 31, on wednesday *March* 28; in the year 32, on monday *Apr.* 14; in the year 33, on friday *Apr.* 3; in the year 34, on friday *Apr.* 23; in the year 35, on wednesday *Apr.* 13, and in the year 36, on saturday *March* 31.

By this computation therefore the year 32 is absolutely excluded, because the Passion cannot fall on friday without making it five days after the full moon, or two days before it; whereas it ought to be upon the day of the full moon, or the next day. For the same reason the years 31 and 35 are excluded, because in them the Passion cannot fall on friday, without making it three days after the full moon, or four days before it: errors so enormous, that they would be very conspicuous in the heavens to every vulgar eye. The year 36 is contended for by few or none, and both this and the year 35 may be thus excluded.

Tiberius in the beginning of his reign made *Valerius Gratus* President of *Judea*; and after 11 years, substituted *Pontius Pilate*, who governed 10 years. Then *Vitellius*, newly made President of *Syria*, deprived him of his honour, substituting *Marcellus*, and at length sent him to *Rome*: but, by reason of delays, *Tiberius* died before *Pilate* got thither. In the mean time *Vitellius*, after he had deposed *Pilate*, came to *Jerusalem* in the time of the Passover, to visit that Province as well as others in the beginning of his office; and in the place of *Caiaphas*, then High Priest, created *Jonathas* the son of *Ananus*, or *Annas* as he is called in scripture. Afterwards, when *Vitellius* was returned to *Antioch*, he received letters from *Tiberius*, to make peace with *Artabanus* king of the *Parthians*. At the same time the *Alans*, by the sollicitation of *Tiberius*, invaded the kingdom of *Artabanus*; and his subjects also, by the procurement of *Vitellius*, soon after rebelled: for *Tiberius* thought that *Artabanus*, thus pressed with difficulties, would more readily accept the conditions of peace. *Artabanus* therefore straightway gathering a greater army, opprest the rebels; and then meeting *Vitellius* at *Euphrates*, made a league with the *Romans*. After this *Tiberius* commanded *Vitellius* to make war upon *Aretas* King of *Arabia*. He therefore leading his army against *Aretas*, went together with *Herod* to *Jerusalem*, to sacrifice at the publick feast which was then to be celebrated. Where being received honourably, he stayed three days, and in the mean while translated the high Priesthood from *Jonathas* to his brother *Theophilus*: and the fourth day, receiving letters of the death of *Tiberius*, made the people swear allegiance to *Caius* the new Emperor; and recalling his army, sent them into quarters. All this is related by *Josephus Antiq. lib.* 18. *c.* 6, 7. Now *Tiberius* reigned 22 years and 7 months, and died *March* 16, in the beginning of the year of *Christ* 37; and the feast of the Passover fell on *April* 20 following, that is, 35 days after the death of *Tiberius*: so that there were about 36 or 38 days, for the news of his death to come from *Rome* to *Vitellius* at *Jerusalem*; which being a convenient time for that message, confirms that the feast which *Vitellius* and *Herod* now went up to was the Passover. For had it been the Pentecost, as is usually supposed, *Vitellius* would have continued three months ignorant of the Emperor's death: which is not to be supposed. However, the things done between this feast and the Passover which *Vitellius* was at before, namely, the stirring up a sedition in *Parthia*, the quieting that sedition, the making a league after that with the *Parthians*, the sending news of that league to *Rome*, the receiving new orders from thence to go against the *Arabians*, and the putting those orders in execution; required much more time than the fifty days between the Passover and Pentecost of the same year: and therefore the Passover which *Vitellius* first went up to, was in the year before. Therefore *Pilate* was deposed before the Passover A.C. 36, and by consequence the passion of *Christ* was before that Passover: for he suffered not under *Vitellius*, nor under *Vitellius* and *Pilate* together, but under *Pilate* alone.

Now it is observable that the high Priesthood was at this time become an annual office, and the Passover was the time of making a new high Priest. For *Gratus* the predecessor of *Pilate*, saith *Josephus*, made *Ismael* high Priest after *Ananus*; and a while after, suppose a year, deposed him, and substituted *Eleazar*, and a year after *Simon*, and after another year *Caiaphas*; and then gave way to *Pilate*. So *Vitellius* at one Passover made *Jonathas* successor to *Caiaphas*, and at the next *Theophilus* to *Jonathas*. Hence *Luke* tells us, that in the 15th year of *Tiberius*, *Annas* and *Caiaphas* were high Priests, that is, *Annas* till the Passover, and *Caiaphas* afterwards. Accordingly *John* speaks of the high Priesthood as an annual office: for he tells us again and again, in the last year of *Christ's* preaching, that *Caiaphas* was high Priest for that year, *John* xi. 49, 51. xviii. 13. And the next year *Luke* tells you, that *Annas* was high Priest, *Acts* iv. 6.

Theophilus was therefore made high Priest in the first year of *Caius*, *Jonathas* in the 22d year of *Tiberius*, and *Caiaphas* in the 21st year of the same Emperor: and therefore, allotting a year to each, the Passion, when *Annas* succeeded *Caiaphas*, could not be later than the 20th year of *Tiberius*, A.C. 34.

Thus there remain only the years 33 and 34 to be considered; and the year 33 I exclude by this argument. In the Passover two years before the Passion, when *Christ* went thro' the corn, and his disciples pluckt the ears, and rubbed them with their hands to eat; this ripeness of the corn shews that the Passover then fell late: and so did the Passover A.C. 32, *April 14*, but the Passover A.C. 31, *March 28th*, fell very early. It was not therefore two years after the year 31, but two years after 32 that *Christ* suffered.

Thus all the characters of the Passion agree to the year 34; and that is the only year to which they all agree.

Notes to Chap. XI

[1] I observe, that *Christ* and his forerunner *John* in their parabolical discourses were wont to allude to things present. The old Prophets, when they would describe things emphatically, did not only draw parables from things which offered themselves, as from the rent of a garment, 1 *Sam.* xv. from the sabbatic year, *Isa.* xxxvii. from the vessels of a Potter, *Jer.* xviii. &c. but also when such fit objects were wanting, they supplied them by their own actions, as by rending a garment, 1 *Kings* xi. by shooting, 2 *Kings* xiii. by making bare their body, *Isa.* xx. by imposing significant names to their sons, *Isa.* viii. *Hos.* i. by hiding a girdle in the bank of *Euphrates*, *Jer.* xiii. by breaking a potter's vessel, *Jer.* xix. by putting on fetters and yokes, *Jer.* xxvii. by binding a book to a stone, and casting them both into *Euphrates*, *Jer.* li. by besieging a painted city, *Ezek.* iv. by dividing hair into three parts, *Ezek.* v. by making a chain, *Ezek.* vii. by carrying out houshold stuff like a captive and trembling, *Ezek.* xii, &c. By such kind of types the Prophets loved to speak. And *Christ* being endued with a nobler prophetic spirit than the rest, excelled also in this kind of speaking, yet so as not to speak by his own actions, that was less grave and decent, but to turn into parables such things as offered themselves. On occasion of the harvest approaching, he admonishes his disciples once and again of the spiritual harvest, *John* iv. 35. *Matth.* ix. 37. Seeing the lilies of the field, he admonishes his disciples about gay clothing, *Matth.* vi. 28. In allusion to the present season of fruits, he admonishes his disciples about knowing men by their fruits, *Matth.* vii. 16. In the time of the Passover, when trees put forth leaves, he bids his disciples *learn a parable from the fig tree: when its branch is yet tender and putteth forth leaves, ye know that summer is nigh,* &c. *Matth.* xxiv. 32. *Luke* xxi. 29. The same day, alluding both to the season of the year and to his passion, which was to be two days after, he formed a parable of the time of fruits approaching, and the murdering of the heir, *Matth.* xxi. 33. Alluding at the same time, both to the money-changers whom he had newly driven out of the Temple, and to his passion at hand; he made a parable of a Noble-man going into a far country to receive a kingdom and return, and delivering his goods to his servants, and at his return condemning the slothful servant because he put not his money to the exchangers, *Matth.* xxv. 14. *Luke* xix. 12. Being near the Temple where sheep were kept in folds to be sold for the sacrifices, he spake many things parabolically of sheep, of the shepherd, and of the door of the sheepfold; and discovers that he alluded to the sheepfolds which were to be hired in the market-place,

by speaking of such folds as a thief could not enter by the door, nor the shepherd himself open, but a porter opened to the shepherd, *John* x. 1, 3. Being in the mount of *Olives, Matth.* xxxvi. 30. *John* xiv. 31. a place so fertile that it could not want vines, he spake many things mystically of the Husbandman, and of the vine and its branches, *John* xv. Meeting a blind man, he admonished of spiritual blindness, *John* ix. 39. At the sight of little children, he described once and again the innocence of the elect, *Matth.* xviii. 2. xix. 13. Knowing that *Lazarus* was dead and should be raised again, he discoursed of the resurrection and life eternal, *John* xi. 25, 26. Hearing of the slaughter of some whom *Pilate* had slain, he admonished of eternal death, *Luke* xiii. 1. To his fishermen he spake of fishers of men, *Matth.* iv. 10. and composed another parable about fishes. *Matth.* xiii. 47. Being by the Temple, he spake of the Temple of his body, *John* ii. 19. At supper he spake a parable about the mystical supper to come in the kingdom of heaven, *Luke* xiv. On occasion of temporal food, he admonished his disciples of spiritual food, and of eating his flesh and drinking his blood mystically, *John* vi. 27, 53. When his disciples wanted bread, he bad them beware of the leven of the Pharisees, *Matth.* xvi. 6. Being desired to eat, he answered that he had other meat, *John* iv. 31. In the great day of the feast of Tabernacles, when the *Jews*, as their custom was, brought a great quantity of waters from the river *Shiloah* into the Temple, *Christ* stood and cried, saying, *If any man thirst let him come unto me and drink. He that believeth in me, out of his belly shall flow rivers of living water*, John vii. 37. The next day, in allusion to the servants who by reason of the sabbatical year were newly set free, he said, *If ye continue in my word, the truth shall make you free.* Which the *Jews* understanding literally with respect to the present manumission of servants, answered, *We be* Abraham's *seed, and were never in bondage to any man: how sayeth thou, ye shall be made free?* John viii. They assert their freedom by a double argument: first, because they were the seed of *Abraham*, and therefore newly made free, had they been ever in bondage; and then, because they never were in bondage. In the last Passover, when *Herod* led his army thro' *Judea* against *Aretas* King of *Arabia*, because *Aretas* was aggressor and the stronger in military forces, as appeared by the event; *Christ* alluding to that state of things, composed the parable of a weaker King leading his army against a stronger who made war upon him, *Luke* xiv. 31. And I doubt not but divers other parables were formed upon other occasions, the history of which we have not.

[2] Joseph. Antiq. lib. 3. c. 10.

CHAP. XII

Of the Prophecy of the Scripture of Truth

T he kingdoms represented by the second and third Beasts, or the Bear and Leopard, are again described by *Daniel* in his last Prophecy written in the third year of *Cyrus* over *Babylon*, the year in which he conquered *Persia*. For this Prophecy is a commentary upon the Vision of the Ram and He-Goat.

Behold, saith [1] he, *there shall stand up yet three kings in* Persia, [*Cyrus, Cambyses*, and *Darius Hystaspes*] *and the fourth* [*Xerxes*] *shall be far richer than they all: and by his strength thro' his riches he shall stir up all against the realm of* Grecia. *And a mighty king* [*Alexander* the great] *shall stand up, that shall rule with great dominion, and do according to his will. And when he shall stand up, his kingdom shall be broken, and shall be divided towards the four winds of heaven; and not to his posterity* [but after their death,] *nor according to his dominion which he ruled: for his kingdom shall be pluckt up, even for others besides those. Alexander* the great having conquered all the *Persian* Empire, and some part of *India*, died at *Babylon* a month before the summer Solstice, in the year of *Nabonassar* 425: and his captains gave the monarchy to his bastard brother *Philip Aridæus*, a man disturbed in his understanding; and made *Perdiccas* administrator of the kingdom. *Perdiccas* with their consent made *Meleager* commander of the army, *Seleucus* master of the horse, *Craterus* treasurer of the kingdom, *Antipater* governor of *Macedon* and *Greece, Ptolemy* governor of *Egypt*; *Antigonus* governor of *Pamphylia, Lycia, Lycaonia*, and *Phrygia major*; *Lysimachus* governor of *Thrace*, and other captains governors of other Provinces; as many as had been so before in the days of *Alexander* the great. The *Babylonians* began now to count by a new *Æra*, which they called the *Æra* of *Philip*, using the years of

Nabonassar, and reckoning the 425th year of *Nabonassar* to be the first year of *Philip*. *Roxana* the wife of *Alexander* being left big with child, and about three or four months after brought to bed of a son, they called him *Alexander*, saluted him King, and joined him with *Philip*, whom they had before placed in the throne. *Philip* reigned three years under the administratorship of *Perdiccas*, two years more under the administratorship of *Antipater*, and above a year more under that of *Polyperchon*; in all six years and four months; and then was slain with his Queen *Eurydice* in *September* by the command of *Olympias* the mother of *Alexander* the great. The *Greeks* being disgusted at the cruelties of *Olympias*, revolted to *Cassander* the son and successor of *Antipater*. *Cassander* affecting the dominion of *Greece*, slew *Olympias*; and soon after shut up the young king *Alexander*, with his mother *Roxana*, in the castle of *Amphipolis*, under the charge of *Glaucias*, *An. Nabonass.* 432. The next year *Ptolemy*, *Cassander* and *Lysimachus*, by means of *Seleucus*, form'd a league against *Antigonus*; and after certain wars made peace with him, *An. Nabonass.* 438, upon these conditions: that *Cassander* should command the forces of *Europe* till *Alexander* the son of *Roxana* came to age; and that *Lysimachus* should govern *Thrace*, *Ptolemy Egypt* and *Lybia*, and *Antigonus* all *Asia*. *Seleucus* had possest himself of *Mesopotamia, Babylonia, Sustana* and *Media*, the year before. About three years after *Alexander*'s death he was made governor of *Babylon* by *Antipater*; then was expelled by *Antigonus*; but now he recovered and enlarged his government over a great part of the *East*: which gave occasion to a new *Æra*, called *Æra Seleucidarum*. Not long after the peace made with *Antigonus*, *Diodorus* saith the same *Olympic* year; *Cassander*, seeing that *Alexander* the son of *Roxana* grew up, and that it was discoursed thro'out *Macedonia* that it was fit he should be set at liberty, and take upon him the government of his father's kingdom, commanded *Glaucias* the governor of the castle to kill *Roxana* and the young king *Alexander* her son, and conceal their deaths. Then *Polyperchon* set up *Hercules*, the son of *Alexander* the great by *Barsinè*, to be king; and soon after, at the sollicitation of *Cassander*, caused him to be slain. Soon after that, upon a great victory at sea got by

Demetrius the son of *Antigonus* over *Ptolemy, Antigonus* took upon himself the title of king, and gave the same title to his son. This was *An. Nabonass.* 441. After his example, *Seleucus, Cassander, Lysimachus* and *Ptolemy*, took upon themselves the title and dignity of kings, having abstained from this honour while there remained any of *Alexander*'s race to inherit the crown. Thus the monarchy of the *Greeks* for want of an heir was broken into several kingdoms; four of which, seated *to the four winds of heaven*, were very eminent. For *Ptolemy* reigned over *Egypt, Lybia* and *Ethiopia; Antigonus* over *Syria* and the lesser *Asia; Lysimachus* over *Thrace;* and *Cassander* over *Macedon, Greece* and *Epirus*, as above.

Seleucus at this time reigned over the nations which were beyond *Euphrates*, and belonged to the bodies of the two first Beasts; but after six years he conquered *Antigonus*, and thereby became possest of one of the four kingdoms. For *Cassander* being afraid of the power of *Antigonus*, combined with *Lysimachus, Ptolemy* and *Seleucus*, against him: and while *Lysimachus* invaded the parts of *Asia* next the *Hellespont, Ptolemy* subdued *Phœnicia* and *Cœlosyria*, with the sea-coasts of *Asia*.

Seleucus came down with a powerful army into *Cappadocia*, and joining the confederate forces, fought *Antigonus* in *Phrygia* and flew him, and seized his kingdom, *An. Nabonass.* 447. After which *Seleucus* built *Antioch, Seleucia, Laodicea, Apamea, Berrhœa, Edessa*, and other cities in *Syria* and *Asia;* and in them granted the *Jews* equal privileges with the *Greeks*.

Demetrius the son of *Antigonus* retained but a small part of his father's dominions, and at length lost *Cyprus* to *Ptolemy;* but afterwards killing *Alexander*, the son and successor of *Cassander* king of *Macedon*, he seized his kingdom, *An. Nabonass.* 454. Sometime after, preparing a very great army to recover his father's dominions in *Asia; Seleucus, Ptolemy, Lysimachus* and *Pyrrhus* king of *Epirus*, combined against him; and *Pyrrhus* invading *Macedon*, corrupted the army of *Demetrius*, put him to flight, seized his kingdom, and shared it with *Lysimachus*. After seven months, *Lysimachus* beating *Pyrrhus*, took *Macedon* from him, and held it five years and a half, uniting the kingdoms of

Macedon and *Thrace*. *Lysimachus* in his wars with *Antigonus* and *Demetrius*, had taken from them *Caria*, *Lydia*, and *Phrygia*; and had a treasury in *Pergamus*, a castle on the top of a conical hill in *Phrygia*, by the river *Caicus*, the custody of which he had committed to one *Philetærus*, who was at first faithful to him, but in the last year of his reign revolted. For *Lysimachus*, having at the instigation of his wife *Arsinoe*, slain first his own son *Agathocles*, and then several that lamented him; the wife of *Agathocles* fled with her children and brothers, and some others of their friends, and sollicited *Seleucus* to make war upon *Lysimachus*; whereupon *Philetærus* also, who grieved at the death of *Agathocles*, and was accused thereof by *Arsinoe*, took up arms, and sided with *Seleucus*. On this occasion *Seleucus* and *Lysimachus* met and fought in *Phrygia*; and *Lysimachus* being slain in the battel, lost his kingdom to *Seleucus*, *An. Nabonass.* 465. Thus the Empire of the *Greeks*, which at first brake into four kingdoms, became now reduced into two notable ones, henceforward called by *Daniel* the kings of the *South* and *North*. For *Ptolemy* now reigned over *Egypt*, *Lybia*, *Ethiopia*, *Arabia*, *Phœnicia*, *Cœlosyria*, and *Cyprus*; and *Seleucus*, having united three of the four kingdoms, had a dominion scarce inferior to that of the *Persian* Empire, conquered by *Alexander* the great. All which is thus represented by *Daniel*:[2] *And the king of the* South [*Ptolemy*] *shall be strong, and one of his Princes* [*Seleucus*, one of *Alexander*'s Princes] *shall be strong above him, and have dominion; his dominion shall be a great dominion.*

After *Seleucus* had reigned seven months over *Macedon*, *Greece*, *Thrace*, *Asia*, *Syria*, *Babylonia*, *Media*, and all the *East* as far as *India*; *Ptolemy Ceraunus*, the younger brother of *Ptolemy Philadelphus* king of *Egypt*, slew him treacherously, and seized his dominions in *Europe*: while *Antiochus Soter*, the son of *Seleucus*, succeeded his father in *Asia*, *Syria*, and most of the *East*; and after nineteen or twenty years was succeeded by his son *Antiochus Theos*; who having a lasting war with *Ptolemy Philadelphus*, at length composed the same by marrying *Berenice* the daughter of *Philadelphus*: but after a reign of fifteen years, his first wife *Laodice* poisoned him, and set her son *Seleucus Callinicus* upon the throne. *Callinicus* in the beginning of his reign, by the impulse of his mother *Laodice*, besieged *Berenice* in *Daphne* near *Antioch*, and slew her with her young son and many of her women. Whereupon *Ptolemy Euergetes*, the son and successor of *Philadelphus*, made war upon *Callinicus*; took from him *Phœnicia*, *Syria*, *Cilicia*, *Mesopotamia*, *Babylonia*, *Sustana*, and some other regions; and carried back into *Egypt* 40000 talents of silver, and 2500 images of the Gods, amongst which were the Gods of *Egypt* carried away by *Cambyses*. *Antiochus Hierax* at first assisted his brother *Callinicus*, but afterwards contended with him for *Asia*. In the mean time *Eumenes* governor of *Pergamus* beat *Antiochus*, and took from them both all *Asia* westward of mount *Taurus*. This was in the fifth year of *Callinicus*, who after an inglorious reign of 20 years was succeeded by his son *Seleucus Ceraunus*; and *Euergetes* after four years more, *An. Nabonass.* 527, was succeeded by his son *Ptolemy Philopator*. All which is thus signified by *Daniel*:[3] *And in the end of years they* [the kings of the *South* and *North*] *shall join themselves together: for the king's daughter of the* South [*Berenice*] *shall come to the king of the* North *to make an agreement, but she shall not retain the power of the arm; neither shall she stand, nor her seed, but she shall be delivered up, and he* [*Callinicus*] *that brought her, and he whom she brought forth, and they that strengthned her in* [those] *times,* [or defended her in the siege of *Daphne*.] *But out of a branch of her roots shall one stand up in his seat* [her brother *Euergetes*] *who shall come with an army, and shall enter into the fortress* [or fenced cities] *of the king of the* North, *and shall act against them and prevail: and shall carry captives into* Egypt, *their Gods with their Princes and precious vessels of silver and gold; and he shall continue some years after the king of the* North.

Seleucus Ceraunus, inheriting the remains of his father's kingdom, and thinking to recover the rest, raised a great army against the governor of *Pergamus*, now King thereof, but died in the third year of his reign. His brother and successor, *Antiochus Magnus*, carrying on the war, took from the King of *Pergamus* almost all the lesser *Asia*, recovering also the Provinces of *Media*, *Persia* and *Babylonia*, from the governors who had revolted: and in the fifth year of his reign invading *Cœlosyria*, he with little opposition possest himself of a good part thereof; and the next year returning to invade the rest of *Cœlosyria* and *Phœnicia*, beat the army of *Ptolemy Philopator* near *Berytus*; he then invaded *Palestine* and the neighbouring parts of *Arabia*, and the third year returned with an army of 78000: but *Ptolemy* coming out of *Egypt* with an army of 75000, fought and routed him at *Raphia* near *Gaza*, between *Palestine* and *Egypt*; and recovered all *Phœnicia* and *Cœlosyria*, *Ann. Nabonass.* 532. Being puffed up with this victory, and living in all manner of luxury, the *Egyptians* revolted, and had wars with him, but were overcome; and in the broils sixty thousand *Egyptian Jews* were slain. All which is thus described by *Daniel*: [4] *But his sons* [*Seleucus Ceraunus*, and *Antiochus Magnus*, the sons of *Callinicus*] *shall be stirred up, and shall gather a great army; and he* [*Antiochus Magnus*] *shall come effectually and overflow, and pass thro' and return, and* [again the next year] *be stirred up* [marching even] *to his fortress,* [the frontier towns of *Egypt*;] *and the King of the* South *shall be moved with choler, and come forth* [the third year] *and fight with him, even with the King of the* North; *and he* [the King of the *North*] *shall lead forth a great multitude, but the multitude shall be given into his hand. And the multitude being taken away, his heart shall be lifted up, and he shall cast down many ten thousands; but he shall not be strengthned by it: for the king of the* North *shall return*, &c.

About twelve years after the battle between *Philopator* and *Antiochus*, *Philopator* died; and left his kingdom to his young son *Ptolemy Epiphanes*, a child of five years old. Thereupon *Antiochus Magnus* confederated with *Philip* king of *Macedon*, that they should each invade the dominions of *Epiphanes* which lay next to them. Hence arose a various war between *Antiochus* and *Epiphanes*, each of them seizing *Phœnicia* and *Cœlosyria* by turns; whereby those countries were much afflicted by both parties. First *Antiochus* seized them; then one *Scopas* being sent with the army of *Egypt*, recovered them from *Antiochus*: the next year, *An. Nabonass.* 550, *Antiochus* fought and routed *Scopas* near the fountains of *Jordan*, besieged him in *Sidon*, took the city, and recovered *Syria* and *Phœnicia* from *Egypt*, the *Jews* coming over to him voluntarily. But about three years after, preparing for a war against the *Romans*, he came to *Raphia* on the borders of *Egypt*; made peace with *Epiphanes*, and gave him his daughter *Cleopatra*: next autumn he passed the *Hellespont* to invade the cities of *Greece* under the *Roman* protection, and took some of them; but was beaten by the *Romans* the summer following, and forced to return back with his army into *Asia*. Before the end of the year the fleet of *Antiochus* was beaten by the fleet of the *Romans* near *Phocœa*: and at the same time *Epiphanes* and *Cleopatra* sent an embassy to *Rome* to congratulate the *Romans* on their success against their father *Antiochus*, and to exhort them to prosecute the war against him into *Asia*. The *Romans* beat *Antiochus* again at sea near *Ephesus*, past their army over the *Hellespont*, and obtain'd a great victory over him by land, took from him all *Asia* westward of mount *Taurus*, gave it to the King of *Pergamus* who assisted them in the war; and imposed a large tribute upon *Antiochus*. Thus the King of *Pergamus*, by the power of the *Romans*, recovered what *Antiochus* had taken from him; and *Antiochus* retiring into the remainder of his kingdom, was slain two years after by the *Persians*, as he was robbing the Temple of *Jupiter Belus* in *Elymais*, to raise money for the *Romans*. All which is thus described by *Daniel*. [5] *For the King of the* North [*Antiochus*] *shall return, and shall set forth a multitude greater than the former; and shall certainly come, after certain years, with a great army and with much riches. And in those times there shall many stand up against the King of the* South, [particularly the *Macedonians*;] *also the robbers of thy people* [the *Samaritans*, &c.] *shall exalt themselves to establish the vision, but they shall fall. So the King of the* North *shall come, and cast up a mount, and take the most fenced cities; and the arms of the* South *shall not withstand, neither his chosen people, neither shall there be any strength to withstand. But he that cometh against him shall do according to his own will, and none shall stand before him: and he shall stand in the glorious land, which shall fail in his hand. He shall also set his face to go with the strength* [or army] *of all his kingdom, and make an agreement with him* [at *Raphia*;] *and he shall give him the daughter of women corrupting her; but she shall not stand his side, neither be for him. After this he shall turn his face unto the Isles, and shall take many: but a Prince for his own behalf* [the *Romans*] *shall cause the reproach offered by him to cease; without his own reproach he shall cause it to turn upon him. Then he shall turn his face towards the fort of his own land: but he shall stumble and fall, and not be found.*

Seleucus Philopator succeeded his father *Antiochus, Anno Nabonass.* 561, and reigned twelve years, but did nothing memorable, being sluggish, and intent upon raising money for the *Romans* to whom he was tributary. He was slain by *Heliodorus*, whom he had sent to rob the Temple of *Jerusalem. Daniel* thus describes his reign. [6] *Then shall stand up in his estate a raiser of taxes in the glory of the kingdom, but within few days he shall be destroyed, neither in anger nor in battle.*

A little before the death of *Philopator*, his son *Demetrius* was sent hostage to *Rome*, in the place of *Antiochus Epiphanes*, the brother of *Philopator*; and *Antiochus* was at *Athens* in his way home from *Rome*, when *Philopator* died: whereupon *Heliodorus* the treasurer of the kingdom, stept into the throne. But *Antiochus* so managed his affairs, that the *Romans* kept *Demetrius* at *Rome*; and their ally the King of *Pergamus* expelled *Heliodorus*, and placed *Antiochus* in the throne, while *Demetrius* the right heir remained an hostage at *Rome. Antiochus* being thus made King by the friendship of the King of *Pergamus* reigned powerfully over *Syria* and the neighbouring nations: but carried himself much below his dignity, stealing privately out of his palace, rambling up and down the city in disguise with one or two of his companions; conversing and drinking with people of the lowest rank, foreigners and strangers; frequenting the meetings of dissolute persons to feast and revel; clothing himself like the *Roman* candidates and officers, acting their parts like a mimick, and in publick festivals jesting and dancing with servants and light people, exposing himself by all manner of ridiculous gestures. This conduct made some take him for a madman, and call him *Antiochus* Επιμενης. In the first year of his reign he deposed *Onias* the high-Priest, and sold the high-Priesthood to *Jason* the younger brother of *Onias*: for *Jason* had promised to give him 440 talents of silver for that office, and 15 more for a licence to erect a place of exercise for the training up of youth in the fashions of the heathen; which licence was granted by the King, and put in execution by *Jason*. Then the King sending one *Apollonius* into *Egypt* to the coronation of *Ptolemy Philometor*, the young son of *Philometor* and *Cleopatra*, and knowing *Philometor* not to be well affected to his affairs in *Phœnicia*, provided for his own safety in those parts; and for that end came to *Joppa* and *Jerusalem*, where he was honourably received; from thence he went in like manner with his little army to the cities of *Phœnicia*, to establish himself against *Egypt*, by courting the people, and distributing extraordinary favours amongst them. All which is thus represented by *Daniel*. [7] *And in his* [*Philometor's*] *estate shall stand up a vile person, to whom they* [the *Syrians* who set up *Heliodorus*] *shall not give the honour of the kingdom. Yet he shall come in peaceably, and obtain the kingdom by flatteries* [made principally to the King of *Pergamus*;] *and the arms* [which in favour of *Heliodorus* oppose him] *shall be overflowed with a food from before him, and be broken; yea also* [*Onias* the high-Priest] *the Prince of the covenant. And after the league made with him,* [the King of *Egypt*, by sending *Apollonius* to his coronation] *he shall work deceitfully* [against the King of *Egypt*,] *for he shall come up and shall become strong* [in *Phœnicia*] *with a small people. And he shall enter into the quiet and plentiful cities of the Province* [of *Phœnicia*;] *and* [to ingratiate himself with the *Jews* of *Phœnicia* and *Egypt*, and with their friends] *he shall do that which his fathers have not done, nor his fathers fathers: he shall scatter among them the prey and the spoil, and the riches* [exacted from other places;] *and shall forecast his devices against the strong holds* [of *Egypt*] *even for a time.*

These things were done in the first year of his reign, *An. Nabonass.* 573. And thenceforward he forecast his devices against the strong holds of *Egypt*, until the sixth year. For three years after, that is in the fourth year of his reign, *Menelaus* bought the high-Priesthood from *Jason*, but not paying the price was sent for by the King; and the King, before he could hear the cause, went into *Cilicia* to appease a sedition there, and left *Andronicus* his deputy at *Antioch*; in the mean time the brother of *Menelaus*, to make up the money, conveyed several vessels out of the Temple, selling some of them at *Tyre*, and sending others to *Andronicus*. When *Menelaus* was reproved for this by *Onias*, he caused *Onias* to be slain by *Andronicus*: for which fact the King at his return from *Cilicia* caused *Andronicus* to be put to death. Then *Antiochus* prepared his second expedition against *Egypt*, which he performed in the sixth year of his reign, *An. Nabonass.* 578: for upon the death of *Cleopatra*, the governors of her son the young King of *Egypt* claimed *Phœnicia* and *Cœlosyria* from him as her dowry; and to recover those countries raised a great army. *Antiochus* considering that his father had not quitted the possession of those countries [8], denied they were her dowry; and with another great army met and fought the *Egyptians* on the borders of *Egypt*, between *Pelusium* and the mountain *Casius*. He there beat them, and might have destroyed their whole army, but that he rode up and down, commanding his soldiers not to kill them, but to take them alive: by which humanity he gained *Pelusium*, and soon after all *Egypt*; entring it with a vast multitude of foot and chariots, elephants and horsemen, and a great navy. Then seizing the cities of *Egypt* as a friend, he marched to *Memphis*, laid the whole blame of the war upon *Eulæus* the King's governor, entred into outward friendship with the young King, and took upon him to order the affairs of the kingdom. While *Aniochus* was thus employ'd, a report being spread in *Phœnicia* that he was dead, *Jason* to recover the high-Priesthood assaulted *Jerusalem* with above a thousand men, and took the city: hereupon the King thinking *Judea* had revolted, came out of *Egypt* in a furious manner, re-took the city, slew forty thousand of the people, made as many prisoners, and sold them to raise money; went into the Temple, spoiled it of its treasures, ornaments, utensils, and vessels of gold and silver, amounting to 1800 talents; and carried all away to *Antioch*. This was done in the year of *Nabonassar* 578, and is thus described by *Daniel.* [9] *And he shall stir up his power, and his courage against the King of the* South *with a great army; and the King of the* South *shall be stirrd up to battle with a very great and mighty army; but he shall not stand: for they,* even *Antiochus* and his friends, *shall forecast devices against him,* as is represented above; *yea, they that feed of the portion of his meat, shall* betray and *destroy him, and his army shall be overthrown, and many shall fall down slain. And both these Kings hearts shall be to do mischief; and they*, being now made friends, *shall speak lyes at one table*, against the *Jews* and against the holy covenant; *but it shall not prosper: for yet the end*, in which the setting up of the abomination of desolation is to prosper, *shall be at the time appointed. Then shall he return into his land with great riches, and his heart shall be against the holy covenant; and he shall act*, against it by spoiling the Temple, *and return into his own land.*

The *Egyptians* of *Alexandria* seeing *Philometor* first educated in luxury by the Eunuch *Eulæus*, and now in the hands of *Antiochus*, gave the kingdom to *Euergetes*, the younger brother of *Philometor*. Whereupon *Antiochus* pretending to restore *Philometor*, made war upon *Euergetes*; beat him at sea, and besieged him and his sister *Cleopatra* in *Alexandria*: while the besieged Princes sent to *Rome* to implore the assistance of the Senate. *Antiochus* finding himself unable to take the city that year, returned into *Syria*, leaving *Philometor* at *Memphis* to govern *Egypt* in his absence. But *Philometor* made friendship with his brother that winter; and *Antiochus*, returning the next spring *An. Nabonass.* 580, to besiege both the brothers in *Alexandria*, was met in the way by the *Roman* Ambassadors, *Popilius Læna, C. Decimius*, and *C. Hostilius*: he offered them his hand to kiss, but *Popilius* delivering to him the tables wherein the message of the Senate was written, bad him read those first. When he had read them, he replied he would consider with his friends what was fit to be done; but *Popilius* drawing a circle about him, bad him answer before he went out of it: *Antiochus*, astonished at this blunt and unusual imperiousness, made answer he would do what the *Romans* demanded; and then *Popilius* gave the King his hand to kiss, and he returned out of *Egypt*. The same year, *An. Nabonass.* 580, his captains by his order spoiled and slaughtered the *Jews*, profaned the Temple, set up the worship of the heathen Gods in all *Judea*, and began to persecute and make war upon those who would not worship them: which actions are thus described by *Daniel*. [10] *At the time appointed he shall come again towards the* South, *but the latter shall not be as the former. For the ships of* Chittim *shall come*, with an embassy from *Rome*, *against him. Therefore he shall be grieved, and return, and have indignation against the holy covenant. So shall he do; he shall even return, and have intelligence with them that forsake the holy covenant.*

In the same year that *Antiochus* by the command of the *Romans* retired out of *Egypt*, and set up the worship of the *Greeks* in *Judea*; the *Romans* conquered the kingdom of *Macedon*, the fundamental kingdom of the Empire of the *Greeks*, and reduced it into a *Roman* Province; and thereby began to put an end to the reign of *Daniel*'s third Beast. This is thus exprest by *Daniel. And after him Arms*, that is the *Romans, shall stand up.* As דלמֹמ signifies *after the King*, Dan. xi. 8; so ונממ may signify *after him. Arms* are every where in this Prophecy of *Daniel* put for the military power of a kingdom: and they stand up when they conquer and grow powerful. Hitherto *Daniel* described the actions of the Kings of the *North* and *South*; but upon the conquest of *Macedon* by the *Romans*, he left off describing the actions of the *Greeks*, and began to describe those of the *Romans* in *Greece*. They conquered *Macedon, Illyricum* and *Epirus*, in the year of *Nabonassar* 580. 35 years after, by the last will and testament of *Attalus* the last King of *Pergamus*, they inherited that rich and flourishing kingdom, that is, all *Asia* westward of mount *Taurus*; 69 years after they conquered the kingdom of *Syria*, and reduced it into a Province, and 34 years after they did the like to *Egypt*. By all these steps the *Roman* Arms stood up over the *Greeks*: and after 95 years more, by making war upon the *Jews, they polluted the sanctuary of strength, and took away the daily sacrifice, and then placed the abomination of desolation.* For this abomination was placed after the days of *Christ, Math.* xxiv. 15. In the 16th year of the Emperor *Adrian*, A.C. 132, they placed this abomination by building a Temple to *Jupiter Capitolinus*, where the Temple of God in *Jerusalem* had stood. Thereupon the *Jews* under the conduct of *Barchochab* rose up in arms against the *Romans*, and in the war had 50 cities demolished, 985 of their best towns destroyed, and 580000 men slain by the sword; and in the end of the war, A.C. 136, were banished *Judea* upon pain of death, and thenceforward the land remained desolate of its old inhabitants.

In the beginning of the *Jewish* war in *Nero's* reign, the Apostles fled out of *Judea* with their flocks; some beyond *Jordan* to *Pella* and other places, some into *Egypt, Syria, Mesopotamia, Asia minor,* and elsewhere. *Peter* and *John* came into *Asia,* and *Peter* went thence by *Corinth* to *Rome*; but *John* staying in *Asia,* was banished by the *Romans* into *Patmos,* as the head of a party of the *Jews,* whose nation was in war with the *Romans.* By this dispersion of the *Christian Jews,* the *Christian* religion, which was already propagated westward as far as *Rome,* spred fast into all the *Roman* Empire, and suffered many persecutions under it till the days of *Constantine* the great and his sons: all which is thus described by *Daniel.* [11] *And such as do wickedly against the covenant, shall he,* who places the abomination, *cause to dissemble,* and worship the heathen Gods; *but the people* among them *who do know their God, shall be strong and act. And they that understand among the people, shall instruct many: yet they shall fall by the sword, and by flame, and by captivity, and by spoil many days. Now when they shall fall, they shall be holpen with a little help,* viz. in the reign of *Constantine* the great; *and* at that time by reason of their prosperity, *many shall* come over to them from among the heathen, and *cleave to them with dissimulation. But of those of understanding there shall* still *fall to try* God's people *by them and to purge* them from the dissemblers, *and to make them white even to the time of the end: because it is yet for a time appointed.*

Hitherto the *Roman* Empire continued entire; and under this dominion, the little horn of the He-Goat continued *mighty, but not by his own power.* But now, by the building of *Constantinople,* and endowing it with a Senate and other like privileges with *Rome*; and by the division of the *Roman* Empire into the two Empires of the *Greeks* and *Latins,* headed by those two cities; a new scene of things commences, in which which [12] *a King,* the Empire of the *Greeks, doth according to his will, and,* by setting his own laws above the laws of God, *exalts and magnifies himself above every God, and speaks marvellous things against the God of Gods, and shall prosper till the indignation be accomplished.—Neither shall he regard the God of his fathers, nor the* lawful *desire of women* in matrimony, *nor any God, but shall magnify himself above all. And in his seat he shall honour* Mahuzzims, that is, strong guardians, the souls of the dead; *even with a God whom his fathers knew not shall he honour them*, in their Temples, *with gold and silver, and with precious stones and valuable things.* All which relates to the overspreading of the *Greek* Empire with Monks and Nuns, who placed holiness in abstinence from marriage; and to the invocation of saints and veneration of their reliques, and such like superstitions, which these men introduced in the fourth and fifth centuries. [13] *And at the time of the end the King of the* South, or the Empire of the *Saracens, shall push at him; and the King of the* North, or Empire of the *Turks, shall come against him like a whirlwind, with chariots and with horsemen, and with many ships; and be shall enter into the countries* of the *Greeks, and shall overflow and pass over. He shall enter also into the glorious land, and many countries shall be overthrown; but these shall escape out of his hand, even* Edom *and* Moab, *and the chief of the children* Ammon: that is, those to whom his Caravans pay tribute. *He shall stretch forth his hand also upon the countries, and the land of* Egypt *shall not escape; but he shall have power over the treasures of gold and silver, and over all the precious things of* Egypt; *and the* Lybians *and* Ethiopians *shall be at his steps.* All these nations compose the Empire of the *Turks*, and therefore this Empire is here to be understood by the King of the *North*. They compose also the body of the He-Goat; and therefore the Goat still reigns in his last horn, but not by his own power.

Notes to Chap. XII

[1] Chap. xi. 2, 3, 4.
[2] Chap. xi. 5.
[3] Chap. xi. 6, 7, 8.
[4] Chap. xi. 10, &c.
[5] Chap. xi. 13-19.
[6] Chap. xi. 20.
[7] Chap. xi. 21, &c.
[8] 2 Maccab. iii. 5, 8. & iv. 4.
[9] Chap. xi. 25, &c.
[10] Chap. xi. 29, 30.
[11] Chap. xi. 32, &c.
[12] Chap. xi. 36, &c.
[13] Chap. xi. 40, &c.

CHAP. XIII

*Of the King who did according to his will, and magnified himself
above every God, and honoured* Mahuzzims,
and regarded not the desire of women.

I n the first ages of the Christian religion the Christians of
every city were governed by a Council of Presbyters, and
the President of the Council was the Bishop of the city. The
Bishop and Presbyters of one city meddled not with the affairs of
another city, except by admonitory letters or messages. Nor did
the Bishops of several cities meet together in Council before the
time of the Emperor *Commodus*: for they could not meet together
without the leave of the *Roman* governors of the Provinces. But
in the days of that Emperor they began to meet in Provincial
Councils, by the leave of the governors; first in *Asia*, in
opposition to the *Cataphrygian* Heresy, and soon after in other
places and upon other occasions. The Bishop of the chief city, or
Metropolis of the *Roman* Province, was usually made President
of the Council; and hence came the authority of Metropolitan
Bishops above that of other Bishops within the same Province.
Hence also it was that the Bishop of *Rome* in *Cyprian*'s days
called himself the Bishop of Bishops. As soon as the Empire
became Christian, the *Roman* Emperors began to call general
Councils out of all the Provinces of the Empire; and by
prescribing to them what points they should consider, and
influencing them by their interest and power, they set up what
party they pleased. Hereby the *Greek* Empire, upon the division
of the *Roman* Empire into the *Greek* and *Latin* Empires, became
the King who, in matters of religion, *did according to his will*;
and, in legislature, *exalted and magnified himself above every
God*: and at length, by the seventh general Council, established
the worship of the images and souls of dead men, here called
Mahuzzims.

The same King placed holiness in abstinence from marriage. *Eusebius* in his Ecclesiastical history [1] tells us, that *Musanus* wrote a tract against those who fell away to the heresy of the *Encratites*, which was then newly risen, and had introduced pernicious errors; and that *Tatian*, the disciple of *Justin*, was the author thereof; and that *Irenæus* in his first book against heresies teaches this, writing of *Tatian* and his heresy in these words: *A Saturnino & Marcione profecti qui vocantur Continentes, docuerunt non contrahendum esse matrimonium; reprobantes scilicet primitivum illud opificium Dei, & tacitè accusantes Deum qui masculum & fœminam condidit ad procreationem generis humani. Induxerunt etiam abstinentiam ab esu eorum quæ animalia appellant, ingratos se exhibentes ergo eum qui universa creavit Deum. Negant etiam primi hominis salutem. Atque hoc nuper apud illos excogitatum est, Tatiano quodam omnium primo hujus impietatis auctore: qui Justini auditor, quamdiu cum illo versatus est, nihil ejusmodi protulit. Post martyrium autem illius, ab Ecclesia se abrumpens, doctoris arrogantia elatus ac tumidus, tanquam præstantior cæteris, novam quandam formam doctrinæ conflavit: Æonas invisibiles commentus perinde ac Valentinus: asserens quoque cum Saturnino & Marcione, matrimonium nihil aliud esse quam corruptionem ac stuprum: nova præterea argumenta ad subvertendam Adami salutem excogitans. Hæc Irenæus de Hæresi quæ tunc viguit Encratitarum.* Thus far *Eusebius*. But altho the followers of *Tatian* were at first condemned as hereticks by the name of *Encratites*, or *Continentes*; their principles could not be yet quite exploded: for *Montanus* refined upon them, and made only second marriages unlawful; he also introduced frequent fastings, and annual, fasting days, the keeping of *Lent*, and feeding upon dried meats. The *Apostolici*, about the middle of the third century, condemned marriage, and were a branch of the disciples of *Tatian*. The *Hierocitæ* in *Egypt*, in the latter end of the third century, also condemned marriage. *Paul* the *Eremite* fled into the wilderness from the persecution of *Decius*, and lived there a solitary life till the reign of *Constantine* the great, but made no disciples. *Antony* did the like in the persecution of *Dioclesian*, or a little before, and made disciples; and many others soon followed his example.

Hitherto the principles of the *Encratites* had been rejected by the Churches; but now being refined by the Monks, and imposed not upon all men, but only upon those who would voluntarily undertake a monastic life, they began to be admired, and to overflow first the *Greek* Church, and then the *Latin* also, like a torrent. *Eusebius* tells us, [2] that *Constantine* the great had those men in the highest veneration, who dedicated themselves wholly to the divine philosophy; and that he almost venerated the most holy company of Virgins perpetually devoted to God; being certain that the God to whom he had consecrated himself did dwell in their minds. In his time and that of his sons, this profession of a single life was propagated in *Egypt* by *Antony*, and in *Syria* by *Hilarion*; and spred so fast, that soon after the time of *Julian* the Apostate a third part of the *Egyptians* were got into the desarts of *Egypt*. They lived first singly in cells, then associated into *cœnobia* or convents; and at length came into towns, and filled the Churches with Bishops, Presbyters and Deacons. *Athanasius* in his younger days poured water upon the hands of his master *Antony*; and finding the Monks faithful to him, made many of them Bishops and Presbyters in *Egypt*: and these Bishops erected new Monasteries, out of which they chose Presbyters of their own cities, and sent Bishops to others. The like was done in *Syria*, the superstition being quickly propagated thither out of *Egypt* by *Hilarion* a disciple of *Antony*. *Spiridion* and *Epiphanius* of *Cyprus*, *James* of *Nisibis*, *Cyril* of *Jerusalem*, *Eustathius* of *Sebastia* in *Armenia*, *Eusebius* of *Emisa*, *Titus* of *Bostra*, *Basilius* of *Ancyra*, *Acacius* of *Cæsarea* in *Palestine*, *Elpidius* of *Laodicea*, *Melitius* and *Flavian* of *Antioch*, *Theodorus* of *Tyre*, *Protogenes* of *Carrhœ*, *Acacius* of *Berrhœa*, *Theodotus* of *Hierapolis*, *Eusebius* of *Chalcedon*, *Amphilochius* of *Iconium*, *Gregory Nazianzen*, *Gregory Nyssen*, and *John Chrysostom* of *Constantinople*, were both Bishops and Monks in the fourth century. *Eustathius, Gregory Nazianzen, Gregory Nyssen, Basil*, &c. had Monasteries of Clergymen in their cities, out of which Bishops were sent to other cities; who in like manner erected Monasteries there, till the Churches were supplied with Bishops out of these Monasteries. Hence *Jerome*, in a Letter written about the year 385, [3] saith of the Clergy:

Quasi & ipsi aliud sint quam Monachi, & non quicquid in Monachos dicitur redundet in Clericos qui patres sunt Monachorum. Detrimentum pecoris pastoris ignominia est. And in his book against *Vigilantius: Quid facient Orientis Ecclesiæ? Quæ aut Virgines Clericos accipiunt, aut Continentes, aut si uxores habuerint mariti esse desistunt.* Not long after even the Emperors commanded the Churches to chuse Clergymen out of the Monasteries by this Law.

Impp. Arcad & Honor. AA. Cæsario PF. P.

[4] *Si quos forte Episcopi deesse sibi Clericos arbitrantur, ex monachorum numero rectius ordinabunt: non obnoxios publicis privatisque rationibus cum invidia teneant, sed habeant jam probatos. Dat. vii. Kal. Aug. Honorio A. iv. & Eutychianio Coss.* A.C. 598. The *Greek* Empire being now in the hands of these *Encratites*, and having them in great admiration, *Daniel* makes it a characteristick of the King who doth according to his will, that *he should not regard the desire of Women.*

Thus the Sect of the *Encratites*, set on foot by the *Gnosticks*, and propagated by *Tatian* and *Montanus* near the end of the second century; which was condemned by the Churches of that and the third century, and refined upon by their followers; overspread the *Eastern* Churches in the fourth century, and before the end of it began to overspread the *Western.* Henceforward the Christian Churches having a form of godliness, but denying the power thereof, came into the hands of the *Encratites*: and the Heathens, who in the fourth century came over in great numbers to the Christians, embraced more readily this sort of Christianity, as having a greater affinity with their old superstitions, than that of the sincere Christians; who by the lamps of the seven Churches of *Asia,* and not by the lamps of the Monasteries, had illuminated the Church Catholic during the three first centuries.

The *Cataphrygians* brought in also several other superstitions: such as were the doctrine of Ghosts, and of their punishment in Purgatory, with prayers and oblations for mitigating that punishment, as *Tertullian* teaches in his books *De Anima* and *De Monogamia.* They used also the sign of the cross as a charm. So *Tertullian* in his book *de Corona militis: Ad omnem progressum atque promotum, ad omnem aditum & exitum, ad vestitum, ad calceatum, ad lavacra, ad mensas, ad lamina, ad cubilia, ad sedilia, quacunque nos conversatio exercet, frontem crucis signaculo terimus.* All these superstitions the Apostle refers to, where he saith: *Now the Spirit speaketh expresly, that in the latter times some shall depart from the faith, giving heed to seducing spirits, and doctrines of devils,* the *Dæmons* and Ghosts worshipped by the heathens, *speaking lyes in hypocrisy,* about their apparitions, the miracles done by them, their reliques, and the sign of the cross, *having consciences seared with a hot iron; forbidding to marry, and commanding to abstain from meats,* &c. 1 Tim. iv. 1,2,3. From the *Cataphrygians* these principles and practices were propagated down to posterity. *For the mystery of iniquity* did *already work* in the *Apostles* days in the *Gnosticks,* continued to work very strongly in their offspring the *Tatianists* and *Cataphrygians,* and was to work *till that man of sin* should *be revealed; whose coming is after the working of Satan, with all power and signs, and lying wonders, and all deceivableness of unrighteousness;* coloured over with a form of *Christian* godliness, but without the power thereof, 2 *Thess.* ii. 7-10.

For tho some stop was put to the *Cataphrygian* Christianity, by Provincial Councils, till the fourth century; yet the *Roman* Emperors then turning *Christians,* and great multitudes of heathens coming over in outward profession, these found the *Cataphrygian* Christianity more suitable to their old principles, of placing religion in outward forms and ceremonies, holy-days, and doctrines of Ghosts, than the religion of the sincere *Christians*: wherefore they readily sided with the *Cataphrygian Christians,* and established that Christianity before the end of the fourth century. By this means those of understanding, after they had been persecuted by the heathen Emperors in the three first centuries, and *were holpen with a little help,* by the conversion of *Constantine* the great and his sons to the *Christian* religion, fell under new persecutions, *to purge them* from the dissemblers, *and to make them white, even to the time of the end.*

Notes to Chap. XIII

[1] Lib. 4. c. 28, 29.
[2] In vita Constantini, l. 4. c. 28.
[3] Epist. 10.
[4] L. 32. de Episcopis.

CHAP. XIV

Of the Mahuzzims, honoured by the King who doth according to his will.

In scripture we are told of some *trusting in God* and others *trusting in idols,* and that *God is our refuge, our strength, our defense.* In this sense God is *the rock of his people,* and false Gods are called *the rock of those that trust in them,* Deut. xxxii. 4, 15, 18, 30, 31, 37. In the same sense the Gods of *the King* who *shall do according to his will* are called *Mahuzzims,* munitions, fortresses, protectors, guardians, or defenders. *In his estate,* saith [1] *Daniel, shall he honour* Mahuzzims; *even with a God whom his fathers knew not, shall he honour them with gold and silver, and with precious stones, and things of value. Thus shall he do in the most strong holds* or temples;—*and he shall cause them to rule over many, and divide the land* among them *for a possession.* Now this came to pass by degrees in the following manner.

Gregory Nyssen [2] tells us, that after the persecution of the Emperor *Decius, Gregory* Bishop of *Neocæsarea* in *Pontus, instituted among all people, as an addition or corollary of devotion towards God, that festival days and assemblies should be celebrated to them who had contended for the faith,* that is, to the *Martyrs.* And he adds this reason for the institution: *When he observed,* saith *Nyssen, that the simple and unskilful multitude, by reason of corporeal delights, remained in the error of idols; that the principal thing might be corrected among them, namely, that instead of their vain worship they might turn their eyes upon God; he permitted that at the memories of the holy Martyrs they might make merry and delight themselves, and be dissolved into joy.* The heathens were delighted with the festivals of their Gods, and unwilling to part with those delights; and therefore *Gregory,* to facilitate their conversion, instituted annual festivals to the

Saints and *Martyrs*. Hence it came to pass, that for exploding the festivals of the heathens, the principal festivals of the *Christians* succeeded in their room: as the keeping of *Christmas* with ivy and feasting, and playing and sports, in the room of the *Bacchanalia* and *Saturnalia*; the celebrating of *May-day* with flowers, in the room of the *Floralia*; and the keeping of festivals to the Virgin *Mary*, *John* the Baptist, and divers of the Apostles, in the room of the solemnities at the entrance of the Sun into the signs of the *Zodiac* in the old *Julian* Calendar. In the same persecution of *Decius*, *Cyprian* ordered the passions of the Martyrs in *Africa* to be registred, in order to celebrate their memories annually with oblations and sacrifices: and *Felix* Bishop of *Rome*, a little after, as *Platina* relates, *Martyrum gloria consulens, constituit at quotannis sacrificia eorum nomine celebrarentur*; "consulting the glory of the Martyrs, ordained that sacrifices should be celebrated annually in their name." By the pleasures of these festivals the *Christians* increased much in number, and decreased as much in virtue, until they were *purged and made white* by the persecution of *Dioclesian*. This was the first step made in the *Christian* religion towards the veneration of the Martyrs: and tho it did not yet amount to an unlawful worship; yet it disposed the *Christians* towards such a further veneration of the dead, as in a short time ended in the invocation of Saints.

The next step was the affecting to pray at the sepulchres of the Martyrs: which practice began in *Dioclesian*'s persecution. The Council of *Eliberis* in *Spain*, celebrated in the third or fourth year of *Dioclesian*'s persecution, A.C. 305, hath these Canons. Can. 34. *Cereos per diem placuit in Cœmeterio non incendi: inquietandi enim spiritus sanctorum non sunt. Qui hæc non observârint, arceantur ab Ecclesiæ communione.* Can. 35. *Placuit prohiberi ne fœminæ in Cœmeterio pervigilent, eò quod sæpe sub obtentu orationis latentèr scelera committant.* Presently after that persecution, suppose about the year 314, the Council of *Laodicea* in *Phrygia*, which then met for restoring the lapsed discipline of the Church, has the following Canons. Can. 9. *Those of the Church are not allowed to go into the* Cœmeteries *or* Martyries, *as they are called, of hereticks, for the sake of prayer or recovery of health: but such as go, if they be of the faithful, shall be excommunicated for a time.* Can. 34. *A* Christian *must not leave the Martyrs of* Christ, *and go to false Martyrs*, that is, to the Martyrs of the hereticks; *for these are alien from God: and therefore let those be anathema who go to them.* Can. 51. *The birth-days of the Martyrs shall not be celebrated in* Lent, *but their commemoration shall be made on the Sabbath-days and Lords days.* The Council of *Paphlagonia*, celebrated in the year 324, made this Canon: *If any man being arrogant, abominates the congregations of the Martyrs, or the Liturgies performed therein, or the memories of the Martyrs, let him be anathema.* By all which it is manifest that the *Christians* in the time of *Dioclesian's* persecution used to pray in the *Cœmeteries* or burying-places of the dead; for avoiding the danger of the persecution, and for want of Churches, which were all thrown down: and after the persecution was over, continued that practice in honour of the Martyrs, till new Churches could be built: and by use affected it as advantageous to devotion, and for recovering the health of those that were sick. It also appears that in these burying-places they commemorated the Martyrs yearly upon days dedicated to them, and accounted all these practices pious and religious, and anathematized those men as arrogant who opposed them, or prayed in the *Martyries* of the hereticks. They also lighted torches to the Martyrs in the day-time, as the heathens did to their Gods; which custom, before the end of the fourth century, prevailed much in the *West*. They sprinkled the worshipers of the Martyrs with holy-water, as the heathens did the worshipers of their Gods; and went in pilgrimage to see *Jerusalem* and other holy places, as if those places conferred sanctity on the visiters. From the custom of praying in the *Cœmeteries* and *Martyries*, came the custom of translating the bodies of the Saints and Martyrs into such Churches as were new built: the Emperor *Constantius* began this practice about the year 359, causing the bodies of *Andrew* the Apostle, *Luke* and *Timothy*, to be translated into a new Church at *Constantinople*: and before this act of *Constantius*, the *Egyptians* kept the bodies of their Martyrs and Saints unburied upon beds in their private houses, and told stories of their souls appearing after death and ascending up to heaven, as *Athanasius* relates in the life of *Antony*. All which gave occasion to the Emperor *Julian*, as *Cyril* relates, to accuse the *Christians* in this manner: *Your adding to that antient dead man, Jesus, many new dead men, who can sufficiently abominate? You have filled all places with sepulchres and monuments, altho you are no where bidden to prostrate yourselves to sepulchres, and to respect them officiously.* And a little after: *Since* Jesus *said that sepulchres are full of filthiness, how do you invoke God upon them?* and in another place he saith, that if *Christians* had adhered to the precepts of the *Hebrews, they would have worshiped one God instead of many, and not a man, or rather not many unhappy men*: And that they *adored the wood of the cross, making its images on their foreheads, and before their houses.*

After the sepulchres of Saints and Martyrs were thus converted into places of worship like the heathen temples, and the Churches into sepulchres, and a certain sort of sanctity attributed to the dead bodies of the Saints and Martyrs buried in them, and annual festivals were kept to them, with sacrifices offered to God in their name; the next step towards the invocation of Saints, was the attributing to their dead bodies, bones and other reliques, a power of working miracles, by means of the separate souls, who were supposed to know what we do or say, and to be able to do us good or hurt, and to work those miracles. This was the very notion the heathens had of the separate souls of their antient Kings and Heroes, whom they worshiped under the names of *Saturn, Rhea, Jupiter, Juno, Mars, Venus, Bacchus, Ceres, Osiris, Isis, Apollo, Diana*, and the rest of their Gods. For these Gods being male and female, husband and wife, son and daughter, brother and sister, are thereby discovered to be antient men and women. Now as the first step towards the invocation of Saints was set on foot by the persecution of *Decius*, and the second by the persecution of *Dioclesian*; so this third seems to have been owing to the proceedings of *Constantius* and *Julian* the Apostate. When *Julian* began to restore the worship of the heathen Gods, and to vilify the Saints and Martyrs; the *Christians* of *Syria* and *Egypt* seem to have made a great noise about the miracles done by the reliques of the *Christian* Saints and Martyrs, in opposition to the powers attributed by *Julian* and the heathens to their Idols. For *Sozomen* and *Ruffinus* tell us, that when he opened the heathen Temples, and consulted the Oracle of *Apollo Daphnæus* in the suburbs of *Antioch*, and pressed by many sacrifices for an answer; the Oracle at length told him that the bones of the Martyr *Babylas* which were buried there hinder'd him from speaking. By which answer we may understand, that some *Christian* was got into the place where the heathen Priests used to speak thro' a pipe in delivering their Oracles: and before this, *Hilary* in his book against *Constantius*, written in the last year of that Emperor, makes the following mention of what was then doing in the *East* where he was. *Sine martyrio persequeris. Plus crudelitati vestræ* Nero, Deci, Maximiane, *debemus. Diabolum enim per vos vicimus. Sanctus ubique beatorum martyrum sanguis exceptus est, dum in his Dæmones mugiunt, dum ægritudines depelluntur, dum miraculorum opera cernuntur, elevari sine laqueis corpora, & dispensis pede fœminis vestes non defluere in faciem, uri sine ignibus spiritus, confiteri sine interrogantis incremento fidei.* And *Gregory Nazianzen*, in his first Oration against the Emperor *Julian* then reigning, writes thus: *Martyres non extimuisti quibus præclari honores & festa constituta, à quibus Dæmones propelluntur & morbi curantur; quorum sunt apparitiones & prædictiones; quorum vel sola corpora idem possunt quod animæ sanctæ, sive manibus contrectentur, sive honorentur: quorum vel solæ sanguinis guttæ atque exigua passionis signa idem possunt quod corpora. Hæc non colis sed contemnis & aspernaris.* These things made the heathens in the reign of the same Emperor demolish the sepulchre of *John* the Baptist in *Phœnicia*, and burn his bones; when several *Christians* mixing themselves with the heathens, gathered up some of his remains, which were sent to *Athanasius*, who hid them in the wall of a Church; foreseeing by a prophetic spirit, as *Ruffinus* tells us, that they might be profitable to future generations.

The cry of these miracles being once set on foot, continued for many years, and encreased and grew more general. *Chrysostom*, in his second Oration on St. *Babylas*, twenty years after the silencing of the Oracle of *Apollo Daphnæus* as above, *viz.* A.C. 382, saith of the miracles done by the Saints and their reliques [3]: *Nulla est nostri hujus Orbis seu regio, seu gens, seu urbs, ubi nova & inopinata miracula hæc non decantentur; quæ quidem si figmenta fuissent, prorsus in tantam hominum admirationem non venissent.* And a little after: *Abunde orationi nostræ fidem faciunt quæ quotidiana à martyribus miracula eduntur, magna affatim ad illa hominum multitudine affluente.* And in his 66th Homily, describing how the Devils were tormented and cast out by the bones of the Martyrs, he adds: *Ob eam causam multi plerumque Reges peregrè profecti sunt, ut hoc spectaculo fruerentur. Siquidem sanctorum martyrum templa futuri judicii vestigia & signa exhibent, dum nimirum Dæmones flagris cæduntur, hominesque torquentur & liberantur. Vide quæ sanctorum vitâ functorum vis sit?* And *Jerom* in his Epitaph on *Paula*, thus [4] mentions the same things. *Paula vidit Samariam: ibi siti sunt Elisæus & Abdias prophetæ, & Joannes Baptista, ubi multis intremuit consternata miraculis. Nam cernebat variis dæmones rugire cruciatibus, & ante sepulchra sanctorum ululare, homines more luporum vocibus latrare canum, fremere leonum, sibilare serpentum, mugire taurorum, alios rotare caput & post tergum terram vertice tangere, suspensisque pede fœminis vestes non defluere in faciem.* This was about the year 384: and *Chrysostom* in his Oration on the *Egyptian* Martyrs, seems to make *Egypt* the ringleader in these matters, saying [5]: *Benedictus Deus quandoquidem ex Ægypto prodeunt martyres, ex Ægypto illa cum Deo pugnante ac insanissima, & unde impia ora, unde linguæ blasphemæ; ex Ægypto martyres habentur; non in Ægypto tantum, nec in finitima vicinaque regione, sed* UBIQUE TERRARUM. *Et quemadmodum in annonæ summa ubertate, cum viderunt urbium incolæ majorem quam usus habitatorum postulat esse proventum, ad peregrinas etiam urbes transmittunt: cum & suam comitatem & liberalitatem ostendant, tum ut præter horum abundantiam cum facilitate res quibus indigent rursus ab illis sibi comparent: sic & Ægyptii, quod attinet ad religionis athletas, fecerunt. Cum apud se multam eorum Dei benignitate copiam cernerent, nequaquam ingens Dei munus sua civitate concluserunt, sed in* OMNES TERRÆ PARTES *bonorum thesauros effuderunt: cum ut suum in fratres amorem ostenderent, tum ut communem omnium dominum honore afficerent, ac civitati suæ gloriam apud omnes compararent, totiusque terrarum* ORBIS *esse* METROPOLIN *declararent.— Sanctorum enim illorum corpora quovis adamantino & inexpugnabili muro tutiùs nobis urbem communiunt, & tanquam excelsi quidam scopuli undique prominentes, non horum qui sub sensus cadunt & oculis cernuntur hostium impetus propulsant tantùm, sed etiam invisibilium dæmonum insidias, omnesque diaboli fraudes subvertunt ac dissipant.—Neque vero tantùm adversus hominum insidias aut adversus fallacias dæmonum utilis nobis est hæc possessio, sed si nobis communis dominus ob peccatorum multitudinem irascatur, his objectis corporibus continuo poterimus eum propitium reddere civitati.* This Oration was written at *Antioch*, while *Alexandria* was yet the Metropolis of the *East*, that is, before the year 381, in which *Constantinople* became the Metropolis: and it was a work of some years for the *Egyptians* to have distributed the miracle-working reliques of their Martyrs over all the world, as they had done before that year. *Egypt* abounded most with the reliques of Saints and Martyrs, the *Egyptians* keeping them embalmed upon beds even in their private houses; and *Alexandria* was eminent above all other cities for dispersing them, so as on that account to acquire glory with all men, and manifest herself to be the *Metropolis* of the world. *Antioch* followed the example of *Egypt*, in dispersing the reliques of the forty Martyrs: and the examples of *Egypt* and *Syria* were soon followed by the rest of the world.

The reliques of the forty Martyrs at *Antioch* were distributed among the Churches before the year 373; for *Athanasius* who died in that year, wrote an Oration upon them. This Oration is not yet published, but *Gerard Vossius* saw it in MS. in the Library of Cardinal *Ascanius* in *Italy*, as he says in his commentary upon the Oration of *Ephræm Syrus* on the same forty Martyrs. Now since the Monks of *Alexandria* sent the reliques of the Martyrs of *Egypt* into all parts of the earth, and thereby acquired glory to their city, and declared her in these matters the Metropolis of the whole world, as we have observed out of *Chrysostom*; it may be concluded, that before *Alexandria* received the forty Martyrs from *Antioch*, she began to send out the reliques of her own Martyrs into all parts, setting the first example to other cities.

This practice therefore began in *Egypt* some years before the death of *Athanasius*. It began when the miracle-working bones of *John* the Baptist were carried into *Egypt*, and hid in the wall of a Church, *that they might be profitable to future generations*. It was restrained in the reign of *Julian* the Apostate: and then it spred from *Egypt* into all the Empire, *Alexandria* being the Metropolis of the whole world, according to *Chrysostom*, for propagating this sort of devotion, and *Antioch* and other cities soon following her example.

In propagating these superstitions, the ring-leaders were the Monks, and *Antony* was at the head of them: for in the end of the life of *Antony*, *Athanasius* relates that these were his dying words to his disciples who then attended him. *Do you take care*, said *Antony*, *to adhere to* Christ *in the first place, and then to the Saints, that after death they may receive you as friends and acquaintance into the everlasting tabernacles, Think upon these things, perceive these things; and if you have any regard to me, remember me as a father*. This being delivered in charge to the Monks by *Antony* at his death, A.C. 356, could not but inflame their whole body with devotion towards the Saints, as the ready way to be received, by them into the eternal Tabernacles after death. Hence came that noise about the miracles, done by the reliques of the Saints in the time of *Constantius*: hence came the dispersion of the miracle-working reliques into all the Empire; *Alexandria* setting the example, and being renowned, for it above all other cities. Hence it came to pass in the days of *Julian*, A.C. 362, that *Athanasius* by a prophetic spirit, as *Ruffinus* tells us, hid the bones of *John* the Baptist from the Heathens, not in the ground to be forgotten, but in the hollow wall of a Church before proper witnesses, that they might *be profitable to future generations*. Hence also came the invocation of the Saints for doing such miracles, and for assisting men in their devotions, and mediating with God. For *Athanasius*, even from his youth, looked upon the dead Saints and Martyrs as mediators of our prayers: in his Epistle to *Marcellinus*, written in the days of *Constantine* the great, he saith that the words of the *Psalms* are not to be transposed or any wise changed, but to be recited and sung without any artifice, as they are written, *that the holy men who delivered them, knowing them to be their own words, may pray with us; or rather, that the Holy Ghost who spake in the holy men, seeing his own words with which he inspired them, may join* with them *in assisting us.*

Whilst *Egypt* abounded with Monks above any other country, the veneration of the Saints began sooner, and spred faster there than in other places. *Palladius* going into *Egypt* in the year 388 to visit the Monasteries, and the sepulchres of *Apollonius* and other Martyrs of *Thebais* who had suffered under *Maximinus*, saith of them: *Iis omnibus Christiani fecerunt œdem unam, ubi nunc multœ virtutes peraguntur. Tanta autem fuit viri gratia, ut de iis quœ esset precatus statim exaudiretur, eum sic honorante servatore: quem etiam nos in martyrio precati vidimus, cum iis qui cum ipso fuerunt martyrio affecti; & Deum adorantes, eorum corpora salutavimus. Eunapius* also, a heathen, yet a competent witness of what was done in his own times, relating how the soldiers delivered the temples of *Egypt* into the hands of the Monks, which was done in the year 389, rails thus in an impious manner at the Martyrs, as succeeding in the room of the old Gods of *Egypt. Illi ipsi,* milites, *Monachos Canobi quoque collocârunt, ut pro Diis qui animo cernuntur, servos & quidem flagitiosos divinis honoribus percolerent, hominum mentibus ad cultum ceremoniasque obligatis. Ii namque condita & salita eorum capita, qui ob scelerum multitudinem à judicibus extremo judicio fuerant affecti, pro Divis ostentabant; iis genua submittebant, eos in Deorum numerum receptabant, ad illorum sepulchra pulvere sordibusque conspurcati. Martyres igitur vocabantur, & ministri quidem & legati arbitrique precum apud Deos; cum fuerint servilia infida & flagris pessimè subacta, quœ cicatrices scelerum ac nequitiœ vestigia corporibus circumferunt; ejusmodi tamen Deos fert tellus.* By these instances we may understand the invocation of Saints was now of some standing in *Egypt,* and that it was already generally received and practised there by the common people.

Thus *Basil* a Monk, who was made Bishop of *Cæsarea* in the year 369, and died in the year 378, in his Oration on the Martyr *Mamas,* saith: *Be ye mindful of the Martyr; as many of you as have enjoyed him in your dreams, as many as in this place have been assisted by him in prayer, as many of you as upon invoking him by name have had him present in your works, as many as he has reduced into the way from wandering, as many as he has restored to health, as, many as have had their dead children restored by him to life, as many as have had their lives prolonged by him*: and a little after, he thus expresses the universality of this superstition in the regions of *Cappadocia* and *Bithynia*: *At the memory of the Martyr*, saith he, *the whole region is moved; at his festival the whole city is transported with joy. Nor do the kindred of the rich turn aside to the sepulchres of their ancestors, but all go to the place of devotion.* Again, in the end of the Homily he prays, that *God would preserve the Church, thus fortified with the great towers of the Martyrs*: and in his Oration on the forty Martyrs; *These are they*, saith he, *who obtaining our country, like certain towers afford us safety against our enemies. Neither are they shut up in one place only, but being distributed are sent into many regions, and adorn many countries.—You have often endeavoured, you have often laboured to find one who might pray for you: here are forty, emitting one voice of prayer.—He that is in affliction flies to these, he that rejoices has recourse to these: the first, that he may be freed from evil, the last that he may continue in happiness. Here a woman praying for her children is heard; she obtains a safe return for her husband from abroad, and health for him in his sickness.—O ye common keepers of mankind, the best companions of our cares, suffragans and coadjutors of our prayers, most powerful embassadors to God*, &c. By all which it is manifest, that before the year 378, the Orations and Sermons upon the Saints went much beyond the bounds of mere oratorical flourishes, and that the common people in the *East* were already generally corrupted by the Monks with Saint-worship.

Gregory Nazianzen a Monk, in his sixth Oration written A.C. 373, when he was newly made Bishop of *Sasima*, saith: *Let us purify ourselves to the Martyrs, or rather to the God of the Martyrs*: and a little after he calls the Martyrs *mediators of obtaining an ascension or divinity.* The same year, in the end of his Oration upon *Athanasius* then newly dead, he thus invokes him: *Do thou look down upon us propitiously, and govern this people, as perfect adorers of the perfect Trinity, which in the Father, Son, and Holy Ghost, is contemplated and worshiped: if there shall be peace, preserve me, and feed my flock with me; but if war, bring me home, place me by thyself, and by those that are like thee; however great my request.* And in the end of the funeral Oration upon *Basil*, written A.C. 378, he thus addresses him: *But thou, O divine and sacred Head, look down upon us from heaven; and by thy prayers either take away that thorn of the flesh which is given us by God for exercise, or obtain that we may bear it with courage, and direct all our life to that which is most fitting for us. When we depart this life, receive us there in your Tabernacles, that living together and beholding the holy and blessed Trinity more purely and perfectly, whereof we have now but an imperfect view, we may there come to the end of our desires, and receive this reward of the wars which we have waged or suffered*: and in his Oration upon *Cyprian*, not the Bishop of *Carthage*, but a *Greek*, he invokes him after the same manner; and tells us also how a pious Virgin named *Justina*, was protected by invoking the Virgin *Mary*, and how miracles were done by the ashes of *Cyprian*.

Gregory Nyssen, another eminent Monk and Bishop, in the life of *Ephræm Syrus*, tells how a certain man returning from a far country, was in great danger, by reason all the ways were intercepted by the armies of barbarous nations; but upon invoking *Ephræm* by name, and saying, *Holy* Ephræm *assist me*, he escaped the danger, neglected the fear of death, and beyond his hope got safe home. In the end of this Oration *Gregory* calls upon *Ephræm* after the following manner: *But thou, O Ephræm, assisting now at the divine altar, and sacrificing to the Prince of life, and to the most holy Trinity, together with the Angels; remember us all, and obtain for us pardon of our sins, that we may enjoy the eternal happiness of the kingdom of heaven.* The same *Gregory*, in his Oration on the Martyr *Theodorus* written A.C. 381, thus describes the power of that Martyr, and the practice of the people. *This Martyr*, saith he, *the last year quieted the barbarous tempest, and put a stop to the horrid war of the fierce and cruel* Scythians.*—If any one is permitted to carry away the dust with which the tomb is covered, wherein the body* *of the Martyr rests; the dust is accepted as a gift, and gathered to be laid up as a thing of great price. For to touch the reliques themselves, if any such prosperous fortune shall at any time happen; how great a favour that is, and not to be obtained without the most earnest prayers, they know well who have obtained it. For as a living and florid body, they who behold it embrace it, applying to it the eyes, mouth, ears, and all the organs of sense; and then with affection pouring tears upon the Martyr, as if he was whole and appeared to them: they offer prayers with supplication, that he would intercede for them as an advocate, praying to him as an Officer attending upon God, and invoking him as receiving gifts whenever he will.* At length *Gregory* concludes the Oration with this prayer: *O Theodorus, we want many blessings; intercede and beseech for thy country before the common King and Lord: for the country of the Martyr is the place of his passion, and they are his citizens, brethren and kindred, who have him, defend, adorn and honour him. We fear afflictions, we expect dangers: the wicked* Scythians *are not far off, ready to make war against us. As a soldier fight for us, as a Martyr use liberty of speech for thy fellow-servants. Pray for peace, that these publick meetings may not cease, that the furious and wicked barbarian may not rage against the temples and altars, that the profane and impious may not trample upon the holy things. We acknowledge it a benefit received from thee, that we are preserved safe and entire, we pray for freedom from danger in time to come: and if there shall be need of greater intercession and deprecation, call together the choir of thy brethren the Martyrs, and in conjunction with them all intercede for us. Let the prayers of many just ones attone for the sins of the multitudes and the people; exhort* Peter, *excite* Paul, *and also* John *the divine and beloved disciple, that they may be sollicitous for the Churches which they have erected, for which they have been in chains, for which they have undergone dangers and deaths; that the worship of idols may not lift up its head against us, that heresies may not spring up like thorns in the vineyard, that tares grown up may not choak the wheat, that no rock void of the fatness of true dew may be against us, and render the fruitful power of the word void of a root; but by the power of the prayers of thyself and thy companions, O admirable man and eminent among the Martyrs, the commonwealth of* Christians *may become a field of corn.* The same *Gregory Nyssen,* in his sermon upon the death of *Meletius* Bishop of *Antioch,* preached at *Constantinople* the same year, A.C. 381, before the Bishops of all the *East* assembled in the second general Council, spake thus of *Meletius. The Bridegroom,* saith he, *is not taken from us: he stands in the midst of us, tho we do not see him: he is a Priest in the most inward places, and face to face intercedes before God for us and the sins of the people.* This was no oratorical flourish, but *Gregory*'s real opinion, as may be understood by what we have cited out of him concerning *Ephræm* and *Theodorus*: and as *Gregory* preached this before the Council of *Constantinople*, you may thence know, saith [6] *Baronius*, that he professed what the whole Council, and therewith the whole Church of those parts believed, namely, that the Saints in heaven offer prayers for us before God.

Ephræm Syrus, another eminent Monk, who was contemporary with *Basil,* and died the same year; in the end of his Encomium or Oration upon *Basil* then newly dead, invokes him after this manner: *Intercede for me, a very miserable man; and recal me by thy intercessions, O father; thou who art strong, pray for me who am weak; thou who art diligent, for me who am negligent; thou who art chearful, for me who am heavy; thou who art wise, for me who am foolish. Thou who hast treasured up a treasure of all virtues, be a guide to me who am empty of every good work.* In the beginning of his Encomium upon the forty Martyrs, written at the same time, he thus invokes them: *Help me therefore, O ye Saints, with your intercession; and O ye beloved, with your holy prayers, that* Christ *by his grace may direct my tongue to speak,* &c. and afterwards mentioning the mother of one of these forty Martyrs, he concludes the Oration with this prayer: *I entreat thee, O holy, faithful, and blessed woman, pray for me to the Saints, saying; Intercede ye that triumph in* Christ, *for the most little and miserable* Ephræm, *that he may find mercy, and by the grace of* Christ *may be saved.* Again, in his second Sermon or Oration on the praises of the holy Martyrs of *Christ,* he thus addresses them: *We entreat you most holy Martyrs, to intercede with the Lord for us miserable sinners, beset with the filthiness of negligence, that he would infuse his divine grace into us*: and afterwards, near the end of the same discourse; *Now ye most holy men and glorious Martyrs of God, help me a miserable sinner with your prayers, that in that dreadful hour I may obtain mercy, when the secrets of all hearts shall be made manifest. I am to day become to you, most holy Martyrs of* Christ, *as it were an unprofitable and unskilful cup-bearer: for I have delivered to the sons and brothers of your faith, a cup of the excellent wine of your warfare, with the excellent table of your victory, replenished with all sorts of dainties. I have endeavoured, with the whole affection and desire of my mind, to recreate your fathers and brothers, kindred and relations, who daily frequent the table. For behold they sing, and with exultation and jubilee glorify God, who has crown'd your virtues, by setting on your most sacred heads incorruptible and celestial crowns; they with excessive joy stand about the sacred reliques of your martyrdoms, wishing for a blessing, and desiring to bear away holy medicines both for the body and the mind. As good disciples and faithful ministers of our benign Lord and Saviour, bestow therefore a blessing on them all: and on me also, tho weak and feeble, who having received strength by your merits and intercessions, have with the whole devotion of my mind, sung a hymn to your praise and glory before your holy reliques. Wherefore I beseech you stand before the throne of the divine Majesty for me* Ephræm, *a vile and miserable sinner, that by your prayers I may deserve to obtain salvation, and with you enjoy eternal felicity by the grace and benignity and mercy of our Lord and Saviour* Jesus Christ, *to whom with the Father and Holy Ghost be praise, honour and glory for ever and ever.* Amen.

By what has been cited out of *Basil*, the two *Gregories* and *Ephræm*, we may understand that Saint-worship was established among the Monks and their admirers in *Egypt, Phœnicia, Syria* and *Cappadocia*, before the year 378, this being the year in which *Basil* and *Ephræm* died. *Chrysostom* was not much later; he preached at *Antioch* almost all the time of *Theodosius* the great, and in his Sermons are many exhortations to this sort of superstition, as may be seen in the end of his Orations on S. *Julia*, on St. *Pelagia*, on the Martyr *Ignatius*, on the *Egyptian* Martyrs, on Fate and Providence, on the Martyrs in general, on St. *Berenice* and St. *Prosdoce*, on *Juventinus* and *Maximus*, on the name of *Cœmetery*, &c. Thus in his Sermon on *Berenice* and *Prosdoce*: *Perhaps*, saith he, *you are inflamed with no small love towards these Martyrs; therefore with this ardour let us fall down before their reliques, let us embrace their coffins. For the coffins of the Martyrs have great virtue, even as the bones of the Martyrs have great power. Nor let us only on the day of this festival, but also on other days apply to them, invoke them, and beseech them to be our patrons: for they have great power and efficacy, not only whilst alive, but also after death; and much more after death than before. For now they bear the marks or brands of* Christ; *and when they shew these marks, they can obtain all things of the King. Seeing therefore they abound with such efficacy, and have so much friendship with him; we also, when by continual attendance and perpetual visitation of them we have insinuated ourselves into their familiarity, may by their assistance obtain the mercy of God.*

Constantinople was free from these superstitions till *Gregory Nazianzen* came thither A.D. 379; but in a few years it was also inflamed with it. *Ruffinus* [7] tells us, that when the Emperor *Theodosius* was setting out against the tyrant *Eugenius*, which was in the year 394, he went about with the Priests and people to all the places of prayer; lay prostrate in haircloth before the shrines of the Martyrs and Apostles, and pray'd for assistance by the intercession of the Saints. *Sozomen* [8] adds, that when the Emperor was marched seven miles from *Constantinople* against *Eugenius*, he went into a Church which he had built to *John* the Baptist, *and invoked the Baptist for his assistance. Chrysostom* [9] says: *He that is clothed in purple, approaches to embrace these sepulchres; and laying aside his dignity, stands supplicating the Saints to intercede for him with God: and he who goes crowned with a diadem, offers his prayers to the tent-maker and the fisherman as his Protestors.* And in [10] another place: *The cities run together to the sepulchres of the Martyrs, and the people are inflamed with the love of them.*

This practice of sending reliques from place to place for working miracles, and thereby inflaming the devotion of the nations towards the dead Saints and their reliques, and setting up the religion of invoking their souls, lasted only till the middle of the reign of the Emperor *Theodosius* the great; for he then prohibited it by the following Edict. *Humatum corpus, nemo ad alterum locum transferat; nemo Martyrem distrahat, nemo mercetur: Habeant verò in potestate, si quolibet in loco sanctorum est aliquis conditus, pro ejus veneratione, quod* Martyrium *vocandum sit, addant quod voluerint fabricarum. Dat. iv. Kal. Mart. Constantinopoli, Honorio nob. puero & Euodio Coss.* A.C. 386. After this they filled the fields and high-ways with altars erected to Martyrs, which they pretended to discover by dreams and revelations: and this occasioned the making the fourteenth Canon of the fifth Council of *Carthage*, A.C. 398. *Item placuit, ut altaria, quæ passim per agros aut vias, tanquam memoriæ Martyrum constituuntur, in quibus nullum corpus aut reliquiæ Martyrum conditæ probantur, ab Episcopis, qui illis locis præsunt, si fieri potest, evertantur. Si autem hoc propter tumultus populares non sinitur, plebes tamen admoneantur, ne illa loca frequentent, ut qui rectè sapiunt, nullâ ibi superstitione devincti teneantur. Et omnino nulla memoria Martyrum probabiliter acceptetur, nisi aut ibi corpus aut aliquæ certæ reliquiæ sint, aut ubi origo alicujus habitationis, vel possessionis, vel passionis fidelissima origine traditur. Nam quæ per somnia, & per inanes quasi revelationes quorumlibet hominum ubique constituuntur altaria, omnimodè reprobentur.* These altars were for invoking the Saints or Martyrs buried or pretended to be buried under them. First they filled the Churches in all places with the reliques or pretended reliques of the Martyrs, for invoking them in the Churches; and then they filled the fields and high-ways with altars, for invoking them every where: and this new religion was set up by the Monks in all the *Greek* Empire before the expedition of the Emperor *Theodosius* against *Eugenius*, and I think before his above-mentioned Edict, A.C. 386.

The same religion of worshiping *Mahuzzims* quickly spred into the *Western Empire* also: but *Daniel* in this Prophecy describes chiefly the things done among the nations comprehended in the body of his third Beast.

Notes to Chap. XIV

[1] Chap. xi. 38, 39
[2] Orat. de vita Greg. Thaumaturg. T. 3. p. 574.
[3] Vide Hom. 47. in. S. Julian.
[4] Epist. 27. ad Eustochium.
[5] Edit. Frontonis Ducæi, Tom. 1.
[6] Ad. an. 381, Sect. 41.
[7] Hist. Eccl. l. 2. c. 23.
[8] L. 4. c. 24.
[9] Hom. 66. ad. populum, circa finem. & Hom. 8, 27. in Matth. Hom. 42, 43. in Gen. Hom. 1. in 1 Thess.
[10] Exposit. in Psal. 114. sub finem.

The end of the first Part

PART II

OBSERVATIONS
upon the
APOCALYPSE *of* St. *John*

CHAP. I

*Introduction, concerning the time
when the* Apocalypse *was written*

*I*renæus introduced an opinion that the *Apocalypse* was written in the time of *Domitian*; but then he also postponed the writing of some others of the sacred books, and was to place the *Apocalypse* after them: he might perhaps have heard from his master *Polycarp* that he had received this book from *John* about the time of *Domitian*'s death; or indeed *John* might himself at that time have made a new publication of it, from whence *Irenæus* might imagine it was then but newly written. *Eusebius* in his *Chronicle* and *Ecclesiastical History* follows *Irenæus*; but afterwards [1] in his *Evangelical Demonstrations*, he conjoins the banishment of *John* into *Patmos*, with the deaths of *Peter* and *Paul*: and so do [2] *Tertullian* and *Pseudo-Prochorus*, as well as the first author, whoever he was, of that very antient fable, that *John* was put by *Nero* into a vessel of hot oil, and coming out unhurt, was banished by him into *Patmos*. Tho this story be no more than a fiction yet was it founded on a tradition of the first churches, that *John* was banished into *Patmos* in the days of *Nero*. *Epiphanius* represents the *Gospel of John* as written in the time of *Domitian*, and the *Apocalypse* even before that of *Nero*. [3] *Arethas* in the beginning of his Commentary quotes the opinion of *Irenæus* from *Eusebius*, but follows it not: for he afterwards affirms the *Apocalypse* was written before the destruction of *Jerusalem*, and that former commentators had expounded the sixth seal of that destruction.

With the opinion of the first Commentators agrees the tradition of the Churches of *Syria*, preserved to this day in the title of the *Syriac* Version of the *Apocalypse*, which title is this: *The Revelation which was made to* John *the Evangelist by God in the Island* Patmos, *into which he was banished by* Nero *the*

Cæsar. The fame is confirmed by a story told by [4] *Eusebius* out of *Clemens Alexandrinus*, and other antient authors, concerning a youth, whom *John* some time after his return from *Patmos* committed to the care of the Bishop of a certain city. The Bishop educated, instructed, and at length baptized him; but then remitting of his care, the young man thereupon got into ill company, and began by degrees first to revel and grow vitious, then to abuse and spoil those he met in the night; and at last grew so desperate, that his companions turning a band of high-way men, made him their Captain: and, saith [5] *Chrysostom*, he continued their Captain a long time. At length *John* returning to that city, and hearing what was done, rode to the thief; and, when he out of reverence to his old master fled, *John* rode after him, recalled him, and restored him to the Church. This is a story of many years, and requires that *John* should have returned from *Patmos* rather at the death of *Nero* than at that of *Domitian*; because between the death of *Domitian* and that of *John* there were but two years and an half; and *John* in his old age was [6] so infirm as to be carried to Church, dying above 90 years old, and therefore could not be then suppos'd able to ride after the thief.

This opinion is further supported by the allusions in the *Apocalypse* to the Temple and Altar, and holy City, as then standing; and to the *Gentiles*, who were soon after to tread under foot the holy City and outward Court. 'Tis confirmed also by the style of the *Apocalypse* itself, which is fuller of *Hebraisms* than his Gospel. For thence it may be gathered, that it was written when *John* was newly come out of *Judea*, where he had been used to the *Syriac* tongue; and that he did not write his Gospel, till by long converse with the *Asiatick* Greeks he had left off most of the *Hebraisms*. It is confirmed also by the many false *Apocalypses*, as those of *Peter*, *Paul*, *Thomas*, *Stephen*, *Elias* and *Cerinthus*, written in imitation of the true one. For as the many false Gospels, false Acts, and false Epistles were occasioned by true ones; and the writing many false *Apocalypses*, and ascribing them to Apostles and Prophets, argues that there was a true Apostolic one in great request with the first *Christians*: so this true one may well be suppos'd to have been written early, that there may be room in the Apostolic age for the writing of so many false ones afterwards, and fathering them upon *Peter, Paul, Thomas* and others, who were dead before *John. Caius,* who was contemporary with *Tertullian,* [7] tells us that *Cerinthus* wrote his Revelations as a great Apostle, and pretended the visions were shewn him by Angels, asserting a *millennium* of carnal pleasures at *Jerusalem* after the resurrection; so that his *Apocalypse* was plainly written in imitation of *John*'s: and yet he lived so early, that [8] he resisted the Apostles at *Jerusalem* in or before the first year of *Claudius,* that is, 26 years before the death of *Nero,* and [9] died before *John.*

These reasons may suffice for determining the time; and yet there is one more, which to considering men may seem a good reason, to others not. I'll propound it, and leave it to every man's judgment. The *Apocalypse* seems to be alluded to in the Epistles of *Peter* and that to the *Hebrews* and therefore to have been written before them. Such allusions in the Epistle to the *Hebrews,* I take to be the discourses concerning the High-Priest in the heavenly Tabernacle, who is both Priest and King, as was *Melchisedec*; and those concerning the *word of God,* with the *sharp two-edged sword,* the σαββατισμος, or *millennial* rest, the *earth whose end is to be burned,* suppose by the lake of fire, *the judgment and fiery indignation which shall devour the adversaries,* the *heavenly City which hath foundations whose builder and maker is God,* the *cloud of witnesses, mount* Sion, *heavenly* Jerusalem, *general assembly, spirits of just men made perfect, viz.* by the resurrection, and *the shaking of heaven and earth, and removing them, that the new heaven, new earth and new kingdom which cannot be shaken, may remain.* In the first of *Peter* occur these: [10] *The Revelation of Jesus Christ,* twice or thrice repeated; [11] the *blood of* Christ *as of a Lamb foreordained before the foundation of the world;* [12] the *spiritual building* in heaven, 1 Pet. ii. 5. *an inheritance incorruptible and undefiled and that fadeth not away, reserved in heaven for us, who are kept unto the salvation, ready to be revealed in the last time,* 1 Pet. i. 4, 5. [13] the *royal Priesthood,* [14] the *holy Priesthood,* [15] the *judgment beginning at the house of God,* and [16] *the Church at* Babylon. These are indeed obscurer allusions; but the second Epistle, from the 19th verse of the first Chapter to the end, seems to be a continued Commentary upon the *Apocalypse*. There, in writing to the *Churches in* Asia, to whom *John* was commanded to send this Prophecy, he tells them, they *have a more sure word of Prophecy*, to be heeded by them, *as a light that shineth in a dark place, until the day dawn, and the day-star arise in their hearts*, that is, until they begin to understand it: for *no Prophecy*, saith he, *of the scripture is of any private interpretation; the Prophecy came not in old time by the will of man, but holy men of God spake, as they were moved by the Holy Ghost. Daniel* [17] himself professes that he understood not his own *Prophecies*; and therefore the Churches were not to expect the interpretation from their Prophet *John*, but to study the Prophecies themselves. This is the substance of what *Peter* says in the first chapter; and then in the second he proceeds to describe, out of this *sure word of Prophecy*, how there should arise in the Church *false Prophets*, or *false teachers*, expressed collectively in the *Apocalypse* by the name of the false Prophet; who should *bring in damnable heresies, even denying the Lord that bought them*, which is the character of *Antichrist*: *And many*, saith he, *shall follow their lusts* [18]; they that dwell on the earth [19] shall be deceived by the false Prophet, and be made drunk with the wine of the Whore's fornication, *by reason of whom the way of truth shall be blasphemed*; for [20] the Beast is full of blasphemy: *and thro' covetousness shall they with feigned words make merchandize of you*; for these are the Merchants of the Earth, who trade with the great Whore, and their merchandize [21] is all things of price, with the bodies and souls of men: *whose judgment—lingreth not, and their damnation* [22] *slumbreth not*, but shall surely come upon them at the last day suddenly, as the flood upon *the old world*, and fire and brimstone upon *Sodom* and *Gomorrha*, when the just shall be delivered [23] like *Lot*; for *the Lord knoweth how to deliver the godly out of temptations, and to reserve the unjust unto the day of judgment to be punished*, in the lake of fire; *but chiefly them that walk after the flesh in the lust of uncleanness*, [24] being made drunk with the wine of the Whore's fornication; who *despise dominion, and are not afraid to blaspheme glories*; for the beast opened his mouth against God [25] to blaspheme his name and his tabernacle, and them that dwell in heaven. *These, as natural brute beasts*, the ten-horned beast and two-horned beast, or false Prophet, *made to be taken and destroyed*, in the lake of fire, *blaspheme the things they understand not*:—they count it pleasure to riot in the day-time—sporting themselves with their own deceivings, while they feast [26] with you, *having eyes full of an* [27] *Adulteress*: for the kingdoms of the beast live deliciously with the great Whore, and the nations are made drunk with the wine of her fornication. They *are gone astray, following the way of* Balaam, *the son of* Beor, *who loved the wages of unrighteousness*, the false Prophet [28] who taught *Balak* to cast a stumbling-block before the children of *Israel. These are*, not fountains of living water, but *wells without water*; not such clouds of Saints as the two witnesses ascend in, but *clouds that are carried with a tempest*, &c. Thus does the author of this Epistle spend all the second Chapter in describing the qualities of the *Apocalyptic* Beasts and false Prophet: and then in the third he goes on to describe their destruction more fully, and the future kingdom. He saith, that because the coming of *Christ* should be long deferred, they should scoff, saying, *where is the promise of his coming?* Then he describes the sudden coming of the day of the Lord upon them, *as a thief in the night*, which is the *Apocalyptic* phrase; and the *millennium*, or *thousand years*, which *are with God but as a day*; the *passing away of the old heavens* and earth, by a conflagration in the lake of fire, and our *looking for new heavens and a new earth, wherein dwelleth righteousness*.

Seeing therefore *Peter* and *John* were Apostles of the circumcision, it seems to me that they staid with their Churches in *Judea* and *Syria* till the *Romans* made war upon their nation, that is, till the twelfth year of *Nero*; that they then followed the main body of their flying Churches into *Asia*, and that *Peter* went thence by *Corinth* to *Rome*; that the *Roman* Empire looked upon those Churches as enemies, because *Jews* by birth; and therefore to prevent insurrections, secured their leaders, and banished *John* into *Patmos*. It seems also probable to me that the *Apocalypse* was there composed, and that soon after the Epistle to the *Hebrews* and those of *Peter* were written to these Churches, with reference to this Prophecy as what they were particularly concerned in. For it appears by these Epistles, that they were written in times of general affliction and tribulation under the heathens, and by consequence when the Empire made war upon the *Jews*; for till then the heathens were at peace with the *Christian Jews*, as well as with the rest. The Epistle to the *Hebrews*, since it mentions *Timothy* as related to those *Hebrews*, must be written to them after their flight into *Asia*, where *Timothy* was Bishop; and by consequence after the war began, the *Hebrews* in *Judea* being strangers to *Timothy*. *Peter* seems also to call *Rome Babylon*, as well with respect to the war made upon *Judea*, and the approaching captivity, like that under old *Babylon*, as with respect to that name in the *Apocalypse*: and in writing *to the strangers scattered thro'out* Pontus, Galatia, Cappadocia, Asia *and* Bithynia, he seems to intimate that they were the strangers newly scattered by the *Roman* wars; for those were the only strangers there belonging to his care.

This account of things agrees best with history when duly rectified. For [29] *Justin* and [30] *Irenæus* say, that *Simon Magus* came to *Rome* in the reign of *Claudius*, and exercised juggling tricks there. *Pseudo-Clemens* adds, that he endeavoured there to fly, but broke his neck thro' the prayers of *Peter*. Whence [31] *Eusebius*, or rather his interpolator *Jerom*, has recorded, that *Peter* came to *Rome* in the second year of *Claudius*: but [32] *Cyril* Bishop of *Jerusalem*, *Philastrius*, *Sulpitius*, *Prosper*, *Maximus Taurinensis*, and *Hegesippus junior*, place this victory of *Peter* in the time of *Nero*. Indeed the antienter tradition was, that *Peter* came to *Rome* in the days of this Emperor, as may be seen in [33] *Lactantius*. *Chrysostom* [34] tells us, that the Apostles continued long in *Judea*, and that then being driven out by the *Jews* they went to the *Gentiles*. This dispersion was in the first year of the *Jewish* war, when the *Jews*, as *Josephus* tells us, began to be tumultuous and violent in all places. For all agree that the Apostles were dispersed into several regions at once; and *Origen* has set down the time, [35] telling us that in the beginning of the *Judaic* war, the Apostles and disciples of our Lord were scattered into all nations; *Thomas* into *Parthia*, *Andrew* into *Scythia*, *John* into *Asia*, and *Peter* first into *Asia*, where he preacht to the dispersion, and thence into *Italy*. [36] *Dionysius Corinthius* saith, that *Peter* went from *Asia* by *Corinth* to *Rome*, and all antiquity agrees that *Peter* and *Paul* were martyred there in the end of *Nero*'s reign. *Mark* went with *Timothy* to *Rome*, 2 *Tim.* iv. 11. *Colos.* iv. 10. *Sylvanus* was *Paul*'s assistant; and by the companions of *Peter*, mentioned in his first Epistle, we may know that he wrote from *Rome*; and the Antients generally agree, that in this Epistle he understood *Rome* by *Babylon*. His second Epistle was writ to the same dispersed strangers with the first, 2 *Pet.* iii. 1. and therein he saith, that *Paul* had writ of the same things to them, and also in his other Epistles, *ver.* 15, 16. Now as there is no Epistle of *Paul* to these strangers besides that to the *Hebrews*, so in this Epistle, chap. x. 11, 12. we find at large all those things which *Peter* had been speaking of, and here refers to; particularly the *passing away of the old heavens and earth*, and *establishing an inheritance immoveable*, with an exhortation to grace, because *God*, to the wicked, *is a consuming fire*, Heb. xii. 25, 26, 28, 29.

Having determined the time of writing the *Apocalyse*, I need not say much about the truth of it, since it was in such request with the first ages, that many endeavoured to imitate it, by feigning *Apocalypses* under the Apostles names; and the Apostles themselves, as I have just now shewed, studied it, and used its phrases; by which means the style of the Epistle to the *Hebrews* became more mystical than that of *Paul*'s other Epistles, and the style of *John*'s Gospel more figurative and majestical than that of the other Gospels. I do not apprehend that *Christ* was called the word of God in any book of the New Testament written before the *Apocalypse*; and therefore am of opinion, the language was taken from this Prophecy, as were also many other phrases in this Gospel, such as those of *Christ*'s being *the light which enlightens the world, the lamb of God which taketh away the sins of the world, the bridegroom, he that testifieth, he that came down from heaven, the Son of God,* &c. *Justin Martyr,* who within thirty years after *John*'s death became a *Christian*, writes expresly that *a certain man among the* Christians *whose name was* John, *one of the twelve Apostles of* Christ, *in the Revelation which was shewed him, prophesied that those who believed in* Christ *should live a thousand years at* Jerusalem. And a few lines before he saith: *But*

I, and as many as are Christians, *in all things right in their opinions, believe both that there shall be a resurrection of the flesh, and a thousand years life at* Jerusalem *built, adorned and enlarged.* Which is as much as to say, that all true *Christians* in that early age received this Prophecy: for in all ages, as many as believed the thousand years, received the *Apocalypse* as the foundation of their opinion: and I do not know one instance to the contrary. *Papias* Bishop of *Hierapolis*, a man of the Apostolic age, and one of *John*'s own disciples, did not only teach the doctrine of the thousand years, but also [37] asserted the *Apocalypse* as written by divine inspiration. *Melito*, who flourished next after *Justin*, [38] wrote a commentary upon this Prophecy; and he, being Bishop of *Sardis* one of the seven Churches, could neither be ignorant of their tradition about it, nor impose upon them. *Irenæus*, who was contemporary with *Melito*, wrote much upon it, and said, that *the number 666 was in all the antient and approved copies; and that he had it also confirmed to him by those who had seen* John *face to face*, meaning no doubt his master *Polycarp* for one. At the same time [39] *Theophilus* Bishop of *Antioch* asserted it, and so did *Tertullian, Clemens Alexandrinus*, and *Origen* soon after; and their contemporary *Hippolytus* the Martyr, Metropolitan of the *Arabians*, [40] wrote a commentary upon it. All these were antient men, flourishing within a hundred and twenty years after *John*'s death, and of greatest note in the Churches of those times. Soon after did *Victorinus Pictaviensis* write another commentary upon it; and he lived in the time of *Dioclesian*. This may surely suffice to shew how the *Apocalypse* was received and studied in the first ages: and I do not indeed find any other book of the New Testament so strongly attested, or commented upon so early as this. The Prophecy said: *Blessed is he that readeth, and they that hear the words of this Prophecy, and keep the things which are written therein.* This animated the first *Christians* to study it so much, till the difficulty made them remit, and comment more upon the other books of the New Testament. This was the state of the *Apocalypse*, till the thousand years being misunderstood, brought a prejudice against it: and *Dionysius* of *Alexandria*, noting how it abounded with barbarisms, that is with *Hebraisms*, promoted that prejudice so far, as to cause many *Greeks* in the fourth century to doubt of the book. But whilst the *Latins*, and a great part of the *Greeks*, always retained the *Apocalypse*, and the rest doubted only out of prejudice, it makes nothing against its authority.

This Prophecy is called *the Revelation*, with respect to *the scripture of truth*, which *Daniel* [41] was commanded to *shut up and seal, till the time of the end. Daniel* sealed it *until the time of the end*; and until that time comes, the Lamb is opening the seals: and afterwards the two Witnesses prophesy out of it a long time in sack-cloth, before they ascend up to heaven in a cloud. All which is as much as to say, that these Prophecies of *Daniel* and *John* should not be understood till the time of the end: but then some should prophesy out of them in an afflicted and mournful state for a long time, and that but darkly, so as to convert but few. But in the very end, the Prophecy should be so far interpreted as to convince many. *Then*, saith *Daniel, many shall run to and fro, and knowledge shall be encreased.* For the Gospel must be preached in all nations before the great tribulation, and end of the world. The palm-bearing multitude, which come out of this great tribulation, cannot be innumerable out of all nations, unless they be made so by the preaching of the Gospel before it comes. There must be a stone cut out of a mountain without hands, before it can fall upon the toes of the Image, and become a great mountain and fill the earth. An Angel must fly thro' the midst of heaven with the everlasting Gospel to preach to all nations, before *Babylon* falls, and the Son of man reaps his harvest. The two Prophets must ascend up to heaven in a cloud, before the kingdoms of this world become the kingdoms of *Christ*. 'Tis therefore a part of this Prophecy, that it should not be understood before the last age of the world; and therefore it makes for the credit of the Prophecy, that it is not yet understood. But if the last age, the age of opening these things, be now approaching, as by the great successes of late Interpreters it seems to be, we have more encouragement than ever to look into these things. If the general preaching of the Gospel be approaching, it is to us and our posterity that those words mainly belong: [42] *In the time of the end the wise shall understand, but none of the wicked shall understand.* [43] *Blessed*

is he that readeth, and they that hear the words of this Prophecy,
and keep those things which are written therein.

The folly of Interpreters has been, to foretel times and things
by this Prophecy, as if God designed to make them Prophets. By
this rashness they have not only exposed themselves, but brought
the Prophecy also into contempt. The design of God was much
otherwise. He gave this and the Prophecies of the Old Testament,
not to gratify men's curiosities by enabling them to foreknow
things, but that after they were fulfilled they might be interpreted
by the event, and his own Providence, not the Interpreters, be
then manifested thereby to the world. For the event of things
predicted many ages before, will then be a convincing argument
that the world is governed by providence. For as the few and
obscure Prophecies concerning *Christ's* first coming were for
setting up the *Christian* religion, which all nations have since
corrupted; so the many and clear Prophecies concerning the
things to be done at *Christ's* second coming, are not only for
predicting but also for effecting a recovery and re-establishment
of the long-lost truth, and setting up a kingdom wherein dwells
righteousness. The event will prove the *Apocalypse*; and this
Prophecy, thus proved and understood, will open the old
Prophets, and all together will make known the true religion, and
establish it. For he that will understand the old Prophets, must
begin with this; but the time is not yet come for understanding
them perfectly, because the main revolution predicted in them is
not yet come to pass. *In the days of the voice of the seventh*
Angel, when he shall begin to sound, the mystery of God shall be
finished, as he hath declared to his servants the Prophets: and
then *the kingdoms of this world shall become the kingdoms of our*
Lord and his Christ, *and he shall reign for ever*, Apoc. x. 7. xi.
15. There is already so much of the Prophecy fulfilled, that as
many as will take pains in this study, may see sufficient instances
of God's providence: but then the signal revolutions predicted by
all the holy Prophets, will at once both turn mens eyes upon
considering the predictions, and plainly interpret them. Till then
we must content ourselves with interpreting what hath been
already fulfilled.

Amongst the Interpreters of the last age there is scarce one of note who hath not made some discovery worth knowing; and thence I seem to gather that God is about opening these mysteries. The success of others put me upon considering it; and if I have done any thing which may be useful to following writers, I have my design.

Notes to Chap. I

[1] Dem. Evang. l. 3.
[2] Vid. *Pamelium* in notis ad *Tertull.* de Præscriptionbus, n. 215 & *Hieron* l. 1. contra *Jovinianum*, c. 14. Edit.*Erasmi.*
[3] Areth. c. 18, 19.
[4] Hist. Eccl. l. 3. c. 23.
[5] Chrysost. ad Theodorum lapsum.
[6] Hieron. in Epist. ad Gal. l. 3. c. 6.
[7] Apud Euseb. Eccl. Hist. l. 3. c. 28. Edit. *Valesii.*
[8] Epiphan. Hæres. 28.
[9] Hieron. adv. Lucif.
[10] 1 Pet. i. 7, 13. iv. 13. & v. 1.
[11] Apoc. xiii. 8.
[12] Apoc. xxi.
[13] Apoc. i. 6. & v. 10.
[14] Apoc. xx. 6.
[15] Apoc. xx. 4, 12.
[16] Apoc. xvii.
[17] Dan. viii. 15, 16, 27. & xii. 8, 9.
[18] ασελγειας, *in many of the best MSS.*
[19] Apoc. xiii. 7, 12.
[20] Apoc. xiii. 1, 5, 6.
[21] Apoc. xviii. 12, 13.
[22] Apoc. xix. 20.
[23] Apoc. xxi. 3, 4.
[24] Apoc. ix. 21. *and* xvii. 2.
[25] Apoc. xiii. 6.
[26] Apoc. xviii. 3, 7, 9.
[27] μοιχαλιδος.
[28] Apoc. ii. 14.
[29] Apol. ad Antonin. Pium.
[30] Hæres. l. 1. c. 20. Vide etiam Tertullianum, Apol. c. 13.

[31] Euseb. Chron.
[32] Cyril Catech. 6. Philastr. de hæres. cap. 30. Sulp. Hist. l. 2. Prosper de promiss. dimid. temp. cap. 13. Maximus serm. 5. in Natal. Apost. Hegesip. l. 2. c. 2.
[33] Lactant de mortib. Persec. c. 2.
[34] Hom. 70. in Matt. c. 22.
[35] Apud Euseb. Eccl. Hist. l. 2. c. 25.
[36] Euseb. Hist. l. 2. c. 25.
[37] Arethas in Proæm. comment. in Apoc.
[38] Euseb. Hist. l. 4. cap. 26. Hieron.
[39] Euseb. Hist. l. 4. c. 24.
[40] Hieron.
[41] Dan. x. 21. xii. 4, 9.
[42] Dan. xii. 4, 10.
[43] Apoc. i. 3.

CHAP. II

Of the relation which the Apocalypse *of* John *hath to the Book of
the Law of* Moses, *and to the worship of God in the Temple*

T he *Apocalypse* of *John* is written in the same style and
language with the Prophecies of *Daniel*, and hath the
same relation to them which they have to one another, so
that all of them together make but one complete Prophecy; and in
like manner it consists of two parts, an introductory Prophecy,
and an Interpretation thereof.

The Prophecy is distinguish'd into seven successive parts, by
the opening of the seven seals of the book which *Daniel* was
commanded to seal up: and hence it is called the *Apocalypse* or
Revelation of *Jesus Christ*. The time of the seventh seal is sub-
divided into eight successive parts by the silence in heaven for
half an hour, and the sounding of seven trumpets successively:
and the seventh trumpet sounds to the battle of the great day of
God Almighty, whereby *the kingdoms of this world become the
kingdoms of the Lord and of his Christ*, and those are destroyed
that destroyed the earth.

The Interpretation begins with the words, *And the temple of
God was opened in heaven, and there was seen in his temple the
Ark of his Testament*: and it continues to the end of the Prophecy.
The Temple is the scene of the visions, and the visions in the
Temple relate to the feast of the seventh month: for the feasts of
the *Jews* were typical of things to come. The Passover related to
the first coming of *Christ*, and the feasts of the seventh month to
his second coming: his first coming being therefore over before
this Prophecy was given, the feasts of the seventh month are here
only alluded unto.

On the first day of that month, in the morning, the High-
Priest dressed the lamps: and in allusion hereunto, this Prophecy
begins with a vision of one like *the Son of man* in the High-

Priest's habit, appearing as it were in the midst of the seven golden candlesticks, or over against the midst of them, dressing the lamps, which appeared like a rod of seven stars in his right hand: and this dressing was perform'd by the sending seven Epistles to the Angels or Bishops of the seven Churches of *Asia*, which in the primitive times illuminated the Temple or Church Catholick. These Epistles contain admonitions against the approaching Apostacy, and therefore relate to the times when the Apostacy began to work strongly, and before it prevailed. It began to work in the Apostles days, and was to continue working *till the man of sin should be revealed*. It began to work in the disciples of *Simon*, *Menander*, *Carpocrates*, *Cerinthas*, and such sorts of men as had imbibed the metaphysical philosophy of the *Gentiles* and *Cabalistical Jews*, and were thence called *Gnosticks*. *John* calls them *Antichrists*, saying that in his days there were many *Antichrists*. But these being condemned by the Apostles, and their immediate disciples, put the Churches in no danger during the opening of the first four seals. The visions at the opening of these seals relate only to the civil affairs of the heathen *Roman* Empire. So long the Apostolic traditions prevailed, and preserved the Church in its purity: and therefore the affairs of the Church do not begin to be considered in this Prophecy before the opening of the fifth seal. She began then to decline, and to want admonitions; and therefore is admonished by these Epistles, till the Apostacy prevailed and took place, which was at the opening of the seventh seal. The admonitions therefore in these seven Epistles relate to the state of the Church in the times of the fifth and sixth seals. At the opening of the fifth seal, the Church is purged from hypocrites by a great persecution. At the opening of the sixth, that which letted is taken out of the way, namely the heathen *Roman* Empire. At the opening of the seventh, the man of sin is revealed. And to these times the seven Epistles relate.

The seven Angels, to whom these Epistles were written, answer to the seven *Amarc-holim*, who were Priests and chief Officers of the Temple, and had jointly the keys of the gates of the Temple, with those of the Treasuries, and the direction, appointment and oversight of all things in the Temple.

After the lamps were dresed, *John* saw *the door* of the Temple *opened*; and by *the voice as it were of a trumpet*, was called up to the eastern gate of the great court, to see the visions: and *behold a throne was set, viz.* the mercy-seat upon the Ark of the Testament, which the *Jews* respected as *the throne of God between the* Cherubims, *Exod.* xxv. 2. *Psal.* xcix. 1. *And he that sat on it was to look upon like* Jasper *and* Sardine *stone*, that is, of an olive colour, the people of *Judea* being of that colour. *And*, the Sun being then in the *East, a rainbow was about the throne*, the emblem of glory. *And round about the throne were four and twenty seats*; answering to the chambers of the four and twenty Princes of the Priests, twelve on the south side, and twelve on the north side of the Priests Court. *And upon the seats were four and twenty Elders sitting, clothed in white rayment, with crowns on their heads*; representing the Princes of the four and twenty courses of the Priests clothed in linen. *And out of the throne proceeded lightnings and thunderings, and voices, viz.* the flashes of the fire upon the Altar at the morning-sacrifice, and the thundering voices of those that sounded the trumpets, and sung at the Eastern gate of the Priests Court; for these being between *John* and the throne appeared to him as proceeding from the throne. *And there were seven lamps of fire burning*, in the Temple, *before the throne, which are the seven spirits of God*, or Angels of the seven Churches, represented in the beginning of this Prophecy by seven stars. *And before the throne was a sea of glass clear as chrystal*; the brazen sea between the porch of the Temple and the Altar, filled with clear water. *And in the midst of the throne, and round about the throne, were four Beasts full of eyes before and behind*: that is, one Beast before the throne and one behind it, appearing to *John* as in the midst of the throne, and one on either side in the circle about it, to represent by the multitude of their eyes the people standing in the four sides of the peoples court. *And the first Beast was like a lion, and the second was like a calf, and the third had the face of a man, and the fourth was like a flying eagle.* The people of *Israel* in the wilderness encamped round about the tabernacle, and on the east side were three tribes under the standard of *Judah,* on the west were three tribes under the standard of *Ephraim,* on the south were three tribes under the standard of *Reuben*, and on the north were three tribes under the standard of *Dan, Numb.* ii. And the standard of *Judah* was a Lion, that of *Ephraim* an Ox, that of *Reuben* a Man, and that of *Dan* an Eagle, as the *Jews* affirm. Whence were framed the hieroglyphicks of *Cherubims* and *Seraphims*, to represent the people of *Israel*. A *Cherubim* had one body with four faces, the faces of a Lion, an Ox, a Man and an Eagle, looking to the four winds of heaven, without turning about, as in *Ezekiel*'s vision, chap. i. And four *Seraphims* had the same four faces with four bodies, one face to every body. The four Beasts are therefore four *Seraphims* standing in the four sides of the peoples court; the first in the eastern side with the head of a Lion, the second in the western side with the head of an Ox, the third in the southern side with the head of a Man, the fourth in the northern side with the head of an Eagle: and all four signify together the twelve tribes of *Israel*, out of whom the hundred forty and four thousand were sealed, *Apoc.* vii. 4. *And the four Beasts had each of them six wings*, two to a tribe, in all twenty and four wings, answering to the twenty and four stations of the people. *And they were full of eyes within*, or under their wings. *And they rest not day and night*, or at the morning and evening-sacrifices, *saying, holy, holy, holy Lord God Almighty, which was, and is, and is to come*. These animals are therefore the Seraphims, which appeared to *Isaiah* [1] in a vision like this of the *Apocalypse*. For there also the Lord sat upon a throne in the temple; and the Seraphims each with six wings cried, *Holy, holy, holy Lord God of hosts. And when those animals give glory and honour and thanks to him that sitteth upon the throne, who liveth for ever and ever, the four and twenty Elders* go into the Temple, and there *fall down before him that sitteth on the throne, and worship him that liveth for ever and ever, and cast their crowns before the throne, saying, Thou art worthy, O Lord, to receive glory and honour and power: for thou hast created all things, and for thy pleasure they are and were created*. At the morning and evening-sacrifices, so soon as the sacrifice was laid upon the Altar, and the drink-offering began to be poured out, the trumpets sounded, and the *Levites* sang by course three times; and every time when the trumpets sounded, the people fell down and worshiped. Three times therefore did the people worship; to express which number, the Beasts cry *Holy, holy, holy*: and the song being ended, the people prayed standing, till the solemnity was finished. In the mean time the Priests went into the Temple, and there fell down before him that sat upon the throne, and worshiped.

And John *saw, in the right hand of him that sat upon the throne, a book written within and on the backside, sealed with seven seals, viz.* the book which *Daniel* was commanded to seal up, and which is here represented by the prophetic book of the Law laid up on the right side of the Ark, as it were in the right hand of him that sat on the throne: for the festivals and ceremonies of the Law prescribed to the people in this book, adumbrated those things which were predicted in the book of *Daniel*; and the writing within and on the backside of this book, relates to the synchronal Prophecies. [2] *And none was found worthy to open the book* but the Lamb of God. *And lo, in the midst of the throne and of the four Beasts, and in the midst of the Elders*, that is, at the foot of the Altar, *stood a lamb as it had been slain*, the morning-sacrifice; *having seven horns*, which are the seven Churches, *and seven eyes, which are the seven spirits of God sent forth into all the earth. And he came, and took the book out of the right hand of him that sat upon the throne: And when he had taken the book, the four Beasts and four and twenty Elders fell down before the Lamb, having every one of them harps, and golden vials full of odours, which are the prayers of saints. And they sung a new song, saying, Thou art worthy to take the book, and to open the seals thereof: for thou wast slain, and hast redeemed us to God by thy blood out of every kindred, and tongue, and people, and nation; and hast made us, unto our God, Kings and Priests, and we shall reign on the earth.* The Beasts and Elders therefore represent the primitive *Christians* of all nations; and the worship of these *Christians* in their Churches is here represented under the form of worshiping God and the Lamb in the Temple: God for his benefaction in creating all things, and the Lamb for his benefaction in redeeming us with his blood: God as sitting upon the throne and living for ever, and the Lamb as exalted above all by the merits of his death. *And I heard*, saith

John, the voice of many Angels round about the throne, and the Beasts and the Elders: and the number of them was ten thousand times ten thousand, and thousands of thousands; saying with a loud voice, Worthy is the Lamb that was slain to receive power, and riches, and wisdom, and strength, and honour, and glory, and blessing. And every creature which is in heaven, and on the earth, and under the earth, and such as are in the sea, and all that are in them, heard I, saying, Blessing, honour, glory, and power, be unto him that sitteth upon the throne, and unto the Lamb for ever and ever. And the four Beasts said, Amen. *And the four and twenty Elders fell down and worshiped him that liveth for ever and ever.* This was the worship of the primitive *Christians.*

It was the custom for the High-Priest, seven days before the fast of the seventh month, to continue constantly in the Temple, and study the book of the Law, that he might be perfect in it against the day of expiation; wherein the service, which was various and intricate, was wholly to be performed by himself; part of which service was reading the Law to the people: and to promote his studying it, there were certain Priests appointed by the *Sanhedrim* to be with him those seven days in one of his chambers in the Temple, and there to discourse with him about the Law, and read it to him, and put him in mind of reading and studying it himself. This his opening and reading the Law those seven days, is alluded unto in the Lamb's opening the seals. We are to conceive that those seven days begin in the evening before each day; for the *Jews* began their day in the evening, and that the solemnity of the fast begins in the morning of the seventh day.

The seventh seal was therefore opened on the day of expiation, and then *there was silence in heaven for half an hour. And an Angel,* the High-Priest, *stood at the Altar, having a golden Censer; and there was given him much incense, that he should offer it with the prayers of all Saints, upon the golden Altar which was before the throne.* The custom was on other days, for one of the Priests to take fire from the great Altar in a silver Censer; but on this day, for the High-Priest to take fire from the great Altar in a golden Censer: and when he was come down from the great Altar, he took incense from one of the

Priests who brought it to him, and went with it to the golden Altar: and while he offered the incense, the people prayed without in silence, which is the silence in heaven for half an hour. When the High-Priest had laid the incense on the Altar, he carried a Censer of it burning in his hand, into the most holy place before the Ark. *And the smoke of the incense, with the prayers of the Saints, ascended up before God out of the Angel's hand.* On other days there was a certain measure of incense for the golden Altar: on this day there was a greater quantity for both the Altar and the most holy Place, and therefore it is called *much incense.* After this *the Angel took the Censer, and filled it with fire from the* great *Altar, and cast it into the earth*; that is, by the hands of the Priests who belong to his mystical body, he cast it to the earth without the Temple, for burning the Goat which was the Lord's lot. *And* at this and other concomitant sacrifices, until the evening-sacrifice was ended, *there were voices, and thundrings, and lightnings, and an earthquake*; that is, the voice of the High-Priest reading the Law to the people, and other voices and thundrings from the trumpets and temple-musick at the sacrifices, and lightnings from the fire of the Altar.

The solemnity of the day of expiation being finished, the seven Angels found their trumpets at the great sacrifices of the seven days of the feast of tabernacles; and at the same sacrifices, the seven thunders utter their voices, which are the musick of the Temple, and singing of the *Levites*, intermixed with the soundings of the trumpets: and the seven Angels pour out their vials of wrath, which are the drink-offerings of those sacrifices.

When six of the seals were opened, *John* said: [3] *And after these things*, that is, after the visions of the sixth seal, *I saw four Angels standing on the four corners of the earth, holding the four winds of the earth, that the wind should not blow on the earth, nor on the sea, nor on any tree. And I saw another Angel ascending from the* East, *having the seal of the living God: and he cried with a loud voice to the four Angels, to whom it was given to hurt the earth and the sea, saying, Hurt not the earth, nor the sea, nor the trees, till we have sealed the servants of our God in their foreheads.* This sealing alludes to a tradition of the *Jews*, that upon the day of expiation all the people of *Israel* are sealed up in the books of life and death. For the *Jews* in their *Talmud* [4] tell us, that in the beginning of every new year, or first day of the month *Tisri*, the seventh month of the sacred year, three books are opened in judgment; the book of life, in which the names of those are written who are perfectly just; the book of death, in which the names of those are written who are Atheists or very wicked; and a third book, of those whose judgment is suspended till the day of expiation, and whose names are not written in the book of life or death before that day. The first ten days of this month they call the penitential days; and all these days they fast and pray very much, and are very devout, that on the tenth day their sins may be remitted, and their names may be written in the book of life; which day is therefore called the day of expiation. And upon this tenth day, in returning home from the Synagogues, they say to one another, *God the creator seal you to a good year*. For they conceive that the books are now sealed up, and that the sentence of God remains unchanged henceforward to the end of the year. The same thing is signified by the two Goats, upon whose foreheads the High-Priest yearly, on the day of expiation, lays the two lots inscribed, *For God* and *For* Azazel; God's lot signifying the people who are sealed with the name of God in their foreheads; and the lot *Azazel*, which was sent into the wilderness, representing those who receive the mark and name of the Beast, and go into the wilderness with the great Whore.

The servants of God being therefore sealed in the day of expiation, we may conceive that this sealing is synchronal to the visions which appear upon opening the seventh seal; and that when the Lamb had opened six of the seals and seen the visions relating to the inside of the sixth, he looked on the backside of the seventh leaf, and then saw *the four Angels holding the four winds of heaven, and another Angel ascending from the* East *with the seal of God*. Conceive also, that the Angels which held the four winds were the first four of the seven Angels, who upon opening the seventh seal were seen standing before God; and that upon their holding the winds, *there was silence in heaven for half an hour*; and that while the servants of God were sealing, the Angel with the golden Censer offered their prayers with incense upon the golden Altar, and read the Law: and that so soon as they were sealed, the winds hurt the earth at the sounding of the first trumpet, and the sea at the sounding of the second; these winds signifying the wars, to which the first four trumpets sounded. For as the first four seals are distinguished from the three last by the appearance of four horsemen towards the four winds of heaven; so the wars of the first four trumpets are distinguished from those of the three last, by representing these by *four winds*, and the others by *three great woes*.

In one of *Ezekiel's* visions, when the *Babylonian* captivity was at hand, *six men* appeared *with slaughter-weapons; and a seventh,* who [5] appeared *among them clothed in white linen and a writer's ink-horn by his side,* is commanded to *go thro' the midst of* Jerusalem, *and set a mark upon the foreheads of the men that sigh and cry for all the abominations done in the midst thereof:* and then the six men, like the Angels of the first six trumpets, are commanded to slay those men who are not marked. Conceive therefore that the hundred forty and four thousand are sealed, to preserve them from the plagues of the first six trumpets; and that at length by the preaching of the everlasting gospel, they grow into *a great multitude, which no man could number, of all nations, and kindreds, and people and tongues:* and at the sounding of the seventh trumpet come out of the great tribulation *with Palms in their hands: the kingdoms of this world,* by the war to which that trumpet sounds, *becoming the kingdoms of God and his* Christ. For the solemnity of the great *Hosannah* was kept by the *Jews* upon the seventh or last day of the feast of tabernacles; the *Jews* upon that day carrying Palms in their hands, and crying *Hosannah.*

After six of the Angels, answering to the six men with slaughter-weapons, had sounded their trumpets, the Lamb in the form of *a mighty Angel cane down from heaven clothed with a cloud, and a rainbow was upon his head, and his face was as it were the Sun, and his feet as pillars of fire,* the shape in which *Christ* appeared in the beginning of this Prophecy; *and he had in his hand a little book open,* the book which he had newly opened; for he received but one book from him that sitteth upon the throne, and he alone was worthy to open and look on this book.

And he set his right foot upon the sea and his left foot on the earth, and cried with a loud voice, as when a lion roareth. It was the custom for the High-Priest on the day of expiation, to stand in an elevated place in the peoples court, at the Eastern gate of the Priests court, and read the Law to the people, while the Heifer and the Goat which was the Lord's lot, were burning without the Temple. We may therefore suppose him standing in such a manner, that his right foot might appear to *John* as it were standing on the sea of glass, and his left foot on the ground of the house; and that he cried with a loud voice, in reading the Law on the day of expiation. *And when he had cried, seven thunders uttered their voices.* Thunders are the voice of a cloud, and a cloud signifies a multitude; and this multitude may be the *Levites,* who sang with thundering voices, and played with musical instruments at the great sacrifices, on the seven days of the feast of Tabernacles: at which times the trumpets also sounded. For the trumpets sounded, and the *Levites* sang alternately, three times at every sacrifice. The Prophecy therefore of the seven thunders is nothing else than a repetition of the Prophecy of the seven trumpets in another form. *And the Angel which I saw stand upon the sea and upon the earth, lifted up his hand to heaven, and sware by him that liveth for ever and ever, that* after the seven thunders *there should be time no longer; but in the days of the voice of the seventh Angel, when he shall begin to sound, the mystery of God should be finished, as he hath declared to his servants the Prophets.* The voices of the thunders therefore last to the end of this world, and so do those of the trumpets.

And the voice which I heard from heaven, saith *John, spake unto me again and said, Go and take the little book, &c. And I took the little book out of the Angel's hand, and ate it up; and it was in my mouth sweet as honey, and as soon as I had eaten it, my belly was bitter. And he said unto me, Thou must prophesy again before many peoples, and nations, and tongues, and kings.* This is an introduction to a new Prophecy, to a repetition of the Prophecy of the whole book; and alludes to *Ezekiel's* eating a roll or book spread open before him, and written within and without, full of lamentations and mourning and woe, but sweet in his mouth. Eating and drinking signify acquiring and possessing; and eating the book is becoming inspired with the Prophecy contained in it. It implies being inspired in a vigorous and extraordinary manner with the Prophecy of the whole book, and therefore signifies a lively repetition of the whole Prophecy by way of interpretation, and begins not till the first Prophecy, that of the seals and trumpets, is ended. It was sweet in *John*'s mouth, and therefore begins not with the bitter Prophecy of the *Babylonian* captivity, and the *Gentiles* being in the outward court of the Temple, and treading the holy city under foot; and the prophesying of the *two Witnesses* in sackcloth, and their smiting the earth with all plagues, and being killed by the Beast; but so soon as the Prophecy of the trumpets is ended, it begins with the sweet Prophecy of the glorious *Woman in heaven*, and the victory of *Michael* over the Dragon; and after that, it is bitter in *John*'s belly, by a large description of the times of the great Apostacy.

And the Angel stood, upon the earth and sea, *saying, Rise and measure the Temple of God and the Altar, and them that worship therein,* that is, their courts with the buildings thereon, *viz.* the square court of the Temple called the separate place, and the square court of the Altar called the Priests court, and the court of them that worship in the Temple called the new court: *but the* great *court which is without the Temple, leave out, and measure it not, for it is given to the* Gentiles, *and the holy city shall they tread under foot forty and two months.* This measuring hath reference to *Ezekiel*'s measuring the Temple *of Solomon*: there the whole Temple, including the outward court, was measured, to signify that it should be rebuilt in the latter days. Here the courts of the Temple and Altar, and they who worship therein, are only measured, to signify the building of a second Temple, for those that are sealed out of all the twelve tribes of *Israel*, and worship in the inward court of sincerity and truth: but *John* is commanded to leave out the outward court, or outward form of religion and Church-government, because it is given to the *Babylonian Gentiles.* For the glorious woman in heaven, the remnant of whole seed kept the commandments of God, and had the testimony of *Jesus*, continued the same woman in outward form after her flight into the wilderness, whereby she quitted her former sincerity and piety, and became the great Whore. She lost her chastity, but kept her outward form and shape. And while the *Gentiles* tread the holy city underfoot, and worship in the outward court, the two witnesses, represented perhaps by the two feet of the Angel standing on the sea and earth, prophesied against them, and *had power*, like *Elijah* and *Moses, to consume their enemies with fire proceeding out of their mouth, and to shut heaven that it rain not in the days of their Prophecy, and to turn the waters into blood, and to smite the earth with all plagues as often as they will*, that is, with the plagues of the trumpets and vials of wrath; and at length they are slain, rise again from the dead, and ascend up to heaven in a cloud; and then the seventh trumpet sounds to the day of judgment.

The Prophecy being finished, *John* is inspired anew by the eaten book, and begins the Interpretation thereof with these words, *And the Temple of God was opened in heaven, and there was seen in his Temple the Ark of the Testament.* By the Ark, we may know that this was the first Temple; for the second Temple had no Ark. *And there were lightnings, and voices, and thundrings, and an earthquake, and great hail.* These answer to the wars in the *Roman* Empire, during the reign of the four horsemen, who appeared upon opening the first four seals. *And there appeared a great wonder in heaven, a woman clothed with the Sun.* In the Prophecy, the affairs of the Church begin to be considered at the opening of the fifth seal; and in the Interpretation, they begin at the same time with the vision of the Church in the form of a woman in heaven: there she is persecuted, and here she is pained in travail. The Interpretation proceeds down first to the sealing of the servants of God, and marking the rest with the mark of the Beast; and then to the day of judgment, represented by a harvest and vintage. Then it returns back to the times of opening the seventh seal, and interprets the Prophecy of the seven trumpets by the pouring out of seven vials of wrath. The Angels who pour them out, come out of the *Temple of the Tabernacle*; that is, out of the second Temple, for the Tabernacle had no outward court. Then it returns back again to the times of measuring the Temple and Altar, and of the *Gentiles* worshiping in the outward court, and of the Beast killing the witnesses in the streets of the great city; and interprets these things by the vision of *a woman sitting on the Beast, drunken with the blood of the Saints*; and proceeds in the interpretation downwards to the fall of the great city and the day of judgment.

The whole Prophecy of the book, represented by the book of the Law, is therefore repeated, and interpreted in the visions which follow those of sounding the seventh trumpet, and begin with that of the Temple of God opened in heaven. Only the things, which the seven thunders uttered, were not written down, and therefore not interpreted.

Notes to Chap. II

[1] Isa. vi.
[2] Apoc. v.
[3] Apoc. vii
[4] Buxtorf in Synogoga Judaica, c. 18, 21.
[5] Ezek. ix.

CHAP. III

Of the relation which the Prophecy of John *hath to those of* Daniel*; and of the Subject of the Prophecy.*

The whole scene of sacred Prophecy is composed of three principal parts: the regions beyond *Euphrates*, represented by the two first Beasts of *Daniel*; the Empire of the *Greeks* on this side of *Euphrates*, represented by the Leopard and by the He-Goat; and the Empire of the *Latins* on this side of *Greece*, represented by the Beast with ten horns. And to these three parts, the phrases of the *third part of the earth, sea, rivers, trees, ships, stars, sun, and moon*, relate. I place the body of the fourth Beast on this side of *Greece*, because the three first of the four Beasts had their lives prolonged after their dominion was taken away, and therefore belong not to the body of the fourth. He only stamped them with his feet.

By the *earth*, the *Jews* understood the great continent of all *Asia* and *Africa*, to which they had access by land: and by the Isles of the *sea*, they understood the places to which they sailed by sea, particularly all *Europe*: and hence in this Prophecy, the *earth* and *sea* are put for the nations of the *Greek* and *Latin* Empires.

The third and fourth Beasts of *Daniel* are the same with the Dragon and ten-horned Beast of *John*, but with this difference: *John* puts the Dragon for the whole *Roman* Empire while it continued entire, because it was entire when that Prophecy was given; and the Beast he considers not till the Empire became divided: and then he puts the Dragon for the Empire of the *Greeks*, and the Beast for the Empire of the *Latins*. Hence it is that the Dragon and Beast have common heads and common horns: but the Dragon hath crowns only upon his heads, and the Beast only upon his horns; because the Beast and his horns reigned not before they were divided from the Dragon: and when the Dragon gave the Beast his throne, the ten horns received power as Kings, the same hour with the Beast. The heads are seven successive Kings. Four of them were the four horsemen which appeared at the opening of the first four seals. In the latter end of the sixth head, or seal, considered as present in the visions, it is said, *five* of the seven Kings *are fallen, and one is, and another is not yet come; and the Beast that was and is not*, being wounded to death with a sword, *he is the eighth, and of the seven*: he was therefore a collateral part of the seventh. The horns are the same with those of *Daniel*'s fourth Beast, described above.

The four horsemen which appear at the opening of the first four seals, have been well explained by Mr. *Mede*; excepting that I had rather continue the third to the end of the reign of the three *Gordians* and *Philip* the *Arabian*, those being Kings from the *South*, and begin the fourth with the reign of *Decius*, and continue it till the reign of *Dioclesian*. For the fourth horseman *sat upon a pale* horse, *and his name was Death; and hell followed with him; and power was given them to kill unto the fourth part of the earth, with the sword, and with famine, and with the plague, and with the Beasts of the earth*, or armies of invaders and rebels: and as such were the times during all this interval. Hitherto the *Roman* Empire continued in an undivided monarchical form, except rebellions; and such it is represented by the four horsemen. But *Dioclesian* divided it between himself and *Maximianus*, A.C. 285; and it continued in that divided state, till the victory of *Constantine* the great over *Licinius*, A.C. 323, which put an end to the heathen persecutions set on foot by *Dioclesian* and *Maximianus*, and described at the opening of the fifth seal. But this division of the Empire was imperfect, the whole being still under one and the same Senate. The same victory of *Constantine* over *Licinius* a heathen persecutor, began the fall of the heathen Empire, described at the opening of the sixth seal: and the visions of this seal continue till after the reign of *Julian* the Apostate, he being a heathen Emperor, and reigning over the whole *Roman* Empire.

The affairs of the Church begin to be considered at the opening of the fifth seal, as was said above. Then she is represented by *a woman* in the Temple of heaven, *clothed with the sun* of righteousness, *and the moon* of *Jewish* ceremonies *under her feet, and upon her head a crown of twelve stars* relating to the twelve Apostles and to the twelve tribes of *Israel.* When she fled from the Temple into the wilderness, she left in the Temple a *remnant of her seed, who kept the commandments of God, and had the testimony of Jesus Christ*; and therefore before her flight she represented the true primitive Church of God, tho afterwards she degenerated like *Aholah* and *Aholibah.* In *Diocesian's* persecution *she cried, travelling in birth, and pained to be delivered.* And in the end of that persecution, by the victory of *Constantine* over *Maxentius* A.C. 312, *she brought forth a man-child,* such a child as *was to rule all nations with a rod of iron,* a *Christian* Empire. *And her child,* by the victory of *Constantine* over *Licinius,* A.C. 323, *was caught up unto God and to his throne. And the woman,* by the division of the *Roman* Empire into the *Greek* and *Latin* Empires, *fled* from the first Temple *into the wilderness,* or spiritually barren Empire of the *Latins,* where she is found afterwards sitting upon the Beast and upon the seven mountains; and is called *the great city which reigneth over the Kings of the earth,* that is, over the ten Kings who give their kingdom to her Beast.

But before her flight there was war in heaven between *Michael* and the Dragon, the *Christian* and the heathen religions; and the Dragon, *that old serpent, called the Devil and Satan, who deceiveth the whole world, was cast out to the earth, and his Angels were cast out with him.* And *John heard a voice in heaven, saying, Now is come salvation and strength, and the kingdom of our God, and the power of his* Christ: *for the accuser of our brethren is cast down. And they overcame him by the blood of the Lamb, and by the word of their testimony. And they loved not their lives unto the death. Therefore rejoice, ye heavens, and ye that dwell in them. Woe be to the inhabiters of the earth and sea,* or people of the *Greek* and *Latin* Empires, *for the devil is come down amongst you, having great wrath, because he knoweth that he hath but a short time.*

And when the Dragon saw that he was cast down from the *Roman* throne, and the man-child caught up thither, he *persecuted the woman which brought forth the man-child; and to her*, by the division of the *Roman* Empire between the cities of *Rome* and *Constantinople* A.C. 330, *were given two wings of a great eagle*, the symbol of the *Roman* Empire, *that she might flee* from the first Temple *into the wilderness* of *Arabia, to her place* at *Babylon* mystically so called. *And the serpent*, by the division of the same Empire between the sons of *Constantine* the great, A.C. 337, *cast out of his mouth water as a flood*, the *Western* Empire, *after the woman; that he might cause her to be carried away by the flood. And the earth*, or *Greek* Empire, *helped the woman, and the earth opened her mouth, and swallowed up the flood*, by the victory of *Constantius* over *Magnentius*, A.C. 353, and thus the Beast was wounded to death with a sword. *And the Dragon was wroth with the woman*, in the reign of *Julian* the Apostate A.C. 361, *and*, by a new division of the Empire between *Valentinian* and *Valens*, A.C. 364, *went* from her into the *Eastern* Empire *to make war with the remnant of her seed*, which she left behind her when she fled: and thus the Beast revived. By the next division of the Empire, which was between *Gratian* and *Theodosius* A.C. 379, the *Beast* with ten horns *rose out of the sea*, and the *Beast* with two horns *out of the earth*: and by the last division thereof, which was between the sons of *Theodosius*, A.C. 395, *the Dragon gave the Beast his power and throne, and great authority*. And the ten horns *received power as Kings, the same hour with the Beast*.

At length the woman arrived at her place of temporal as well as spiritual dominion upon the back of the Beast, where she is nourished *a time, and times, and half a time, from the face of the serpent*; not in his kingdom, but at a distance from him. She is nourished by *the merchants of the earth*, three times or years and an half, or 42 months, or 1260 days: and in these Prophecies days are put for years. During all this time the Beast acted, and *she sat upon him*, that is, reigned over him, and over the ten Kings *who gave their power and strength*, that is, their kingdom *to the Beast*; and she was *drunken with the blood of the Saints*. By all these circumstances she is the eleventh horn of *Daniel*'s fourth Beast, who reigned with *a look more stout than his fellows*, and was of a different kind from the rest, and had eyes *and a mouth* like the woman; *and made war with the saints, and prevailed against them*, and *wore them out*, and *thought to change times and laws*, and had them *given into his hand, until a time, and times, and half a time*. These characters of the woman, and little horn of the Beast, agree perfectly: in respect of her temporal dominion, she was a horn of the Beast; in respect of her spiritual dominion, she rode upon him in the form of a woman, and was his Church, and committed fornication with the ten Kings.

The second Beast, which *rose up out of the earth*, was the Church of the *Greek* Empire: for it *had two horns like those of the Lamb*, and therefore was a Church; and it *spake as the Dragon*, and therefore was of his religion; and it *came up out of the earth*, and by consequence in his kingdom. It is called also *the false Prophet* who wrought miracles before the first Beast, by which he deceived them that received his mark, and worshiped his image. When the Dragon went from the woman to make war with the remnant of her seed, this Beast arising out of the earth assisted in that war, and *caused the earth and them which dwell therein to worship* the authority of *the first Beast, whose mortal wound was healed*, and to *make an Image to him*, that is, to assemble a body of men like him in point of religion. He had also *power to give life* and authority *to the Image*, so that it could *both speak, and* by dictating *cause that all* religious bodies of men, *who would not worship* the authority of *the Image, should be* mystically *killed. And he causeth all men to receive a mark in their right hand or in their forehead, and that no man might buy or sell save he that had the mark, or the name of the Beast, or the number of his name*; all the rest being excommunicated by the Beast with two horns. His mark is ✝✝✝, and his name ΛΑΤΕΙΝΟΣ, and the number of his name 666.

Thus the Beast, after he was wounded to death with a sword and revived, was deified, as the heathens used to deify their Kings after death, and had an Image erected to him; and his worshipers were initiated in this new religion, by receiving the mark or name of this new God, or the number of his name. By killing all that will not worship him and his Image, the first Temple, illuminated by the lamps of the seven Churches, is demolished, and a new Temple built for them who will not worship him; and the outward court of this new Temple, or outward form of a Church, is given to the *Gentiles*, who worship the Beast and his Image: while they who will not worship him, are sealed with the name of God in their foreheads, and retire into the inward court of this new Temple. These are the 144000 sealed out of all the twelve tribes of *Israel*, and called the *two Witnesses*, as being derived from the two wings of the woman while she was flying into the wilderness, and represented by two of the seven candlesticks. These appear to *John* in the inward court of the second Temple, standing on mount *Sion* with the Lamb, and as it were on the sea of glass. These are *the Saints of the most High*, and *the host of heaven*, and *the holy people* spoken of by *Daniel*, as worn out and trampled under foot, and destroyed in the latter times by the little horns of his fourth Beast and He-Goat.

While the *Gentiles* tread the holy city under foot, God *gives power to his two Witnesses, and they prophesy a thousand two hundred and threescore days clothed in sackcloth.* They are called *the two Olive-trees*, with relation to the two Olive-trees, which in *Zechary*'s vision, chap. iv. stand on either side of the golden candlestick to supply the lamps with oil: and Olive-trees, according to the Apostle *Paul*, represent Churches, *Rom.* xi. They supply the lamps with oil, by maintaining teachers. They are also called *the two candlesticks*; which in this Prophecy signify Churches, the seven Churches of *Asia* being represented by seven candlesticks. Five of these Churches were found faulty, and threatned if they did not repent; the other two were without fault, and so their candlesticks were fit to be placed in the second Temple. These were the Churches in *Smyrna* and *Philadelphia*. They were in a state of tribulation and persecution, and the only two of the seven in such a state: and so their candlesticks were fit to represent the Churches in affliction in the times of the second Temple, and the only two of the seven that were fit. The *two Witnesses* are not new Churches: they are the posterity of the primitive Church, the posterity of the two wings of the woman, and so are fitly represented by two of the primitive candlesticks. We may conceive therefore, that when the first Temple was destroyed, and a new one built for them who worship in the inward court, two of the seven candlesticks were placed in this new Temple.

The affairs of the Church are not considered during the opening of the first four seals. They begin to be consider'd at the opening of the fifth seal, as was said above; and are further considered at the opening of the sixth seal; and the seventh seal contains the times of the great Apostacy. And therefore I refer the Epistles to the seven Churches unto the times of the fifth and sixth seals: for they relate to the Church when she began to decline, and contain admonitions against the great Apostacy then approaching.

When *Eusebius* had brought down his *Ecclesiatical History* to the reign of *Dioclesian*, he thus describes the state of the Church: *Qualem quantamque gloriam simul ac libertatem doctrina veræ erga supremum Deum pietatis à Christo primùm hominibus annunciata, apud omnes Græcos pariter & barbaros ante persecutionem nostrâ memoriâ excitatam, consecuta sit, nos certè pro merito explicare non possumus. Argumento esse possit Imperatorum benignitas erga nostros: quibus regendas etiam provincias committebant, omni sacrificandi metu eos liberantes ob singularem, qua in religionem nostram affecti erant, benevolentiam.* And a little after: *Jam vero quis innumerabilem hominum quotidiè ad fidem Christi confugientium turbam, quis numerum ecclesiarum in singulis urbibus, quis illustres populorum concursus in ædibus sacris, cumulatè possit describere? Quo factum est, ut priscis ædificiis jam non contenti, in singulis urbibus spatiosas ab ipsis fundamentis exstruerent ecclesias. Atque hæc progressii temporis increscentia, & quotidiè in majus & melius proficiscentia, nec livor ullus atterere, nec malignitas dæmonis fascinare, nec hominum insidiæ prohibere unquam potuerunt, quamdiu omnipotentis Dei dextra populum suum, utpote tali dignum præsidio, texit atque custodiit. Sed cum ex nimia libertate in negligentiam ac desidiam prolapsi essemus; cum alter alteri invidere atque obtrectare cœpisset; cum inter nos quasi bella intestina gereremus, verbis, tanquam armis quibusdam hastisque, nos mutuò vulnerantes; cum Antistites adversus Antistites, populi in populos collisi, jurgia ac tumultus agitarent; denique cum fraus & simulatio ad summum malitiæ culmen adolevisset: tum divina ultio, levi brachio ut solet, integro adhuc ecclesiæ statu, & fidelium turbis liberè convenientibus, sensim ac moderatè in nos cœpit animadvertere; orsà primùm persecutione ab iis qui militabant. Cum verò sensu omni destituti de placando Dei numine ne cogitaremus quidem; quin potius instar impiorum quorundam res humanas nullâ providentiâ gubernari rati, alia quotidiè crimina aliis adjiceremus: cum Pastores nostri spretâ religionis regulâ, mutuis inter se contentionibus decertarent, nihil aliud quam jurgia, minas, œmulationem, odia, ac mutuas inimicitias amplificare studentes; principatum quasi tyrannidem quandam contentissimè sibi vindicantes: tunc demùm juxta dictum Hieremiœ,* obscuravit Dominus in ira sua filiam Sion, & dejecit de cælo gloriam Israel,—*per Ecclesiarum scilicet subversionem,* &c. This was the state of the Church just before the subversion of the Churches in the beginning of *Dioclesian*'s persecution: and to this state of the Church agrees the first of the seven Epistles to the Angel of the seven Churches, [1] that to the Church in *Ephesus*. *I have something against thee,* saith *Christ* to the Angel of that Church, *because thou hast left thy first love. Remember therefore from whence thou art fallen, and repent, and do the first works; or else I will come unto thee quickly, and will remove thy candlestick out of its place, except thou repent. But this thou hast, that thou hatest the deeds of the* Nicolaitans, *which I also hate.* The *Nicolaitans* are the *Continentes* above described, who placed religion in abstinence from marriage, abandoning their wives if they had any. They are here called *Nicolaitans*, from *Nicolas* one of the seven deacons of the primitive Church of *Jerusalem*; who having a beautiful wife, and being taxed with uxoriousness, abandoned her, and permitted her to marry whom she pleased, saying that we must disuse the flesh; and thenceforward lived a single life in continency, as his children also. The *Continentes* afterwards embraced the doctrine of *Æons* and Ghosts male and female, and were avoided by the Churches till the fourth century; and the Church of *Ephesus* is here commended for hating their deeds.

The persecution of *Dioclesian* began in the year of *Christ* 302, and lasted ten years in the *Eastern* Empire and two years in the *Western*. To this state of the Church the second Epistle, to the Church of *Smyrna*, agrees. *I know,* saith [2] *Christ, thy works, and tribulation, and poverty, but thou art rich; and I know the blasphemy of them, which say they are* Jews *and are not, but are the synagogue of Satan. Fear none of those things which thou shalt suffer: Behold, the Devil shall call some of you into prison, that ye may be tried; and ye shall have tribulation ten days. Be thou faithful unto death, and I will give thee a crown of life.* The tribulation of ten days can agree to no other persecution than that of *Dioclesian,* it being the only persecution which lasted ten years. By *the blasphemy of them which say they are* Jews *and are not, but are the synagogue of Satan,* I understand the Idolatry of the *Nicolaitans,* who falsly said they were *Christians.*

The *Nicolaitans* are complained of also in [3] the third Epistle, as men that *held the doctrine of* Balaam, *who taught* Balac *to cast a stumbling-block before the children of* Israel, *to eat things sacrificed to Idols, and* [4] *to commit* spiritual *fornication.* For *Balaam* taught the *Moabites* and *Midianites* to tempt and invite *Israel* by their women to commit fornication, and to feast with them at the sacrifices of their Gods. The Dragon therefore began now to come down among the inhabitants of the earth and sea.

The *Nicolaitans* are also complained of in the fourth Epistle, under the name of the *woman* Jezabel, *who calleth herself a Prophetess, to teach and to seduce the servants of* Christ *to commit fornication, and to eat things sacrificed to Idols.* The woman therefore began now to fly into the wilderness.

The reign of *Constantine* the great from the time of his conquering *Licinius,* was monarchical over the whole *Roman* Empire. Then the Empire became divided between the sons of *Constantine*: and afterwards it was again united under *Constantius,* by his victory over *Magnentius.* To the affairs of the Church in these three successive periods of time, the third, fourth, and fifth Epistles, that is, those to the Angels of the Churches in *Pergamus, Thyatira,* and *Sardis,* seem to relate. The next Emperor was *Julian* the Apostate.

In the sixth Epistle, [5] to the Angel of the Church in *Philadelphia, Christ* saith: *Because* in the reign of the heathen Emperor *Julian, thou hast kept the word of my patience, I also will keep thee from the hour of temptation, which* by the woman's flying into the wilderness, and the Dragon's making war with the remnant of her seed, and the killing of all who will not worship the Image of the Beast, *shall come upon all the world, to try them that dwell upon the earth*, and to distinguish them by sealing the one with the name of God in their foreheads, and marking the other with the mark of the Beast. *Him that overcometh, I will make a pillar in the Temple of my God; and he shall go no more out* of it. *And I will write upon him the name of my God* in his forehead. So the *Christians* of the Church of *Philadelphia*, as many of them as overcome, are sealed with the seal of God, and placed in the second Temple, and go no more out. The same is to be understood of the Church in *Smyrna*, which also kept the word of God's patience, and was without fault. These two Churches, with their posterity, are therefore the *two Pillars*, and the *two Candlesticks*, and the *two Witnesses* in the second Temple.

After the reign of the Emperor *Julian,* and his successor *Jovian* who reigned but five months, the Empire became again divided between *Valentinian* and *Valens*. Then the Church Catholick, in the Epistle to the Angel of the Church of *Laodicea*, is reprehended as *lukewarm*, and [6] threatned to be *spewed out of* Christ's *mouth*. She said, that she was *rich and increased with goods, and had need of nothing*, being in outward prosperity; *and knew not that she was* inwardly *wretched, and miserable, and poor, and blind, and naked*. She is therefore *spewed out of* Christ's *mouth* at the opening of the seventh seal: and this puts an end to the times of the first Temple.

About one half of the *Roman* Empire turned *Christians* in the time of *Constantine* the great and his sons. After *Julian* had opened the Temples, and restored the worship of the heathens, the Emperors *Valentinian* and *Valens* tolerated it all their reign; and therefore the Prophecy of the sixth seal was not fully accomplished before the reign of their successor *Gratian*. It was the custom of the heathen Priests, in the beginning of the reign of every sovereign Emperor, to offer him the dignity and habit of the *Pontifex Maximus*. This dignity all Emperors had hitherto accepted: but *Gratian* rejected it, threw down the idols, interdicted the sacrifices, and took away their revenues with the salaries and authority of the Priests. *Theodosius* the great followed his example; and heathenism afterwards recovered itself no more, but decreased so fast, that *Prudentius*, about ten years after the death of *Theodosius*, called the heathens, *vix pauca ingenia & pars hominum rarissima*. Whence the affairs of the sixth seal ended with the reign of *Valens*, or rather with the beginning of the reign of *Theodosius*, when he, like his predecessor *Gratian*, rejected the dignity of *Pontifex Maximus*. For the *Romans* were very much infested by the invasions of foreign nations in the reign of *Valentinian* and *Valens*: *Hoc tempore*, saith *Ammianus*, *velut per universum orbem Romanum bellicum canentibus buccinis, excitæ gentes sævissimæ limites sibi proximos persultabant: Gallias Rhœtiasque simul Alemanni populabantur: Sarmatæ Pannonias & Quadi: Picti, Saxones, & Scoti & Attacotti Britannos ærumnis vexavere continuis: Austoriani, Mauricæque aliæ gentes Africam solito acriùs incursabant: Thracias diripiebant prædatorii globi Gotthorum: Persarum Rex manus Armeniis injectabat*. And whilst the Emperors were busy in repelling these enemies, the *Hunns* and *Alans* and *Goths* came over the *Danube* in two bodies, overcame and slew *Valens*, and made so great a slaughter of the *Roman* army, that *Ammianus* saith: *Nec ulla Annalibus præter Cannensem ita ad internecionem res legitur gesta*. These wars were not fully stopt on all sides till the beginning of the reign of *Theodosius*, A.C. 379 & 380: but thenceforward the Empire remained quiet from foreign armies, till his death, A.C. 395. So long the four winds were held: and so long there was silence in heaven. And the seventh seal was opened when this silence began.

Mr. *Mede* hath explained the Prophecy of the first six trumpets not much amiss: but if he had observed, that the Prophecy of pouring out the vials of wrath is synchronal to that of sounding the trumpets, his explanation would have been yet more complete.

The name of *Woes* is given to the wars to which the three last trumpets sound, to distinguish them from the wars of the four first. The sacrifices on the first four days of the feast of Tabernacles, at which the first four trumpets sound, and the first four vials of wrath are poured out, are slaughters in four great wars; and these wars are represented by four winds from the four corners of the earth. The first was an east wind, the second a west wind, the third a south wind, and the fourth a north wind, with respect to the city of *Rome*, the metropolis of the old *Roman* Empire. These four plagues fell upon *the third part of the Earth, Sea, Rivers, Sun, Moon and Stars*; that is, upon the Earth, Sea, Rivers, Sun, Moon and Stars of the third part of the whole scene of these Prophecies of *Daniel* and *John*.

The plague of the eastern wind [7] at the sounding of the first trumpet, was to fall upon the *Earth*, that is, upon the nations of the *Greek* Empire. Accordingly, after the death of *Theodosius* the great, the *Goths, Sarmatians, Hunns, Isaurians*, and *Austorian* Moors invaded and miserably wasted *Greece, Thrace, Asia minor, Armenia, Syria, Egypt, Lybia*, and *Illyricum*, for ten or twelve years together.

The plague of the western wind at the sounding of the second trumpet, was to fall upon the *Sea*, or *Western* Empire, by means of *a great mountain burning with fire* cast into it, and *turning it to blood*. Accordingly in the year 407, that Empire began to be invaded by the *Visigoths, Vandals, Alans, Sueves, Burgundians, Ostrogoths, Heruli, Quadi, Gepides*; and by these wars it was broken into ten kingdoms, and miserably wasted: and *Rome* itself, the burning mountain, was besieged and taken by the *Ostrogoths*, in the beginning of these miseries.

The plague of the southern wind at the sounding of the third trumpet, was to cause *a great star, burning as it were a lamp, to fall from heaven upon the rivers and fountains of waters*, the *Western* Empire now divided into many kingdoms, and to turn them to *wormwood* and *blood*, and make them *bitter*. Accordingly *Genseric*, the King of the *Vandals* and *Alans* in *Spain*, A.C. 427, enter'd *Africa* with an army of eighty thousand men; where he invaded the *Moors*, and made war upon the *Romans*, both there and on the sea-coasts of *Europe*, for fifty years together, almost without intermission, taking *Hippo* A.C. 431, and *Carthage* the capital of *Africa* A.C. 439. In A.C. 455, with a numerous fleet and an army of three hundred thousand *Vandals* and *Moors*, he invaded *Italy*, took and plundered *Rome, Naples, Capua*, and many other cities; carrying thence their wealth with the flower of the people into *Africa*: and the next year, A.C. 456, he rent all *Africa* from the Empire, totally expelling the *Romans*. Then the *Vandals* invaded and took the Islands of the *Mediterranean, Sicily, Sardinia, Corsica, Ebusus, Majorca, Minorca,* &c. and *Ricimer* besieged the Emperer *Anthemius* in *Rome*, took the city, and gave his soldiers the plunder, A.C. 472. The *Visigoths* about the same time drove the *Romans* out of *Spain*: and now the *Western* Emperor, the *great star which fell from heaven, burning as it were a lamp*, having by all these wars gradually lost almost all his dominions, was invaded, and conquered in one year by *Odoacer* King of the *Heruli*, A.C. 476. After this the *Moors* revolted A.C. 477, and weakned the *Vandals* by several wars, and took *Mauritania* from them. These wars continued till the *Vandals* were conquered by *Belisarius*, A.C. 534. and by all these wars *Africa* was almost depopulated, according to *Procopius*, who reckons that above five millions of men perished in them. When the *Vandals* first invaded *Africa*, that country was very populous, consisting of about 700 bishopricks, more than were in all *France, Spain* and *Italy* together: but by the wars between the *Vandals, Romans* and *Moors*, it was depopulated to that degree, that *Procopius* tells us, it was next to a miracle for a traveller to see a man.

In pouring out the third vial it is [8] said: *Thou art righteous, O Lord,—because thou hast judged thus: for they have shed the blood of thy Saints and Prophets, and thou hast given them blood to drink, for they are worthy.* How they shed the blood of Saints, may be understood by the following Edict of the Emperor *Honorius*, procured by four Bishops sent to him by a Council of *African* Bishops, who met at *Carthage* 14 *June*, A.C. 410.

Impp. Honor. &. Theod. AA. Heracliano Com. Afric.

Oraculo penitus remoto, quo ad ritus suos hæreticæ superstitionis abrepserant, sciant omnes sanctæ legis inimici, plectendos se pœna & proscriptionis & sanguinis, si ultra convenire per publicum, execrandâ sceleris sui temeritate temptaverint. Dat. viii. Kal. Sept. Varano V.C. Cons. A.C. 410.

Which Edict was five years after fortified by the following.

Impp. Honor. & Theod. AA. Heracliano Com. Afric.

Sciant cuncti qui ad ritus suos hæresis superstitionibus obrepserant sacrosanctæ legis inimici, plectendos se pœnâ & proscriptionis & sanguinis, si ultra convenire per publicum exercendi sceleris sui temeritate temptaverint: ne quâ vera divinaque reverentia contagione temeretur. Dat. viii. *Kal. Sept. Honorio* x. *& Theod.* vi. *AA. Coss.* A.C. 415.

These Edicts being directed to the governor of *Africa*, extended only to the *Africans*. Before these there were many severe ones against the *Donatists*, but they did not extend to blood. These two were the first which made their meetings, and the meetings of all dissenters, capital: for by *hereticks* in these Edicts are meant all dissenters, as is manifest by the following against *Euresius* a *Luciferan* Bishop.

Impp. Arcad. & Honor. AA. Aureliano Proc. Africæ.

Hæreticorum vocabulo continentur, & latis adversus eos sanctionibus debent succumbere, qui vel levi argumento à judicio Catholicæ religionis & tramite detecti fuerint deviare: ideoque experientia tua Euresium hæreticum esse cognoscat. Dat. iii. *Non. Sept. Constantinop. Olybrio & Probino Coss.* A.C. 395.

The *Greek* Emperor *Zeno* adopted *Theoderic* King of the *Ostrogoths* to be his son, made him master of the horse and *Patricius*, and Consul of *Constantinople*; and recommending to him the *Roman* people and Senate, gave him the *Western* Empire, and sent him into *Italy* against *Odoacer* King of the *Heruli*. *Theoderic* thereupon led his nation into *Italy*, conquered *Odoacer*, and reigned over *Italy*, *Sicily*, *Rhœtia*, *Noricum*, *Dalmatia*, *Liburnia*, *Istria*, and part of *Suevia*, *Pannonia* and *Gallia*. Whence *Ennodius* said, in a Panegyric to *Theoderic*: *Ad limitem suum Romana regna remeâsse. Theoderic* reigned with great prudence, moderation and felicity; treated the *Romans* with singular benevolence, governed them by their own laws, and restored their government under their Senate and Consuls, he himself supplying the place of Emperor, without assuming the title. *Ita sibi parentibus præfuit*, saith *Procopius*, *ut vere*

Imperatori conveniens decus nullum ipsi abesset: Justitiæ magnus ei cultus, legumque diligens custodia: terras à vicinis barbaris servavit intactas, &c. Whence I do not reckon the reign of this King, amongst the plagues of the four winds.

The plague of the northern wind, at the sounding of the fourth trumpet, was to cause *the Sun, Moon and Stars*, that is, the King, kingdom and Princes of the *Western* Empire, *to be darkned*, and to continue some time in darkness. Accordingly *Belisarius*, having conquered the *Vandals*, invaded *Italy* A.C. 535, and made war upon the *Ostrogoths* in *Dalmatia, Liburnia, Venetia, Lombardy, Tuscany*, and other regions northward from *Rome*, twenty years together. In this war many cities were taken and retaken. In retaking *Millain* from the *Romans*, the *Ostrogoths* slew all the males young and old, amounting, as *Procopius* reckons, to three hundred thousand, and sent the women captives to their allies the *Burgundians*. *Rome* itself was taken and retaken several times, and thereby the people were thinned; the old government by a Senate ceased, the nobles were ruined, and all the glory of the city was extinguish'd: and A.C. 552, after a war of seventeen years, the kingdom of the *Ostrogoths* fell; yet the remainder of the *Ostrogoths*, and an army of *Germans* called in to their assistance, continued the war three or four years longer. Then ensued the war of the *Heruli*, who, as *Anastasius* tells us, *perimebant cunctam Italiam*, slew all *Italy*. This was followed by the war of the *Lombards*, the fiercest of all the *Barbarians*, which began A.C. 568, and lasted for thirty eight years together; *factâ tali clade*, saith *Anastasius, qualem à sæculo nullus meminit*; ending at last in the Papacy of *Sabinian*, A.C. 605, by a peace then made with the *Lombards*. Three years before this war ended, *Gregory* the great, then Bishop of *Rome*, thus speaks of it: *Qualiter enim & quotidianis gladiis & quantis Longobardorum incursionibus, ecce jam per triginta quinque annorum longitudinem premimur, nullis explere vocibus suggestionis valemus*: and in one of his Sermons to the people, he thus expresses the great consumption of the *Romans* by these wars: *Ex illa plebe innumerabili quanti remanseritis aspicitis, & tamen adhuc quotidiè flagella urgent, repentini casus opprimunt, novæ res & improvisæ clades affligunt*. In another Sermon he thus describes the desolations: *Destructæ urbes, eversa sunt castra, depopulati agri, in solitudinem terra redacta est. Nullus in agris incola, penè nullus in urbibus habitator remansit. Et tamen ipsæ parvæ generis humani reliquiæ adhuc quotidiè & sine cessatione feriuntur, & finem non habent flagella cælestis justitiæ. Ipsa autem quæ aliquando mundi Domina esse videbatur, qualis remansit Roma conspicimus innumeris doloribus multipliciter attrita, defolatione civium, impressione hostium, frequentiâ ruinarum.—Ecce jam de illa omnes hujus fæculi potentes ablati sunt.—Ecce populi defecerunt.—Ubi enim Senatus? Ubi jam populus? Contabuerunt ossa, consumptæ sunt carnes. Omnis enim sæcularium dignitatum ordo extinctus est, & tamen ipsos vos paucos qui remansimus, adhuc quotidié gladii, adhuc quotidié innumeræ tribulationes premunt.—Vacua jam ardet Roma. Quid autem ista de hominibus dicimus? Cum ruinis crebrescentibus ipsa quoque destrui ædificia videmus. Postquam defecerunt homines etiam parietes cadunt. Jam ecce desolata, ecce contrita, ecce gemitibus oppressa est,* &c. All this was spoken by *Gregory* to the people of *Rome*, who were witnesses of the truth of it. Thus by *the plagues of the four winds*, the Empire of the *Greeks* was shaken, and the Empire of the *Latins* fell; and *Rome* remained nothing more than the capital of a poor dukedom, subordinate to *Ravenna*, the seat of the Exarchs.

The fifth trumpet sounded to the wars, which the *King of the South*, as he is called by *Daniel*, made *in the time of the end*, in *pushing at the King who did according to his will*. This plague began with the *opening of the bottomless pit*, which denotes the letting out of a false religion: the *smoke which came out of the pit*, signifying the multitude which embraced that religion; and the *locusts which came out of the smoke*, the armies which came out of that multitude. This pit was opened, to let out smoke and locusts into the regions of the four monarchies, or some of them. *The King of these locusts* was the *Angel of the bottomless pit*, being chief governor as well in religious as civil affairs, such as was the Caliph of the *Saracens*. Swarms of locusts often arise in *Arabia fælix*, and from thence infest the neighbouring nations: and so are a very fit type of the numerous armies of *Arabians* invading the *Romans*. They began to invade them A.C. 634, and to reign at *Damascus* A.C. 637. They built *Bagdad* A.C. 766, and reigned over *Persia*, *Syria*, *Arabia*, *Egypt*, *Africa* and *Spain*. They afterwards lost *Africa* to *Mahades*, A.C. 910; *Media*, *Hircania*, *Chorasan*, and all *Persia*, to the *Dailamites*, between the years 927 and 935; *Mesopotamia* and *Miafarekin* to *Nasiruddaulas*, A.C. 930; *Syria* and *Egypt* to *Achsjid*, A.C. 935, and now being in great distress, the Caliph of *Bagdad*, A.C. 936, surrendred all the rest of his temporal power to *Mahomet* the son of *Rajici*, King of *Wasit* in *Chaldea*, and made him Emperor of Emperors. But *Mahomet* within two years lost *Bagdad* to the *Turks*; and thenceforward *Bagdad* was sometimes in the hands of the *Turks*, and sometimes in the hands of the *Saracens*, till *Togrul-beig*, called also *Togra*, *Dogrissa*, *Tangrolipix*, and *Sadoc*, conquered *Chorasan* and *Persia*; and A.C. 1055, added *Bagdad* to his Empire, making it the seat thereof. His successors *Olub-Arflan* and *Melechschah*, conquered the regions upon *Euphrates*; and these conquests, after the death of *Melechschah*, brake into the kingdoms of *Armenia*, *Mesopotamia*, *Syria*, and *Cappadocia*. The whole time that the Caliphs of the *Saracens* reigned with a temporal dominion at *Damascus* and *Bagdad* together, was 300 years, *viz.* from the year 637 to the year 936 inclusive. Now locusts live but five months; and therefore, for the decorum of the type, these locusts are said to *hurt men five months and five months*, as if they had lived about five months at *Damascus*, and again about five months at *Bagdad*; in all ten months, or 300 prophetic days, which are years.

The sixth trumpet sounded to the wars, which *Daniel*'s King of the *North* made against the King above-mentioned, *who did according to his will*. In these wars the King of the *North*, according to *Daniel*, conquered the Empire of the *Greeks*, and also *Judea*, *Egypt*, *Lybia*, and *Ethiopia*: and by these conquests the Empire of the *Turks* was set up, as may be known by the extent thereof. These wars commenced A.C. 1258, when the four kingdoms of the *Turks* seated upon *Euphrates*, that of *Armenia major* seated at *Miyapharekin*, *Megarkin* or *Martyropolis*, that of *Mesopotamia* seated at *Mosul*, that of all *Syria* seated at *Aleppo*, and that of *Cappadocia* seated at *Iconium*, were invaded by the *Tartars* under *Hulacu*, and driven into the western parts of *Asia minor*, where they made war upon the *Greeks*, and began to erect the present Empire of the *Turks*. Upon the sounding of the sixth trumpet, [9] *John heard a voice from the four horns of the golden Altar which is before God, saying to the sixth Angel which had the trumpet, Loose the four Angels which are bound at the great river* Euphrates. *And the four Angels were loosed, which were prepared for an hour and a day, and a month and a year, for to slay the third part of men.* By the four horns of the golden Altar, is signified the situation of the head cities of the said four kingdoms, *Miyapharekin, Mosul, Aleppo,* and *Iconium,* which were in a quadrangle. They slew the third part of men, when they conquered the *Greek* Empire, and took *Constantinople,* A.C. 1453. and they began to be prepared for this purpose, when *Olub-Arslan* began to conquer the nations upon *Euphrates,* A.C. 1063. The interval is called an hour and a day, and a month and a year, or 391 prophetic days, which are years. In the first thirty years, *Olub-Arslan* and *Melechschah* conquered the nations upon *Euphrates,* and reigned over the whole. *Melechschah* died A.C. 1092, and was succeeded by a little child; and then this kingdom broke into the four kingdoms above-mentioned.

Notes to Chap. III

[1] Apoc. ii. 4, &c.
[2] Apoc. ii. 9, 10.
[3] Ver. 14.
[4] Numb. xxv. 1, 2, 18, & xxi. 16.
[5] Apoc. iii. 10, 12.
[6] Apoc. iii. 16, 17.
[7] Apoc. viii. 7, &c.
[8] Apoc. xvi. 5, 6.
[9] Apoc. ix. 13, &c.

THE END

Advertisement

The last pages of these Observations having been differently drawn up by the Author in another copy of his Work; they are here inserted as they follow in that copy, after the 22d line of the 261st page foregoing.

And none was found worthy to open the book till the Lamb of God appeared; the great High-Priest represented by a lamb slain at the foot of the Altar in the morning-sacrifice. *And he came, and took the book out of the hand of him that sat upon the throne.* For the High-Priest, in the feast of the seventh month, went into the most holy place, and took the book of the law out of the right side of the Ark, to read it to the people: and in order to read it well, he studied it seven days, that is, upon the fourth, fifth, sixth, seventh, eighth, ninth and tenth days, being attended by some of the priests to hear him perform. These seven days are alluded to, by the Lamb's opening the seven seals successively.

Upon the tenth day of the month, a young bullock was offered for a sin-offering for the High-Priest, and a goat for a sin-offering for the people: and lots were cast upon two goats to determine which of them should be God's lot for the sin-offering; and the other goat was called *Azazel,* the scape-goat. The High-Priest in his linen garments, took a censer full of burning coals of fire from the Altar, his hand being full of sweet incense beaten small; and went into the most holy place within the veil, and put the incense upon the fire, and sprinkled the blood of the bullock with his finger upon the mercy-seat and before the mercy-seat seven times; and then he killed the goat which fell to God's lot, for a sin-offering for the people, and brought his blood within the veil, and sprinkled it also seven times upon the mercy-seat and before the mercy-seat. Then he went out to the Altar, and sprinkled it also seven times with the blood of the bullock, and as often with the blood of the goat. After this *he laid both his hands upon the head of the live goat; and confessed over him all the iniquities of the children of* Israel, *and all their transgressions in all their sins, putting them upon the head of the goat; and sent him away into the wilderness by the hands of a fit man: and the goat bore upon him all their iniquities into a land not inhabited,* Levit. chap. iv. & chap. xvi. While the High-Priest was doing these things in the most holy place and at the Altar, the people continued at their devotion quietly and in silence. Then the High-Priest went into the holy place, put off his linen garments, and put on other garments; then came out, and sent the bullock and the goat of the sin-offering to be burnt without the camp, with fire taken in a censer from the Altar: and as the people returned home from the Temple, they said to one another, *God seal you to a good new year.*

In allusion to all this, *when he had opened the seventh seal, there was silence in heaven about the space of half an hour. And an Angel stood at the Altar having a golden Censer, and there was given unto him much incense, that he should offer it with the prayers of all Saints, upon the golden Altar which was before the throne. And the smoke of the incense with the prayers of the Saints ascended up before God out of the Angel's hand. And the Angel took the Censer, and filled it with fire of the Altar, and cast it to the earth,* suppose without the camp, for sacrificing the goat which fell to God's lot. For the High-Priest being *Christ* himself, the bullock is omitted. At this sacrifice *there were voices and thundrings,* of the musick of the Temple, *and lightnings* of the sacred fire, *and an earthquake*: and synchronal to these things was the sealing of *the 144000 out of all the twelve tribes of the children of* Israel *with the seal of God in their foreheads,* while the rest of the twelve tribes received the mark of the Beast, and the Woman fled from the Temple into the wilderness to her place upon this Beast. For this sealing and marking was represented by casting lots upon the two goats, sacrificing God's lot on mount *Sion,* and sending the scape-goat into the wilderness loaden with the sins of the people.

Upon the fifteenth day of the month, and the six following days, there were very great sacrifices. And in allusion to the sounding of trumpets, and singing with thundring voices, and pouring out drink-offerings at those sacrifices, *seven trumpets are sounded,* and *seven thunders utter their voices,* and *seven vials of wrath are poured out.* Wherefore the sounding of the *seven trumpets*, the voices of the *seven thunders*, and the pouring out of the *seven vials of wrath*, are synchronal, and relate to one and the same division of the time of the seventh seal following the silence, into seven successive parts. The seven days of this feast were called the feast of Tabernacles; and during these seven days the children of *Israel* dwelt in booths, and rejoiced with palm-branches in their hands. To this alludes *the multitude with palms in their hands*, which appeared after the sealing of the 144000, and *came out of the great tribulation* with triumph at the battle of the great day, to which the seventh trumpet sounds. The visions therefore of the 144000, and of the palm-bearing multitude, extend to the sounding of the seventh trumpet, and therefore are synchronal to the times of the seventh seal.

When the 144000 *are sealed out of all the twelve tribes of* Israel, and the rest receive *the mark of the Beast*, and thereby the first temple is destroyed; *John* is bidden to *measure the temple and altar*, that is, their courts, *and them that worship therein*, that is, the 144000 standing on mount *Sion* and on the sea of glass: *but the court that is without the temple*, that is, the peoples court, to *leave out and measure it not, because it is given to the* Gentiles, those who receive the mark of the Beast; *and the holy city they shall tread under foot forty and two months*, that is, all the time that the Beast acts under the woman *Babylon*: and *the two witnesses prophesy 1260 days*, that is, all the same time, *clothed in sackcloth. These have power*, like *Elijah, to shut heaven that it rain not*, at the sounding of the first trumpet; and, like *Moses, to turn the waters into blood* at the sounding of the second; *and to smite the earth with all plagues*, those of the trumpets, *as often as they will*. These prophesy at the building of the second temple, like *Haggai* and *Zechary*. These are *the two Olive-trees*, or Churches, which *supplied the lamps with oil*, Zech. iv. These are *the two candlesticks*, or Churches, *standing before the God of the earth*. Five of the seven Churches of *Asia*, those in prosperity, are found fault with, and exhorted to repent, and threatned to be *removed out of their places*, or *spewed out of* Christ's *mouth*, or *punished with the sword of* Christ's *mouth, except they repent*: the other two, the Churches of *Smyrna* and *Philadelphia*, which were under persecution, remain in a state of persecution, to illuminate the second temple. When the primitive Church catholick, represented by *the woman in heaven*, apostatized, and became divided into two corrupt Churches, represented by the *whore of* Babylon and the *two-horned Beast*, the 144000 *who were sealed out of all the twelve tribes*, became the *two Witnesses*, in opposition to those two false Churches: and the name of *two Witnesses* once imposed, remains to the true Church of God in all times and places to the end of the Prophecy.

In the interpretation of this Prophecy, *the woman in heaven clothed with the sun*, before she flies into the wilderness, represents the primitive Church catholick, illuminated with the *seven lamps* in the *seven golden candlesticks*, which are the *seven Churches of Asia*. The Dragon signifies the same Empire with *Daniel's* He-goat in the reign of his last horn, that is, the whole *Roman* Empire, until it became divided into the *Greek* and *Latin* Empires; and all the time of that division it signifies the *Greek* Empire alone: and the Beast is *Daniel's* fourth Beast, that is, the Empire of the *Latins*. Before the division of the *Roman* Empire into the *Greek* and *Latin* Empires, the Beast is included in the body of the Dragon; and from the time of that division, the Beast is the *Latin* Empire only. Hence the Dragon and Beast have the same heads and horns; but the heads are crowned upon the Dragon, and the horns upon the Beast. The horns are ten kingdoms, into which the Beast becomes divided presently after his separation from the Dragon, as hath been described above. The heads are seven successive dynasties, or parts, into which the *Roman* Empire becomes divided by the opening of the seven seals. Before the woman fled into the wilderness, *she being with child* of a Christian Empire, *cried travelling, viz.* in the ten years persecution of *Dioclesian, and pained to be delivered: and the Dragon*, the heathen *Roman* Empire, *stood before her, to devour her child as soon as it was born. And she brought forth a man child, who* at length *was to rule all nations with a rod of iron. And her child was caught up unto God, and to his throne* in the Temple, by the victory of *Constantine* the great over *Maxentius: and the woman fled* from the Temple *into the wilderness* of *Arabia* to *Babylon, where she hath a place* of riches and honour and dominion, upon the back of the Beast, *prepared of God, that they should feed her there 1260 days. And there was war in heaven*, between the heathens under *Maximinus* and the new Christian Empire; *and the great Dragon was cast out, that old serpent, which deceiveth the whole world*, the spirit of heathen idolatry; *he was cast out* of the throne *into the earth. And they overcame him by the blood of the Lamb, and by the word of their testimony; and they loved not their lives unto the death.*

And when the Dragon saw that he was cast unto the earth, he persecuted the woman which brought forth the man child, stirring up a new persecution against her in the reign of *Licinius. And to the woman*, by the building of *Constantinople* and equalling it to *Rome, were given two wings of a great eagle, that she might flee into the wilderness into her place* upon the back of her Beast, *where she is nourished for a time, and times, and half a time, from the face of the serpent. And the serpent*, upon the death of *Constantine* the great, *cast out of his mouth water as a flood, viz.* the *Western* Empire under *Constantine junior* and *Constans, after the woman: that he might cause her to be carried away of the flood. And the earth*, the nations of *Asia* now under *Constantinople, helped the woman*; and by conquering the *Western* Empire, now under *Magnentius, swallowed up the flood which the Dragon cast out of his mouth. And the Dragon was wroth with the woman, and went to make war with the remnant of her seed, which keep the commandments of God, and have the testimony of* Jesus Christ, *which* in that war *were sealed out of all the twelve tribes of* Israel, and remained upon mount *Sion* with the Lamb, being in number 144000, and having their father's name written in their foreheads.

When the earth had swallowed up the flood, and the Dragon was gone to make war with the remnant of the woman's seed, *John stood upon the sand of the sea, and saw a Beast rise out of the sea, having seven heads and ten horns. And the Beast was like unto a Leopard, and his feet were as the feet of a Bear, and his mouth as the mouth of a Lion. John* here names *Daniel's* four Beasts in order, putting his Beast in the room of *Daniel's* fourth Beast, to shew that they are the same. *And the Dragon gave this Beast his power and his seat and great authority*, by relinquishing the *Western* Empire to him. *And one of his heads,* the sixth, was *as it were wounded to death, viz.* by the sword of the earth, which swallowed up the waters cast out of the mouth of the Dragon; *and his deadly wound was healed,* by a new division of the Empire between *Valentinian* and *Valens, An.* 364. *John* saw the Beast rise out of the sea, at the division thereof between *Gratian* and *Theodosius, An.* 379. The Dragon gave the Beast his power, and his seat and great authority, at the death of *Theodosius,* when *Theodosius* gave the *Western* Empire to his son *Honorius.* After which the two Empires were no more united: but the *Western* Empire became presently divided into ten kingdoms, as above; and these kingdoms at length united in religion under the woman, and reign with her *forty and two months.*

And I beheld, saith *John, another Beast coming up out of the earth.* When the woman fled from the Dragon into the kingdom of the Beast, and became his Church, this other Beast rose up out of the earth, to represent the Church of the Dragon. For *he had two horns like the Lamb,* such as were the bishopricks of *Alexandria* and *Antioch: and he spake as the Dragon* in matters of religion: *and he causeth the earth,* or nations of the Dragon's kingdom, *to worship the first Beast, whose deadly wound was healed,* that is, to be of his religion. *And he doth great wonders, so that he maketh fire come down from heaven on the earth in the sight of men*; that is, he excommunicateth those who differ from him in point of religion: for in pronouncing their excommunications, they used to swing down a lighted torch from above. *And he said to them that dwell on the earth, that they should make an image to the Beast, which had the wound by a sword, and did live*; that is, that they should call a Council of men of the religion of this Beast. *And he had power to give life unto the image of the Beast, that the image of the Beast should both speak, and cause that as many as would not worship the image of the Beast should be killed, viz.* mystically, by dissolving their Churches. *And he causeth all both small and great, rich and poor, free and bond, to receive a mark in their right band or in their foreheads, and that no man might buy or sell, save he that had the mark, or the name of the Beast, or the number of his name*; that is, the mark ✠, or the name ΛΑΤΕΙΝΟΣ, or the number thereof χξς, 666. All others were excommunicated.

When the seven Angels had poured out the seven vials of wrath, and *John* had described them all in the present time, he is called up from the time of the seventh vial to the time of the sixth seal, to take a view of the woman and her Beast, who were to reign in the times of the seventh seal. In respect of the latter part of time of the sixth seal, then considered as present, the Angel tells *John*: *The Beast that thou sawest, was and is not, and shall ascend out of the abyss, and go into perdition*; that is, he was in the reign of *Constans* and *Magnentius*, until *Constantius* conquered *Magnentius*, and re-united the *Western* Empire to the *Eastern*. He is not during the reunion, and he shall ascend out of the abyss or sea at a following division of the Empire. The Angel tells him further: *Here is the mind which hath wisdom: the seven heads are seven mountains, on which the woman sitteth*; *Rome* being built upon seven hills, and thence called the seven-hilled city. *Also there are seven Kings: five are fallen, and one is, and the other is not yet come; and when he cometh, he must continue a short space: and the Beast that was and is not, even he is the eighth, and is of the seven, and goeth into perdition*. Five are fallen, the times of the five first seals being past; and one is, the time of the sixth seal being considered as present; and another is not yet come, and when he cometh, which will be at the opening of the seventh seal, he must continue a short space: and the Beast that was and is not, even he is the eighth, by means of the division of the *Roman* Empire into two collateral Empires; and is of the seven, being one half of the seventh, and shall go into perdition. The words, *five are fallen, and one is, and the other is not yet come*, are usually referred by interpreters to the time of *John* the Apostle, when the Prophecy was given: but it is to be considered, that in this Prophecy many things are spoken of as present, which were not present when the Prophecy was given, but which would be present with respect to some future time, considered as present in the visions. Thus where it is said upon pouring out the seventh vial of wrath, that *great* Babylon *came in remembrance before God, to give unto her the cup of the wine of the fierceness of his wrath*; this relates not to the time of *John* the

Apostle, but to the time of pouring out the seventh vial of wrath. So where it is said, *Babylon is fallen, is fallen*; and *thrust in thy sickle and reap, for the time is come for thee to reap*; and *the time of the dead is come, that they should be judged*; and again, *I saw the dead small and great stand before God*: these sayings relate not to the days of *John* the Apostle, but to the latter times considered as present in the visions. In like manner the words, *five are fallen, and one is, and the other is not yet come*, and *the Beast that was and is not, he is the eighth*, are not to be referred to the age of *John* the Apostle, but relate to the time when the Beast was to be wounded to death with a sword, and shew that this wound was to be given him in his sixth head: and without this reference we are not told in what head the Beast was wounded. *And the ten horns which thou sawest, are ten Kings, which have received no kingdom as yet, but receive power as Kings one hour with the Beast. These have one mind*, being all of the whore's religion, *and shall give their power and strength unto the Beast. These shall make war with the Lamb*, at the sounding of the seventh trumpet; *and the Lamb shall overcome them: for he is Lord of Lords and King of Kings; and they that are with him are called and chosen and faithful. And he saith unto me, the waters which thou sawest where the whore sitteth, are peoples and multitudes and nations and tongues*, composing her Beast. *And the ten horns which thou sawest upon the Beast, these shall hate the whore, and shall make her desolate and naked, and shall eat her flesh, and burn her with fire*, at the end of the 1260 days. *For God hath put in their hearts to fulfil his will, and to agree and give their kingdom unto the Beast, until the words of God shall be fulfilled. And the woman which thou sawest, is that great city which reigneth over the Kings of the earth*, or the great city of the *Latins*, which reigneth over the ten Kings till the end of those days.

FINIS